Surviving Teenage Motherhood

Studies in Childhood and Youth

Series Editors: **Allison James** and **Adrian L. James**

Titles include:

Kate Bacon
TWINS IN SOCIETY
Parents, Bodies, Space and Talk

David Buckingham and Vebjørg Tingstad (*editors*)
CHILDHOOD AND CONSUMER CULTURE

Allison James, Anne Trine Kjørholt and Vebjørg Tingstad (*editors*)
CHILDREN, FOOD AND IDENTITY IN EVERYDAY LIFE

Helen Stapleton
SURVIVING TEENAGE MOTHERHOOD
Myths and Realities

Studies in Childhood and Youth
Series Standing Order ISBN 978–0–230–21686–0 hardback
(outside North America only)

You can receive future titles in this series as they are published by placing a standing order. Please contact your bookseller or, in case of difficulty, write to us at the address below with your name and address, the title of the series and the ISBN quoted above.

Customer Services Department, Macmillan Distribution Ltd, Houndmills, Basingstoke, Hampshire RG21 6XS, England

Surviving Teenage Motherhood

Myths and Realities

Helen Stapleton
Australian Catholic University & Mater Mothers' Hospitals, Australia

palgrave
macmillan

First published 2010 by
PALGRAVE MACMILLAN

Palgrave Macmillan in the UK is an imprint of Macmillan Publishers Limited, registered in England, company number 785998, of Houndmills, Basingstoke, Hampshire RG21 6XS.

Palgrave Macmillan in the US is a division of St Martin's Press LLC, 175 Fifth Avenue, New York, NY 10010.

Palgrave Macmillan is the global academic imprint of the above companies and has companies and representatives throughout the world.

Palgrave® and Macmillan® are registered trademarks in the United States, the United Kingdom, Europe and other countries.

ISBN 978–0–230–57920–0   hardback

This book is printed on paper suitable for recycling and made from fully managed and sustained forest sources. Logging, pulping and manufacturing processes are expected to conform to the environmental regulations of the country of origin.

A catalogue record for this book is available from the British Library.

A catalog record for this book is available from the Library of Congress.

10   9   8   7   6   5   4   3   2   1
19   18   17   16   15   14   13   12   11   10

Printed and bound in Great Britain by
CPI Antony Rowe, Chippenham and Eastbourne

For Liana

Contents

Acknowledgements

With appreciations to Penny and Allison, and Richard, Jenny and Mavis.

And grateful thanks to the teenagers, their mothers and boyfriends, and midwives for sharing intimate, and sometimes difficult, aspects of their lives and experiences.

Introduction

This book is about the experiences of 17 teenagers, their significant others and some midwives, from pregnancy realisation through the early years of motherhood. The agency-centred accounts from the teenagers and these selected others provide a counterbalance, and indeed something of an antidote, to the usual pathologising of young people who opt to 'do' their adolescent years differently from their mainstream peer groups. These narratives reflect trends in academic circles which increasingly favour methodologies for accessing participants' voices, especially those considered marginalised. The need to actively pursue such approaches is imperative to the research enterprise, not least because they help to expose the 'classed' dimensions of participants' experiences which, eventually, may provide something of a challenge to conventional, and majority, viewpoints.

Although the data were collected in the UK (England and Wales), I hope that my findings will have international appeal and resonance for both specialist and lay audiences. Taking an ethnographic approach, I chart the changes to significant relationships (as defined by the teenagers themselves) and major life-cycle transitions over a discrete period of adolescence. I also examine changing attitudes to female sexuality and moral discourses on adolescent subjectivity especially as these pertain to teenage motherhood; the intergenerational transmission of childbearing and rearing knowledges and practices is of central importance. My aim is to provide a snapshot of how a selected group of contemporary teenagers 'do' maternity in contemporary Western culture. In so doing, I hope to raise questions about the significance of class in determining the development of mothering trajectories, representations of female adolescence, and the ubiquitous sexualisation and objectification of teenage girls in the media and in popular culture.

Medical discourses play a significant role in policing and regulating women's bodies, in defining 'appropriate' female behaviours and in authorising socio-cultural constructions of femininity. Pregnancy and childbirth signalled the beginning of a different corporeal relationship for the teenagers in this study. In keeping with their peer group, the majority of the teenagers who participated in my research had little previous contact with medical services and personnel, with the possible exception of sexual health/family planning services. Becoming a mother heralded an unaccustomed emphasis on the body, and an expectation of submission to maternity staff for regular monitoring and assessment. Their experiences of these encounters provide another lens through which to examine the interplay of power and personal agency in the lives of these young mothers and their children, and the relationship between the body and self-identity. This book also briefly mentions midwives and other maternity professionals, and describes the 'workings' of hierarchically organised institutions; the discourses of choice and control in the contested arenas of female reproduction are repeatedly emphasised.

The genesis of this book was a research project evaluating the impact of a set of evidence-based leaflets on decision-making in maternity care (Kirkham and Stapleton, 2001). An important aspect of the study involved many hours observing interactions between maternity professionals and their clients. I was especially interested in the attitudes and behaviours of these professionals, particularly the differences I observed in their approaches to their middle-class and working-class clients, including pregnant teenagers. I also began to appreciate how radically the presentation of pregnancy in adolescence had changed. In their tight jeans, crop tops, stretch lycra clothing and exposed midriffs, the teenagers I observed seemed to take up more visual 'space'; their piercings and tattoos were not hidden but rather displayed as identity statements. They appeared more *embodied*. But it was their 'rebellious' stance and their nonconformist presentations of 'self' which particularly interested me; these pregnant teenagers seemed to have a very different 'take' on their situation than the midwives and others involved in their maternity care provision. I became increasingly aware that the 'real' stories, and the 'real' meanings about their lives, could not be conveyed in 'one-off' interviews, no matter how 'in depth' they purported to be. I wanted to know more about the outcomes of the teenagers' childbearing experiences: whether 'A' managed to birth her baby at home as she intended; whether 'B' managed to avoid the midwife she disliked; whether 'C's' baby turned from a breech position to head down before she went into labour. I also became more curious about major life events beyond those associated with pregnancy, and the teenagers' relationships with their significant others (especially their mothers). My data suggested that health professionals tended to view pregnant teenagers as a homogeneous group of (bad or, at least, immature) girls. And, while many midwives had teenage daughters themselves, few made direct reference to their sexuality, including how they negotiated a sexual identity. In contrast, the midwives' teenage sons were presented as relatively immune from the consequences of their emerging sexuality, as illustrated by one midwife's comment: 'Thank God I've only got boys!' My curiosity was further aroused as many of the midwives shared the same social status and milieu as their teenage clients and families and, indeed, some also had sisters or nieces, and/or were closely associated with other young women who had birthed babies as teenagers. Additionally, a small number of midwives confided that they too had become pregnant as teenagers and had 'put the baby up' (for adoption), mainly to avoid bringing their families into disrepute. I was bothered, and intrigued, by these double standards, especially from those whose professional role concerned the sexual health and well-being of pregnant teenagers/young mothers.

Encounters I observed between pregnant teenagers and midwives and/or obstetricians suggested that these professionals held a single, and unitary, perspective on adolescent pregnancy: it was ill-advised. 'Respectable' girls appreciated the importance of educational, rather than sexual, attainment and orientated themselves accordingly. More importantly perhaps, they appreciated that emergency contraception, and termination, were the preferred options should they find themselves pregnant. The teenagers I observed, however, were rarely given the opportunity to tell their own stories about how they became pregnant. I would later discover that their accounts were not dissimilar to those I had heard from older childbearing women and included unprotected sex (sometimes fuelled by excess alcohol), contraceptive failure and/or coerced sex. Perhaps because the focus of contemporary maternity 'care' has increasingly focused on the well-being of the foetus, the welfare of the (teenage) mother is frequently overlooked and, hence, the often traumatic events preceding pregnancy are unavailable to care providers.

There were many, and varied, ways in which health professionals disregarded the childbearing teenagers in their care, who they often seemed to view as unreliable witnesses to their own circumstances and life events. For instance, many practitioners did not introduce themselves, did not look up when the teenagers entered the consulting room, did not acknowledge their boyfriends, directed conversation to the teenager's mother and otherwise infantilised them. Pregnant teenagers were seldom offered opportunities for self-disclosure and only very rarely did discussion focus on their concerns; pregnancy and impending motherhood were the only permitted conversation topics, whereas with older women they joked, inquired about other family members, and offered advice about maternity leave and their male partner's potential involvement in the birth. While other categories of pregnant women were also marginalised by health professionals, the plight of the teenagers got under my skin. It was something about their physical vulnerability, their youth and lack of experience in an unfamiliar setting, combined with the discrimination and hostility they faced accessing 'care' in a supposedly 'safe' environment, which angered me. That many of them attended antenatal clinics unaccompanied also concerned me.

Youth, gender and notions of 'risk'

The category 'youth' has been subjected to public scrutiny in recent years, perhaps because teenagers and their (diverse) cultures have come to symbolise both the scale, and the dynamics, of wider social change. Moral outrage and 'panics' about the activities of adolescents, particularly as regards their sexual behaviours and practices, regularly punctuate the (textual) landscape. Regardless of the meanings teenagers themselves ascribe to their behaviours, the visual images they project are prone to misinterpretation. Bodily gestures, clothing, hairstyles and other fashion trends may all be construed as anti-establishment displays requiring the institution of remedial action in order to curb 'quantum leaps' (Osgerby, 1998: 10) in the scale of their purported delinquency. In the public imagination, periods of social upheaval and displacement have a long association with subsequent 'crime waves', as was evident in the immediate post-war period when the 'war babies' of absent fathers and working mothers reappeared some years later as a generation of juvenile delinquents.

However, social and political responses to youth have never been uniform. Typically adolescents are vilified for being morally and culturally bankrupt, while simultaneously lauded for their future potential. The 'youth as trouble/youth as fun' dichotomy (Hebdige, 1988: 28) is thus a key motif around which social change in adolescence may be both organised and understood. This is perhaps most obvious in economic analyses explaining youth employment patterns and opportunities.

In the post-war years, for example, teenagers were referred to as the 'bulge generation' (Ashton and Seymour, 1993: 118), who enjoyed full employment status on account of an unprecedented, and widespread, shortage of unskilled labour. Economic independence facilitated social and sexual independence, which coincided with the development and marketing of the oral contraceptive pill. Hence, adolescents became an easy target for commercial exploitation and their new-found affluence gave rise to the social construction of the 'teenager', who embodied the mythology of classlessness and carefreeness.

The distinguishing features of youth as a discrete group, on the trajectory from childhood to adulthood, have varied across cultures and throughout historical periods, although there is general agreement that the physical changes associated with puberty are cross-culturally and historically universal. While certain biological markers indicate tangible moments in this transition, such physical indicators are themselves subject to social, economic and cultural influences. The identification of adolescence as a distinctive stage in the life cycle, characterised by turbulences and crises, advanced the development of adolescent medicine and adolescent psycho-pathology as medical sub-specialties. Indeed, the specificity of behaviours, attitudes and developmental responses of adolescents in Western cultures are such that adolescence has been referred to as a 'culture-bound syndrome' (Hill and Fortenberry, 1992: 73).

Despite the universality of adolescent milestones, teenage girls, especially those who become pregnant, generally have a much tougher time than their male counterparts. Visible evidence of sexual prowess among girls is usually met with opprobrium, with greater restrictions imposed on their freedom and access to public spaces, especially those considered to be unsafe. See, for example, Dwyer (2006); Kukla (2006); Longhurst (2001); and Valentine (2008), for accounts of spatial restrictions imposed on women's (pregnant) bodies. Girls' socialisation processes often engender a sense of fearfulness which acts to further constrain their activities, especially at the corporeal level, while ideological constructs tend to reinforce mistaken beliefs that crimes against women's bodies are more likely to occur in public spaces than in the home or workplace. Boys, meanwhile, are expected (encouraged?) to 'cast their seed', 'sow their oats' and otherwise 'be' (hetero)sexual; they are rarely chastised for rule-breaking behaviours unless they violate the law. The aggressive sexual socialisation of adolescent males (Murnen and Wright, 2002) can thus be described as supporting risk-taking behaviours, encouraging them to exploit and manipulate their environment to best advantage. In short, boys develop the very skills and attributes which are most esteemed in male-dominated, capitalist, industrial societies.

In many cultures, all major transitions, from being born to dying, involve initiation rites requiring demonstrable acts of individual bravery and courage. Risk-taking in this context is viewed as inevitable. The opposite focus is evident in contemporary Western societies, where survival (at any cost) is viewed as the most valued outcome, even if this is only achievable by (state) interventions that closely monitor and regulate health and related behaviours. Risk-taking in this context is viewed as anathema. The (health) risks to contemporary youth may be said to mirror those of 'any inexperienced person exploring new worlds' (Ashton and Seymour, 1993: 117), although in Western societies risk-taking must subscribe to normative (class-based) notions of appropriateness if individuals wish to avoid being stigmatised. Hence the opprobrium attached to young women engaging in sex without using contraception and/or continuing a pregnancy which 'should' have been terminated.

Since the concept of 'safety' has been valorised and widely promoted as an achievable and laudable aim, health-related risk management has become big business. Healthcare settings, and the personnel who work within them, are now routinely assessed from a risk perspective. In post-modern societies, markers which regulate the boundaries of safety and risk have given new meaning to an ever-expanding range of human activities and, in this landscape, 'safe sex' becomes a more labile term which may be equally applied within libertarian discourses and those which espouse the politics of fear. The myth of the 'zipless fuck', and the implication that sex practised 'healthily' will not result in infection or pregnancy, is thus counterbalanced by the 'precautionary principle' (Furedi, 1998: 9) which, in turn, may be seen as a metaphor encapsulating 'an entire attitude to life' (ibid.). Coined by Erica Mann Jong in her popular 1973 novel *Fear of Flying*, a 'zipless fuck' referred to a sexual encounter between two previously unacquainted persons, without emotional involvement or intentions towards commitment. The consequences of pregnancy and sexually transmitted disease were rather overlooked within this discourse, although the latter are all too easily acquired, with one highly regarded source suggesting that a female adolescent who engages in a single act of unprotected sex with an infected partner has a 1 per cent chance of acquiring HIV, a 30 per cent chance of contracting genital herpes and a 50 per cent chance of acquiring gonorrhoea (Alan Guttmacher Institute, 1999). Early childbearing for teenagers from disadvantaged backgrounds, however, turns the concept of risk on its head, reconfiguring this event as a relatively low-risk undertaking when compared with the continuous and substantial threats to personal safety and psychological integrity which many endure throughout their formative years.

Although the discursive space of teenage pregnancy has been identified, the 'politics of naming' (Cain, 1989: 15), and the disassembling of female adolescent experience are only beginning. Finding words to talk about difficult experiences such as forced sex, or an abortion kept secret from parents, requires a consciousness capable of articulating the memory of distress and a culture that gives adolescents access to adult language, rather than that limited to a 'subculture'. This is a complex undertaking because, despite adult rights in some areas, young people are denied full adult status in many Western societies. Working-class girls face particular difficulties, not least because their voices are often perceived as neither authoritative nor credible. Furthermore, adolescent sexuality cannot be discussed in isolation from the troubled relationship which many teenage girls have with their bodies, as evidenced by the substantial literature on self-harming behaviours and body dysmorphic disorders (or imagined ugliness syndrome), more recently referred to as 'body hatred' (Frost, 2001: 10).

Feminists researching non-feminists: round pegs in square holes?

Although I employed a feminist approach to this research, I do not wish to imply that I adopted a single, universally accepted, set of techniques or position to which all feminists would subscribe but rather to acknowledge the cacophony of 'feminisms', so often evident in qualitative research methodologies. Some would indeed argue whether a 'feminist' ethnography is achievable or even desirable because ethnographic methods *per se* may expose research subjects 'to greater risk of exploitation, betrayal and abandonment' (Stacey, 1988: 21) than might be the case if they participated in research projects employing traditional 'positivist' approaches. Methodological pluralism is now widely accepted and not all feminists share a common standpoint, or a 'totalizing theory' (Smith, 1992: 88). It is reasonable to suggest, however, that all feminists believe in the importance of describing women's diverse experiences and the need to challenge oppressive practices.

Interpretation, a critical aspect of the feminist ethnographic endeavour, demands an 'ethnographic attitude (incorporating) a mode of practice and theoretical attention, a way of remaining mindful and accountable' (Haraway, 1997: 39). Hence, a feminist understanding of epistemology seeks to understand not only 'what' is known but 'who' can be a knower and hence who might be regarded as a legitimate producer of knowledge(s) (Harding, 1987). This raises obvious questions about power in research relationships, an area in which I experienced difficulty not least because although I was attempting to *do* feminist research, the majority of my participants would not have identified as being aligned with feminist ideals. The degree to which I was able to accurately interpret the teenagers' worlds, while simultaneously acknowledging the very real differences between us, especially regarding our understandings of gendered experience, was a constant worry.

Research which claims a feminist basis, then, is not so much concerned with the methods used to generate and analyse data, as with the lens through which the researcher views underlying epistemological, methodological and philosophical issues. The kaleidoscopic nature of the researcher's viewfinder is such that there is no distinct (anthropological) point of view but that rather 'there are as many perspectives as there are anthropologists' (Peacock, 1986: viii). Even if the subjective lens of the ethnographer were to remain constant, social groups can themselves undergo change, and thus it is most unlikely that an ethnography of any particular group can ever be replicated in its entirety.

An insistence on naming and making visible the intersections of power and privilege is, however, an essential aspect of the feminist 'plot'. As with this study of teenage pregnancy, the researcher undertaking a feminist enquiry is no invisible, nameless voice of authority, but rather a 'real, historical individual with concrete, specific desires and interests' (Harding, 1987: 9), which originate within a precise socio-cultural context. Acknowledging the ethnographer as a (female) human being means acknowledging limitations and accepting idiosyncrasies and shortcomings which may effect a less than perfect performance. As one eminent anthropologist suggests: 'We cannot rid ourselves of the cultural self we bring with us into the field any more than we disown the eyes, ears and skin through which we take in our intuitive perceptions about the new and strange world we have entered' (Scheper-Hughes, 1992: 28). If we accept then, that the purpose of a 'good-enough' ethnography is not the production of a complete and 'objective' account but rather a narrative capable of portraying and communicating human 'truths', then we may consider it has as much in common with literature as science. Despite efforts to 'write into' the research processes the gendered, classed and raced identity of the researcher, crises of representation inevitably frustrate our ability to produce a 'good-enough' ethnographic text. I hope readers will judge this book as adequate in this respect.

The stigmatised 'other' and the research process

A study of teenage pregnancy takes the researcher (and the reader) into terrain which is widely acknowledged as emotionally charged, where those affected are often stigmatised and socially excluded. The concept of stigma is based on understandings of social relationships wherein individuals or groups are signified as 'different', often on account of behaviours judged as failing to meet socially prescribed norms of morality. Stigmatised relationships are neither exceptional nor atypical; indeed, as the late Susan Sontag observed, one of the largest stigmatised groups comprises the 'kingdom of the ill' (Sontag, 1983: 3). The size of group membership, however, does little to dilute the discrimination and prejudice which separates the 'normal' from the discredited self.

For the purposes of this study, I have expanded the concept of the stigmatised and socially excluded 'other' to take account of a peculiar kind of muteness which marked my interactions with some of the teenagers and their families. I borrow from John Berger (1989) here as I suspect this trait may be similar to what he referred to as the 'inarticulateness' of patients served by Dr John Sassall, the country doctor whose life he profiles. Sassall's patients struggled to communicate their experiences, 'to translate what they know into thoughts which they can think' (ibid.: 99), and this was linked to a sense of (cultural) dispossession originating in shame about their lowly place in the class hierarchy. Like Sassall, I also struggled when my enquiries met with long silences, monosyllabic responses and/or 'blanking' behaviours from the teenagers and/or their significant others and I sometimes felt frustrated when they did not (could not?) express themselves verbally with any degree of fluency. Conversational gaps and hesitations were unsettling, especially in the early days of my research when I was tempted to formulate 'answers' to my own questions which I might subsequently insinuate into the conversation and later recover as 'authentic' data. While it is not my intention to disavow personal responsibility for the omissions and failings in my research techniques, nor to suggest that those who contributed to the research were inadequate in any way, I would like to illuminate some of the difficulties involved when attempting to see, and describe, things from the 'native's' viewpoint (Geertz, [1983] 2000).

An individual's standing as a 'knower' is allied to, and dependent upon, their credibility within society. This is largely a matter of how they are seen by significant others: whether they are deemed capable of representing themselves truthfully, and whether coherence and factuality can be adduced from their account(s). Credibility may be influenced by sex, age, religion, class and ethnicity, but it is also inseparable from less well-defined factors such as 'reputation' and/or social standing. For example, the credibility of a female rape victim may be disputed if her persona and testimony do not accord with the stereotype of an 'innocent' woman, but instead convey an impression that she 'asked for it'. Teenagers have little credibility in the public imagination; their low status is especially noticeable in the case of young mothers. This echoes what Miranda Fricker (2003) has termed 'epistemic injustice', whereby the person telling the story is designated as unreliable because of a preconceived, although not necessarily intentional, prejudice on the part of the hearer. The speaker thus receives less credibility than s/he would receive if the hearer was operating from a position of openness.

Being ranked as inferior actually *makes* one inferior (by way of expectations); this has been understood for many years. Empirical studies have confirmed that the 'Pygmalion effect' operates in educational, judicial and healthcare settings demonstrating that preconceived ideas about individuals may significantly influence outcomes. The values of powerholders may thus transform 'social inputs (class) into educational outputs (marks, scholarships, university places) through the mediation of those stereotypical categories of judgement [...] which enable *class*ification to be euphemised as *academic* classification' (Jenkins, 2004: 168–70; original emphasis). The pervasiveness of stereotyping practices is such that young childbearing women are routinely scripted to become welfare-dependent, inadequate mothers of unruly children who, in turn, are destined to repeat the cycle. The role of more powerful others in shaping events, and ensuring that outcomes for particular (stigmatised) groups are *always* negative, is thus routinely overlooked.

A brief synopsis of the study design and methodology

This was a qualitative study involving 17 teenagers and their significant others, including mothers and other family members, boyfriends and midwives. The sample comprised two groups: I initially carried out 11 'one-off', opportunistic, interviews with pregnant teenagers and some of their mothers living in South Wales; a further two follow-up interviews were undertaken with two of these young mothers within the first two years following birth. The remaining six teenagers, all of whom lived in South Yorkshire, participated in the longitudinal phase of the study; four of their biological mothers were also recruited. One teenager, who was estranged from her mother, allowed me to enrol the female manager of the hostel where she was living – she referred to her as her 'dream' mother. The mother of another young woman suffered from serious mental health problems which occasionally resulted in displays of extreme violence, especially towards her daughter. I decided not to invite her to join the study as I was concerned about compromising her daughter's welfare.

The teenagers were aged 14 to 17 at the time of conception, with those in the Welsh cohort at the upper end of the range; the majority were white British and all were working-class. Participation in the study varied between 18 months to just over two years. Family members of both cohorts lived in close proximity to one another; 20 miles (approx. 30 kilometres) was considered a fair distance, and 40 miles (approx. 64 kilometres) a long way to travel. Perception of distance may have been exaggerated by a widespread lack of access to private transport and generally poor public transport links. Both research areas are economically deprived and report traditionally high rates of teenage pregnancy. Some teenagers (n=6) were attending school at the time pregnancy was confirmed; many had considerable experience of social exclusion. All but three of the teenagers were pregnant for the first time; two from the South Yorkshire cohort (Jade and Tracey) became mothers for the second time during the study period.

Data were generated through one-off and serial interviews, and selected observations of interactions between midwives and teenagers, and their families, in a range of settings including hospital, community-based (shopping malls, fast-food outlets and mother–baby clinics) and domiciliary. An additional data stream was generated by the teenager–mother dyads mapping their support networks, both at the time they joined the study, and at the point of exit. I acknowledge that narratives may refer to practices and viewpoints in operation over a particular time span and in discrete geographical locations; the text cannot, of course, describe, nor account for, changes which may have taken place since.

In order to maximise the potential for anonymity, all identifying data have been changed. Everyone who participated in the research was invited to nominate a pseudonym of their choice and some accepted this invitation with alacrity. On the occasions names were selected which were already in use, or where these were the real names of others who participated in the study, I chose an alternative name. As the interviews were transcribed verbatim, quotations reflect local conventions with respect to the use of (colloquial) language.

Theoretical underpinnings

In writing this book, I have drawn upon two broad theoretical perspectives: social constructionism and embodiment. The solidity of the term 'social construction' has been challenged in recent years with suggestions made for the adoption of an alternative terminology, which more cogently describes how human experience may be 'packed' and 'unpacked', and how conceptual frameworks may thus be released from their 'encrustations' (Wong and Checkland, 1999). Arguing that the term, as metaphor and as statement of fact, is overused, Ian Hacking (1999, 2003) urges authors who claim a constructionist orientation to clearly and precisely explicate the 'what' of the construction enterprise. Hacking also argues that the word 'social' is redundant, because the social context is implicit whenever 'any idea that is debated, assessed, applied, and developed is situated in a social setting' (1999: 423). The social component of human interaction is always and everywhere present; without this we cannot create meaning. Furthermore, Hacking says that the 'construction' element of the term is misleading because it conflates several discrete items, including experiences, memories, discourses and behaviours, into a unitary concept. He suggests the word 'shaping' is a more accurate description of the processes by which ideas, beliefs and attitudes about categories of people (he cites abused children, pregnant teenagers and women refugees) are translated into theoretical propositions. Other authors propose that words such as 'making' (Wong, 1997: 273), 'fabricating' (Armstrong, 1983: 457) and/or 'inventing' (Oyĕwùmí, 2006: 540) more accurately reflect the 'construction' element of human experience.

This book draws on a diverse literature. The orientation is feminist, concerned with women's lives and experiences, especially childbearing and rearing. I take account of on-going debates about (gendered) power relations and the role of medicine as an agent of social control (Lupton, 1994), the social construction of gender in medical discourses (Martin, 1987) and the significance of social class as a significant determinant of health outcomes (Doyal, 1995; Graham 1993a, 1993b). The contribution from cross-cultural studies of childbirth practices (Davis-Floyd and Sargent, 1997; Jordan, 1978) is highlighted as the experience of becoming a mother was a defining factor, metaphorically and literally, in the female relationships which are the main focus of this study: between the teenagers and their own mothers, between teenagers and their own babies, and between mothers, teenagers, boyfriends and midwives. Hence, motherhood and mothering practices are central themes linking the first three chapters.

The following chapter explores historical and contemporary understandings of mothers in the context of 'doing' family life and kinship relations which, in turn, provides an overview of the multiple ways in which practices have changed. I explore how competing accounts of teenage pregnancy – as a 'disaster' or a 'crisis' requiring effective management and damage limitation, or as 'lightning rods for stigma' (Kelly, 2000: 20) – reflect current tensions associated with this life-course transition. I also discuss contested representations of teenage sexuality and young motherhood and relate these to discourses on 'illegitimacy', 'unmarried mothers' and/or 'promiscuous women'. I then link these discourses to readings of nonconformist pregnancy and demonstrate how they have informed political debates and social policy initiatives.

In particular, I ask why teenagers who are biologically at the 'peak age of reproductive functioning' (Morgan et al., 1999: 135), and therefore physiologically well endowed for childbearing, have come to be labelled and perceived as a deviant category. I consider legislation regulating adolescent sexual behaviours before briefly summarising recent UK policy developments, and associated critical commentary, in the interrelated areas of teenage pregnancy, social exclusion and childhood poverty.

1
Teenage Pregnancy, Motherhood and Family Life

Because adolescence has only recently been identified as a separate phase between childhood and adulthood, childbearing accounts from teenage mothers have hitherto been inseparable from the narratives of other disadvantaged mothers. These accounts generally make for poignant reading, describing the cruel treatment of nonconformist mothers who, despite circumstances beyond their control, were shunned by society. Any discussion of contemporary teenage pregnancy is necessarily defined by reference to its antecedents and hence the need to summarise key historical events and arguments which have shaped current discourses.

Conceptualising 'family': trends and current practices

The concept of mothering and family life is acknowledged as a 'complex historical, social and cultural phenomenon' (Christensen, 2004: 380) and this is nowhere more fluently described than in *The World We Have Lost* – a historical account of family life and household structures by the social historian Peter Laslett ([1965] 2000). Laslett challenges long-held assumptions about family groupings and age at marriage, including the widely held belief that marriage rules during earlier periods condoned unions between teenagers – although, that said, it was relatively common practice for young people to be *espoused*, sometimes from childhood. He also debunks the notion of the nuclear family as a modern invention, suggesting that our ancestors mostly lived within small family groupings.

Research examining changing notions of family and kinship in contemporary society (Silva and Smart, 1999; Smart et al., 2001) suggests that attempts to portray family units as predetermined or representative is untenable. With a shift in focus from studies of 'the family' as

14

a social institution under a capitalist/patriarchal organising system, to closer scrutiny of the interiority of family life and the personal relationships of individual family members, the diversity of family structures and their individually constructed arrangements for self-management have emerged. For example, when single motherhood is examined from a life-course perspective, it emerges 'less as a distinct family form and more as an experience coloured by the lone mother's place in a network of relationships, as well as her place in her broader personal, social and historical context' (May, 2004: 401). Hence, post-modern understandings of 'family' view these social arrangements as fluid and flexible sites for constructing 'webs of relationships' (ibid.) between ever more diverse groupings of (unrelated) adults and children. As the macro elements of family structures have changed, so have the micro-structures, with intergenerational research revealing a greater emphasis on children's emotional well-being in contrast to a previous focus on their physical and material needs (Wade, 2005). Changing perceptions of safety and risk also mean that contemporary children and young people are subjected to an ever more intensive parental 'gaze' intended to protect them from 'stranger danger' (Valentine, 1997: 42) and other possible threats, but which nonetheless inevitably restricts their autonomy and freedom.

So while the contours and contexts of Western family life have undergone considerable change in recent decades, this is not to imply that diversity in kinship relations is a recent phenomenon nor that, until recently, it described *normative* patterns of family life. That said, although there appears to be general agreement that family relationships, patterns and practices have changed substantially, the *rate* and *extent* of change have been contested. Indeed, some would argue (Silva and Smart, 1999) that any such alterations are all too often framed in alarmist terms and frequently (and negatively) exaggerated for political expediency. In her moving ethnography of the 'violence' embedded in discourses of mothering in Brazil, Nancy Scheper-Hughes (1992) usefully reminds us, however, that *any* demographic change inevitably affects social arrangements and sentiments, including the intimate bonds between mothers and their children.

The percolation of feminist ideas, a more sexually permissive climate and a more liberal understanding of 'family' have contributed to an undermining of the conjugal 'rights' previously claimed by men (and which contributed to unwanted pregnancies in women). While marriage was once perceived as protective against a disreputable sexual reputation, by the late 1960s women were employing alternative reproductive and relationship scripts to those promulgated by adherents of the nuclear family. Oppressive, patriarchal structures were challenged, threatening the institution of marriage that had previously exerted such a powerful control over female sexuality. A more tolerant view of coupling was adopted, with 'de facto' and 'common law' relationships increasingly viewed as routine rather than exotic. In this apparently liberated climate, illegitimacy *per se* was viewed as less of a threat to the social order than economically unsupported mothers. Reconstructing pregnant teenagers as problematic, rather than 'simply' morally deficient, paved the way for legislation which has attached ever more stringent criteria to welfare claimants.

Throughout the industrialised world, pregnant teenagers are routinely described 'in the language of stigmatised dependency' (Davies et al., 1999: 45), consistently portrayed in terms of a 'deficit' model, reinforcing negative stereotypes of 'troubled' and 'troublesome' girls (Dennison and Coleman, 1998; Hudson, 1989; Lees, 1989). Although the illegal status of illegitimacy has been widely abolished, the use of the term 'illegitimate' has been replaced with more 'morally neutral' (Reekie, 1998: 10) terminology; official discourses continue to employ terms such as extra-nuptial or extra-marital, the prefix 'extra' signifying exclusion and otherness.

Contested representations of teenage sexuality and motherhood

The shift in phraseology from 'illegitimate' to 'teenage' motherhood diluted the association with marriage. What had been portrayed as a *moral* problem was now (re)presented as a technical, or scientific, problem. Around this time the mechanistic model of the post-war welfare state encouraged people to believe that medical experts could define, and manage, health and illness (and birth/death). In conjunction with this shift in practice and values, the Western model of childbirth was redefined as 'technological' and its practices as 'technocratic'. Resolving technical as opposed to moral problems requires different approaches: where the latter discourage rational discourse, technical problems 'are those for which solutions are imaginable' (Arney and Bergen, 1984: 15) – and which attract research funding and demand evidence-based reasons for interventions. Technical problems may be deviations from the 'natural' order, but rather than being censured for their lack of conformity, they tend to be subjected to 'technologies of correction and normalisation' (ibid.: 11). But while moral and scientific/technical problems may pose different challenges, I suggest that *any* maternity occurring outside conventional structures offends against the 'natural' order, raises questions about parenting capacity and is therefore vulnerable to exclusionary practices.

The theory of 'communitarianism', as advanced by the sociologist Amitai Etzioni (1993), has been hailed by some politicians and policy makers as the answer to the 'parenting deficit' which he claims is responsible for many of the ills besetting modern society. Etzioni posits that many parents, but especially mothers, fail to provide adequate parenting for their children because they privilege their own needs for rewarding careers and financial security over their children's needs for sustained emotional attachment and physical contact. Critics, including Lynne Murray (1995), have rejected Etzioni's claims, asserting that, on the contrary, work outside the home is crucial to women's health and well-being because it is preventive against maternal depression which, in turn, is injurious to child health. Furthermore, research confirms the complex relationship between maternal well-being and paid employment (Klumb and Lampert, 2004) and the continued failure to effectively challenge the gendered division of household labour (Summers, 2003; Everingham et al., 2007). Of course, teenage mothers are exempt from these debates because their (inconsequential) status confirms their parental inadequacies, regardless of whether they choose to mother full-time or pursue educational or employment opportunities.

Disapproving judgements of non-normative childbearing women (lesbians and the voluntarily childless, although excluding those in religious orders), often from privileged and authoritative elders whose social status 'celebrate(s) the idea of being in control' (Arai, 2003: 212), generally fail to take account of the circumstances and preferences of others, especially pregnant teenagers. When their perspectives are sought, qualitative research in particular suggests that parenthood is less of a problem for those concerned than for society in general, and for policy makers in particular. This may partially explain the only modest successes of interventions intended to curb adolescent sexual risk-taking and reduce rates of teenage maternity (Owen et al., 2010). Adolescent sexual health interventions have historically been gender-oriented, targeting girls, perhaps because pregnancy is often portrayed as the ultimate health risk for this group. However, in failing to consider the health and related concerns of young people as a whole, instead of as 'epidemiologically defined elements' (Ashton and Seymour, 1993: 117), the negative aspects of this particular stage in the female life course are simply reinforced.

Reference to young people's sexuality and sexual preferences is generally absent in discussions of adolescent sex, although there is evidence to suggest that curiosity is a significant driver for the first sexual experience (Dickson et al., 1998). Accounts from teenage girls who actively engage in, and enjoy, sex are scarce and, hence, the potential for alternative readings of female adolescent sexuality is restricted. The 'discourse of desire' (Fine, 1988: 29) does not sit comfortably with current policy, however, which, perforce, 'ideologically separates the female sexual agent, or subject, from her counterpart, the female sexual victim' (ibid.: 30). Entrenched beliefs about women's passivity, and lack of understanding about the constituents of female desire and pleasure, make it difficult for teenage girls to assert their sexual preferences, while the pleasurable physicality of teenage sex remains largely undocumented in research texts. Societal attitudes largely uphold a 'sex-negative' attitude towards female adolescent sexuality, whereby girls are expected to take the initiative in protecting themselves against male predatory behaviours and sexual pressures. At transition to puberty, they are pressured to be 'nice girls and ultimately good women' (Tolman, 1994: 324), containing their (hetero)sexual impulses until they are older and, ideally, married. Indeed, girls are socialised into accepting that sexual restraint is a positive female attribute.

Finally, there is little detailed documentation of non-coital sexual practices, all of which are low risk for pregnancy. Indeed, the narrow focus on mapping the adult-derived, normatively ascribed, components of adolescent sexuality may disregard what young people themselves consider sex (or, indeed, abstinence) to be. Semantic diversity in relation to 'sex talk' was perhaps most famously captured by President Clinton, who claimed that the oral sex he enjoyed with Monica Lewinski did not constitute 'proper' sexual relations. The phrase 'sexually active', then, generates multiple understandings that are always contextually bound – which perhaps suggests that attempting to portray the sexual practices of others with any degree of accuracy may not be possible.

Pre-existing factors contributing to young motherhood

Growing up in poverty is arguably the most critical determinant of adult experience, including age at first conception; daughters of unskilled manual workers are almost ten times more likely to become pregnant than those whose parents have professional qualifications. Poverty contributes to increased fertility because 'the greater a population's disadvantage, the less difference childbearing in adolescence makes in determining long-term success' (Treffers et al., 2001: 112). Hence, poor teenagers have fewer reasons to delay childbearing. Within the UK, a north–south divide demonstrates the clear geographical link between teenage conceptions and deprivation indices, with the (industrialised, poorer) northern counties returning above average pregnancy rates (Hardill et al., 2001). Higher conception rates are also associated with living in seaside and surrounding rural locations (Bell et al., 2004), and with selected black and ethnic minority populations (Berthoud, 2001; Higginbottom et al., 2005), while lower rates may indicate the presence of a young, female GP, and/or more available nurse time (Hippisley-Cox et al., 2000; Lee et al., 2004).

Teenage motherhood is correlated with family disruption, including parental marital breakdown, sexual abuse and exploitation, experience of statutory care and foster or kinship care; increased vulnerability to pregnancy has also been linked with exiting statutory care arrangements (Biehal et al., 1995). Similar factors have long been implicated in teenage fatherhood (Kiernan, 1992), although anthropological research has emphasised the ways in which 'culture and social organization may influence contraceptive patterns and men's influences on those patterns' (Dudgeon and Inhorn, 2004: 1383).

Changes in household family structure, and the adaptive responses required to integrate these events, have been noted as particularly stressful for daughters, reinforcing a propensity to earlier childbearing. Motherhood during adolescence has also been linked to homelessness (Joseph Rowntree Foundation, 1995), criminality (Botting et al., 1998), lower educational attainment, dislike of school and failure to participate in post-compulsory education (Hobcraft and Keirnan, 1999; Bonell et al., 2003); the culmination of reduced occupational prospects is thought to create greater reliance on social security benefits (SEU, 1999).

Longitudinal studies reveal intergenerational transmission of parenting norms, as evidenced by the substantial numbers of teenage mothers who are daughters of teenage mothers. Peter Laslett (1977) makes the same point in his historical study of illegitimacy when he refers to the 'perduring sub-society of the illegitimacy-prone' (ibid.: 4); a more recent publication (Levene et al., 2005) expands these ideas. Female siblings of teenage parents are also at higher risk of becoming pregnant in their adolescent years and this risk appears to increase over time; a significant proportion of young mothers become pregnant more than once during adolescence.

Some outcomes associated with early childbearing

Early childbearing is generally understood to be associated with adverse medical outcomes, and concerns have been repeatedly expressed about the resources required to support teenagers and their children. Indeed, (inequitable) resource allocation is a major criticism levelled at teenage parenthood, although other groups of childbearing women, including those undergoing assisted reproduction, also require considerable financial investment (Shennan and Bewley, 2006; Bewley, 2005; Jacobsson et al., 2004). Older age at conception is also linked to a range of adverse maternal and neonatal outcomes, with associated increased economic costs (Bewley et al., 2009; Wellesley et al., 2002).

Low birth weight, prematurity and infant mortality are traditionally associated with early motherhood (Ancel et al., 1999; Botting et al., 1998; SEU, 1999), although only some very young mothers (ten to 13 years) appear to be vulnerable. Of note is the relationship between premature births to adolescent mothers and low gynaecological age (GA) – defined as the time lapse between the onset of menarche and first delivery; a low GA (<2years) is linked to a 50 per cent increase in premature births (Treffers et al., 2001). These findings support claims made that as the majority of teenage births are to adolescents at the older end of the age spectrum, there is little overall evidence of harm (Smith and Pell, 2001). Absence of paternal involvement at the time of antenatal booking – as evidenced, perhaps, by a lack of paternal details in maternity records – significantly increases the risks of prematurity and low birthweight (Knight et al., 2006). Older infants of teenage mothers appear to be more accident prone, require more hospital admissions in childhood and make more use of health services overall (Tripp and Viner, 2005).

Suggestions that childbearing in adolescence is linked with pregnancy-induced hypertension and eclampsia remain unproven, although the aetiology of eclampsia (of which raised blood pressure is symptomatic) as an immunologic disorder arising from insufficient exposure to sperm, is now generally accepted as theoretically sound (Dekker et al., 1998). Eclampsia commonly affects 'first' pregnancies (including those resulting from a new partner, artificial donor insemination and/or oocyte donation); women who are consistently exposed to one partner's sperm are thus better protected. Teenage pregnancy often results from a new and short-term relationship and, hence, a relatively short exposure time to the male partner's semen, and it is this reduced exposure which is linked to an increased risk of eclampsia and the need to expedite (premature) delivery. Adolescents who enjoy trouble-free pregnancies are less likely than older women to encounter problems in labour, although there is some evidence that immaturity of the pelvic bones may cause obstructed labour in very young girls (Treffers et al., 2001).

Poorer pregnancy outcomes may partly result from teenagers being less likely to experience a trusting relationship with a healthcare provider or access appropriate antenatal care, especially in countries where this must be paid for (Sarri and Phillips, 2004; Treffers et al., 2001). Teenage mothers are more likely to be lone mothers, to live in poorer quality housing and, due to poverty, to have poorer mental and physical health (Allen et al., 1998; Hardill et al., 2001; Hobcraft and Keirnan, 1999). Early childbearing (rather than early abortion) may negatively influence adult women's marriage prospects, their potential for home ownership and their ability to attract a male partner with good employment prospects (Ermisch and Pevalin, 2003).

An alternative view, however, proposes that teenage pregnancy may actually confer health *benefits*, including protection against breast cancer and diabetes (Bingley et al., 2000; McPherson et al., 2000). Indeed, it has been argued that some of the negative outcomes of teenage pregnancy have been exaggerated and that many young mothers and their children fare actually reasonably well in the long term (Ermisch and Pevalin, 2003; Shaw et al., 2006). This may reflect the availability of support networks within working-class communities where mothers and grandmothers traditionally assist with childcare, including 'cushioning' individual young mothers against financial hardship (Mitchell and Green, 2002). In this sense many are better supported by kinship networks than their older, more affluent, contemporaries. If teenage women are at the biological pinnacle for reproductive functioning then it may be to their advantage to assume motherhood earlier rather than later, especially in view of the accelerated health deterioration experienced by poorer people (Fessler, 2003).

There are many reasons why the spotlight remains focused on the limitations of young motherhood, although this may have less do with qualms about their welfare and more to do with sexual double standards. Given that 'successful' parenting appears to depend more on adequate material resources and social support than maternal age alone, the persistence of negative views of teen parenting suggests a need for societal scapegoats. This may partly explain why young mothers continue to be harshly judged when remedial action might be taken to address poverty and discrimination.

Trends in adolescent fertility and sexual health

The UK has consistently returned one of the highest teenage conception and birth rates of all Western countries, although this must be set in the context of a recent, but sustained, downward turn (ONS, 2006). Any decline in the teenage birth rate may, however, simply reflect higher termination rates, with worse health consequences for adolescents who delay help-seeking (or whose attempts are thwarted) and are consequently ineligible for less invasive termination procedures. The USA has experienced a 27 per cent overall decline since the early 1990s (Irwin, 2006), mostly among older African-American teenagers for whom early childbearing was previously normative but who increasingly appear to be deferring childbearing because of expanded employment opportunities (Colen et al., 2006). Statistics suggest that teenage pregnancy rates have increased differentially in line with local levels of deprivation, although opinions vary as to whether the UK trend over the past decade is upward, downward or essentially unchanged (Jewell et al., 2000; Nicoll et al., 1999; Tripp and Viner, 2005; TPU, 2007). Lack of consensus may be partly explained by the fact that although statistical data on conception, abortion and birth rates are widely available, there is no universally accepted baseline for assessing data quality, nor how it is aggregated. Accurate interpretation, especially at a local population level, is therefore extremely difficult, and this is further aggravated because of the difficulties in accurately recording the number of pregnancies which miscarry early (and which do not necessitate hospital admission), or indeed in women who do not even realise conception has occurred.

Disquiet about adolescent fertility in Western societies is not new. Historically, however, state intervention in the lives of the (reproducing) poorer classes was available only if they agreed to be monitored and supervised 'by an inspector from the prefecture whom they fear but whose advice they heed' (Donzelot, 1979: 31). In the UK, as in other Western countries, the setting of national targets for teenage conceptions and births politicised the issue and hence transferred it to the public health agenda, with successive governments introducing ever more stringent criteria for accessing state aid. These measures guaranteed an overall reduction in welfare provision for the most disadvantaged sectors of the population.

The sexual health of UK adolescents continues to be an area of concern (Royal College of Psychiatrists, 2003), with some authorities claiming it is the worst in Europe (Boseley, 1999); rates of chlamydia, syphilis, genital warts and genital herpes have increased substantially (Health Protection Agency, 2006), with some strains showing resistance to conventional treatments (Hardill et al., 2001). More relaxed public attitudes may have positively influenced the provision and uptake of adolescent sexual health services in the UK, although recent research (Owen et al., 2010) also suggests that health professionals' tendencies to disregard and infantilise young people, especially men, remains problematic.

The majority of teenage conceptions are purportedly unintended (Ashton and Seymour, 1993; Henshaw, 1998), occurring as a result of contraceptive failure, a sense of personal invulnerability, and/or impulsive behaviour fuelled by alcohol and/or drugs (Churchill et al., 2000; Dickson et al., 1998; Free et al., 2002; Paton, 2004). Reports from some teenagers, however, suggest that early childbearing is a 'positive life choice' (Tripp and Viner, 2005: 592) and/or a rite of passage to adulthood in the absence of middle-class aspirations and opportunities (SmithBattle, 2000). Indeed, some teenagers plan to become pregnant, are pleased when they do, and hold affirmative views on motherhood (Baker, 1999; Seamark and Lings, 2004; Skuse, 1997). These findings echo those of my study: that teenage pregnancy is not always 'bad news', although I also acknowledge that these alternative perspectives may simply reflect the fact that young women with poor employment prospects have less reason to defer motherhood. Growing up with adversity appears to be coupled with accelerated maturation (Wallace, 1987), which may be an additional reason why working-class girls assume a maternal role at an earlier age (Arai, 2003).

The age at which young people in Western societies become sexually active has been falling for some decades (Wellings et al., 1994), and the gender gap also appears to be declining, or even reversing (Dennison and Coleman, 2000), possibly due to young people growing up in a more sexualised society; earlier sexual activity, however, is associated with earlier childbearing, which is also linked to ethnicity and social class (Wellings et al., 1994; SEU, 1999). The percentage of teenage girls engaging in sexual intercourse at an earlier age has steadily increased (Wellings et al., 1994); age at first intercourse is around 16 years for both sexes (Tripp and Viner, 2005).

Young people from less advantaged backgrounds commence their sexual careers on average two years earlier than more privileged adolescents, while those residing in seaside resorts are more likely to engage in unprotected sex due partly to the 'hedonistic' and 'carnivalised' environments created by local leisure industries (Bell et al., 2004: 1). In addition to socio-economic disadvantage, cultural determinants, such as arranged marriage and the requirement to demonstrate early fertility, exert pressures on teenagers from some black and minority ethnic backgrounds (Higginbottom et al., 2005); female 'honour' thus serves as a marker of the social control of sexuality and female reproductive power.

Adolescent sexual health service provision and legal constraints

The provision of, and access to, appropriate health services for young people is widely seen as fundamental to reducing teenage conception and birth rates (Smith and Jacobson, 1988; Wellings and Mitchell, 1998). Pregnant teenagers are very likely to consult a health professional in the year preceding pregnancy, however, with one study reporting that almost 75 per cent of such consultations were in order to obtain contraceptive advice (Churchill et al., 2000). Better provision of sexual health services, however, does not appear to have empowered teenage girls to negotiate sexual relationships on their own terms. In this respect, their experiences may be compared with their eighteenth-century counterparts, who 'had no or little control over their reproduction (hence) the result of sexual relationships outside marriage was often the misfortune of illegitimate pregnancy' (Evans, 2005: 204).

The relationship between providing contraception and reducing conception rates is complex. Significant numbers of adolescents are thought to use ineffective/inconsistent methods of contraception, while a previous pregnancy, including a termination, is associated with an increased likelihood of using hormonal methods; promoting oral/injectable contraceptive methods over barrier methods may inadvertently encourage the very kind of sexual activities associated with acquiring an STI (Paton, 2004). The negative effects of hormonal contraceptives on adolescent bone density has also raised concerns, not least because the teenagers most susceptible to bone loss (and consequently to bone fractures) are unlikely to access the optimal nutrition known to be preventive (Gold and Bachrach, 2004). Limited knowledge about emergency birth control has been identified as an obstacle to its effective use, especially among teenagers from disadvantaged backgrounds, many of whom lack the resources to seek appropriate guidance.

While I acknowledge that legal constraints on teenagers' access to sexual experiences are universal, the following points (1–4) describe the UK context where this study was conducted.

1 The legal age of sexual consent

The legal age of consent for females and males in the UK is 16. The same laws apply to heterosexual and homosexual activity and apply to everyone over the age of ten, which is the age of criminal responsibility in England and Wales (different laws apply in Scotland). The UK Sex Offenders Act (2003) became law in May 2004, aiming to reform existing law regarding sex offences (explicitly paedophilia and related crimes such as grooming young children via the internet), to remove existing discrimination against homosexuals and to provide additional support for victims of sexually motivated crimes. While the Act abolished gender differences between underage teenagers, it potentially criminalised *all* under 16-year-olds engaging in consensual sexual activity.

Where 'visible' evidence of intercourse was available, for example pregnancy or an STI, the law provided for young men to be pursued through the courts on charges of statutory rape or assault, regardless of the wishes of their young female partners. The Act now recognises, however, that mutually agreed, non-exploitative, sexual activity between under 16-year-olds does occur, and as of April 2006, professionals are not obliged to report such teenagers to the police. The guidance developed by the UK Department for Education and Skills (DfES, 2006b) advises that decisions concerning possible referral to child protection agencies should be considered on a case-by-case basis, but that pre-teen (under 13 years) sex will continue to be viewed as a potentially serious offence under the Sexual Offences Act, not least because minors cannot legally consent to sex. These issues highlight the contradictions and uncertainties embedded in policy directives which consider sexual responsibility in isolation from other adult responsibilities, and which separate sexual maturity from sexual responsibility.

2 Sex education

In 1943, a perceived rise in both illegitimate pregnancies and venereal diseases prompted the then UK Board of Education to recommend the provision of sex education in schools. Amendments to the 1996 Education Act removed responsibility for sex education provision from local authorities, investing accountability with head-teachers and school governors. Even though the UK has one of the highest divorce rates in Europe, government policy requires state-maintained pupils to receive sex education which emphasises the importance of marriage for family life and the appropriateness of this environment for raising children. A study of the sex educational needs of young people revealed that 32 per cent of the sample received no information from home-based sources and a further 33 per cent reported that what they received at school was insufficient (Salihi and Melrose, 2002). The same study found that boys were generally less well informed than girls about sex and related matters. Another survey agrees that young people fare badly in domestic settings, with almost half (46 per cent) receiving 'nothing' or 'not a lot' of sex and relationship information from parents and, although slightly more than half (52 per cent) reported finding it easy to talk to mothers, only just over a quarter (26 per cent) reported the same easiness with fathers (BMRB International, 2003). Recent international research (Wynn et al., 2009) confirms that sexual misconceptions among teenagers are widespread.

3 Accessing contraception

Young people under the age of 16 may access family planning services in order to obtain contraception if they are deemed competent to make their own decisions and they fully understand the implications (Wheeler, 2006). This requires the young person to demonstrate that they are sufficiently mature to understand the advice offered; parental consent for contraception provision is no longer required providing certain conditions (known as the 'Gillick' criteria) are satisfied. Confusion about the confidentiality of sexual health service provision persists, however, with approximately 33 per cent of UK teenagers not appreciating that they can access contraception without parental consent (Wellings et al., 2005). Indeed, the 'confidentiality clause' was cited as the reason why a school outreach worker arranged for a 14-year-old girl to have an abortion without parental knowledge (Townsend, 2004); concerns have been raised in this respect that provision of confidential family planning advice is detrimental to parental relationships, especially between mothers and adolescent daughters.

These principles notwithstanding, young people have as much right to confidentiality in their interactions with health professionals as any other client, and even when those under 16 are deemed insufficiently mature to consent to treatment, or to make decisions on their own behalf, the law permits that the consultation itself remains confidential.

4 Abortion

Two Acts of Parliament – the Abortion Act (1967) and the Human Fertilisation and Embryology Act (1990) – regulate the provision of abortion in the UK. This requires two registered medical practitioners to agree that an abortion is indicated and that it will be undertaken by a registered practitioner in an NHS hospital, or in alternative premises approved by the Department of Health; staff may refuse to participate on moral or religious grounds. A number of points must be satisfied before an abortion can be sanctioned, including observance of the 24-week upper-time limit, proof that continuation of the pregnancy poses a grave and permanent threat to the health of the pregnant woman, and/or substantial evidence that the unborn foetus is seriously damaged. The use of emergency contraception is not considered to be a form of abortion because it is generally accepted that there is no established pregnancy to terminate.

Policy developments in the interrelated areas of teenage pregnancy, social exclusion and child poverty: a UK perspective

From 1997, when it came to power, the ('New') Labour government introduced a continual stream of social policy initiatives designed to reform the welfare agenda. A considerable swathe of these programmes (for example, the Working Tax Credit, the Child Tax Credit, Health/Education Action Zones; New Deal for Communities; Sure Start and Sure Start Plus programmes; Health Living Centres, Connexions) had particular relevance for pregnant teenagers and young mothers and, hence, were integral to the Teenage Pregnancy Strategy (SEU, 1999). Selected initiatives are summarised below.

Teenage pregnancy

Unacceptable economic cost, calculated at more than £65 million annually, was a major driver prompting the launch of the UK Teenage Pregnancy Strategy (SEU, 1999). This initiative sought to achieve two main goals: to reduce (more specifically to halve) the rate of under-18 conceptions by 2010, and to reduce the long-term social exclusion of teenage parents by involving them in education, training and/or employment schemes. However, despite substantial investment, at the time of writing only very modest reductions in teenage conceptions have been achieved (approx. 13 per cent against the baseline figure of 50 per cent), although these fail to reflect the considerable geographical variation, with some areas reporting reductions of up to 26 per cent (DCSF, 2009). The UK Labour government responded to these results with the publication of a further strategy document which encouraged parents and schools to take more responsibility for educating children about sex, relationships and contraception (DCSF, 2010b). For example, an overall reduction in conceptions of less than 10 per cent has been achieved (ONS, 2006), with some areas, including South Yorkshire (from where my main sample was recruited), showing little change (TPU, 2007). Although the majority of young people use contraception at first sexual intercourse, an increase in unprotected sex among adolescents has been reported: from 78 per cent in 2001 to 88 per cent in 2004 for women, and from 81 per cent to 86 per cent for men. Failure to achieve educational targets, especially for the most marginalised children and young people, has also been noted (New Policy Institute, 2006).

Directives for midwives (DfES, 2007) and Local Authorities and Primary Care Trusts (DfES, 2006a) were introduced with the aim of max-imising opportunities for the most effective delivery of the Teenage Pregnancy Strategy over the remainder of the programme. Research findings (Cater and Coleman, 2006; MacDonald and Marsh, 2005), how-ever, have questioned a central tenet of the strategy document: that teenage pregnancy is 'accidental' and, hence, 'the first conscious deci-sion that many teenagers make [...] is whether to have an abortion or to continue with the pregnancy' (SEU, 1999: 28). As I have previously suggested, some teenagers choose motherhood and sooner or later do actually embark on a chosen career trajectory, although the nature and significance of such choices have been largely overlooked by both policy makers and academics. Furthermore, New Labour's emphasis on interventions which stressed self-regulation, responsible citizenship, and participation through education, training and/or employment was problematic because it disregarded multiple, and pre-existing, levels of exclusion. It also dismissed teenagers' preferences to be full-time moth-ers to their infants and ultimately attached a moral 'weighting' to their already keenly felt sense of stigma and isolation (Kidger, 2004). That said, discourses of sexuality persistently exercised a powerful influence on policy development, and New Labour policies repeatedly empha-sised 'modernizing the social and remoralizing welfares' (Carabine, 2000: 952).

The focus of the Teenage Pregnancy Strategy assumed that attention to single, linear, themes, including improved access to contraception and provision of better (sex) education, would contribute to the 'celebra-tory discourse of opportunity and achievement [...] From being assumed to be headed towards marriage, motherhood and limited economic participation, the girl is now a social category understood primarily as being endowed with economic capacity' (McRobbie, 2007: 722). These assumptions have been criticised, not least because decision-making processes in adolescence, particularly with respect to reproduction, are multifactorial and complex, and it is these issues that recent critiques of teenage parenthood have begun to address (Cater and Coleman, 2006; MacDonald and Marsh, 2005). Finally, while the Teenage Pregnancy Strategy emphasised the strong association of young motherhood with worsening material deprivation, further (longitudinal) research suggests that it is the cumulative, and inherited, aspects of poverty, rather than early childbearing *per se*, which impacts most negatively on the lives of young mothers and their children (Ermisch and Pevalin, 2003; Dennison, 2004; DfES, 2005). While the strategy is officially reported as a 'model of joint working and inter-agency collaboration' (Wellings et al., 2005: 6), the results have also been described as 'disappointing' (O'Hara, 2009).

Social exclusion

Definitions of social exclusion typically incorporate structures, processes and characteristics of society as a whole, as well as the experiences of individuals within discrete communities. On account of its divisive connotations (the included majority v. the excluded minority), the term is widely regarded as 'intrinsically problematic' (Levitas, 2005: 7), although it is generally acknowledged to involve 'multi-dimensional disadvantage' (Levitas et al., 2007: 117). Macro-drivers, including demographic change, variations in the labour market and social policy directives, may aggravate individual risk factors for social exclusion, although establishing causation for social scientists is far from straightforward. Structural factors, including power, and polarisation processes whereby individuals are detached from their communities by the exclusionary practices of the socially included, contribute to 'a postindustrial social order dominated by globalizing capital and the superclass associated with that globalizing capital' (Byrne, 2005: 182). Poverty and social exclusion tend to be viewed as an 'inseparable dyad' (Levitas et al., 2007: 3), although what it means to *be* poor is extremely variable. Differences in individual circumstances, and in socio-cultural interpretations, may be considerable and, hence, the finely nuanced understandings of the term 'social exclusion' suggest that clear-cut distinctions can never be absolutely applied. An operational definition of social exclusion, which incorporates most factors described in the literature, reads thus:

> Social exclusion is a complex and multidimensional process. It involves the lack or denial of resources, rights, goods and services, and the inability to participate in the normal relationships and activities, available to the majority of people in our society, whether in

economic, social, cultural or political arenas. It affects both the quality of life of individuals and the equity and cohesion of society as a whole. (Levitas et al., 2007: 9)

The same authors describe gradations in the severity of exclusion, including that of 'deep' exclusion which is 'across more than one domain [...] resulting in severe negative consequences for quality of life, well-being and future life chances' (Levitas et al., 2007: 9). In 1999, Sure Start Local Programmes (SSLPs) were introduced into deprived neighbourhoods throughout England as a potential vehicle for reducing the social exclusion of the poorest families; by 2004 a total of 524 such schemes were in existence. Recent policy has continued to endorse the contributions these schemes make to the enhancement of children's well-being, and that of their families, and their positive value has been commented on by independent researchers in this area (Higginbottom et al., 2005; Attree, 2004). Sure Start has been described as operating on two distinct, but interrelated, levels: reducing health and socio-economic risks, and facilitating the development of supportive environments which stimulate future capacity building. The small, and some would say limited, effects of SSLPs appear to vary, however, with the degree of social deprivation: children from relatively less socially deprived families (for example, non-teenage mothers) benefit from living in SSLP communities, while children from the most socially deprived families (teenage mothers, lone parents, unemployed households) are adversely affected (Belsky et al., 2007). Criticism has been levelled at the organisational elements of local programmes which, because of their local autonomous status, are neither required to produce, nor adhere to, protocols modelled on examples of best practice (ibid.).

The Sure Start Plus (SSP) programmes, which commenced in 2001, were charged with reducing the social exclusion specifically associated with teenage pregnancy and young parenthood (the inclusion of young fathers was a central objective of SSP). A core aspect of the initiative stressed the importance of a co-ordinated, multi-agency, approach provided through the aegis of personal advisers offering one-to-one support to their young clients. Although some aspects of service delivery have achieved modest success, for example in reducing the risk of conduct disorder in preschool children, and providing crisis support for pregnant adolescents and increased educational participation for under 16-year-olds, there appears to have been little impact on maternal health-related objectives, including smoking cessation and improvements in breastfeeding rates. Most schemes also failed to attract young fathers, largely due to lack of resources and clear inclusion strategies. The fact that both the Sure Start and Sure Start Plus interventions have failed to achieve government targets, however, should not obscure the fact that both these initiatives were generally well received at a local level and most managed to avoid generating the stigmatising reputations associated with state interventions targeting poor communities, especially those with significant populations of adolescent parents. Besides, precise measurement of the 'impact' factor of these interventions was always likely to be problematic, not least because of the difficulty of disentangling the effects of the intervention from the multiple stresses this client group already experience on a regular, and on-going, basis.

Childhood poverty

The links between early parenthood, social exclusion and child poverty are well established and, while successive governments have suggested various eradication measures, it has remained firmly, and contentiously, on the policy agenda. A comparative study of child support policies in the UK and Australia reported that the UK (1991) Act was 'hugely controversial, administratively inept and essentially flawed' (Ridge, 2005: 123). Rather than it being lauded as an intervention to benefit children, particularly those who were already disadvantaged, this policy was widely perceived as a somewhat crude response to the then Conservative government's concerns about the perceived economic burden on the state caused by lone mothers, many of whom were adolescent. Speeches from successive Labour prime ministers exposed a fundamental flaw underlying policy strategy to reduce child poverty: a 'belief in the labour market as the primary agent of social inclusion' (Lister, 2002: 33), a focus which privileges paid work and incentivises welfare-to-work schemes as routes out of poverty. The repeated emphasis on employment as a route to inclusion belies the evidence that, for the most marginalised and stigmatised families (aka teenage parents), regular, paid and secure, employment is rarely an available option.

Although some overall progress has been made in reducing child poverty, the UK Labour government failed to achieve its policy objective of a 25 per cent reduction by 2004/05, and in the absence of substantial additional funds, will fall well short of targets set for 2010 (Brewer et al., 2009). The effects of the current UK/global economic recession have exacerbated the difficulties and fuelled demands for much bolder policies for the eradication of childhood poverty by 2020 (ibid.). Final legislation by the outgoing Labour government in the shape of the Child Poverty Act (2010) will set national targets and strategies (DCSF, 2010a). It is too early to know what the new coalition government will propose. Furthermore, class-related health inequalities persist and are evident in all aspects of health; the limited information available on change over time (for example as demonstrated by low birth weights, and neonatal and infant deaths) provides further evidence that inequalities are not reducing. The risk of birthing a low weight infant may be determined as early as 12 weeks of pregnancy (Bukowski et al., 2007), with economic disadvantage associated with intrauterine growth retardation (Reagan et al., 2007); these findings clearly expose the effects of poverty from the very beginning of the life cycle. Rather than age at first parenthood, then, poverty is most damaging on health and life opportunities, and unless more potent and redistributive polices are implemented, the negative effects are likely to be transmitted to, and magnified by, future generations.

Failure to achieve national targets reflects, at least in part, the legacy of existing policies which reinforce, rather than alleviate, trajectories of disadvantage (Sutherland et al., 2003). The psychological impact of being born and growing up in poor, socially excluded, communities has also been a neglected consideration in policy development. For marginalised populations, escape from poverty and social exclusion will not be easy, not least because the corrosive effects of chronic low self-esteem and a sense of hopelessness resulting from the cumulative, and intergenerational, effects of wide-ranging discrimination are deeply ingrained. Hence, presenting disenfranchised young people with new opportunities for education and training may be insufficient to convince them of the benefits of taking control over their own lives and developing the necessary skills which may provide them and their families with a more optimistic future.

Similar weaknesses may be identified in the major policy directives which have informed interventions in teenage pregnancy, social exclusion and child poverty. As I hope this book will clearly demonstrate, the prospects for the infants born of, and into, the most disadvantaged circumstances appear grim. Hence, it would be unsurprising if their future adolescent/adult identities failed to reflect this legacy – typically in the form of repeated truancy from school, an early exit from formal education, and early parental responsibilities in the absence of stable relationships and failure to locate meaningful and secure employment. It is these continuities in disadvantage which remain most intractable and which, therefore, present the biggest challenges to politicians and those charged with generating social policy initiatives.

In the next chapter I introduce the teenagers, and some of their mothers and boyfriends. In so doing I wish to acknowledge their multiple and generous contributions, without which this book could not have happened. I hope I have managed to interpret and re-present their sometimes painful and distressing life stories with sufficient insight and sensitivity. The Wales-based cohort is listed first (in alphabetical order), followed by the South Yorkshire cohort, with whom I had substantially more contact.

2
Introducing the Teenagers and their Significant Others

The Wales-based cohort

Alys

Alys was aged 15 at recruitment and 20 weeks pregnant with her first baby boy (Aled) who weighed 8lb (3.6kg) at birth; he was formula-fed. For the duration of the study period Alys lived in the family home with her widowed mother (Angharad), two older brothers and the family's elderly dog; her eldest brother lived locally with his girlfriend. They were a close-knit bilingual (Welsh–English) family; the household income was benefit derived and the home rented from the council. Alys's father had died suddenly 18 months prior to her becoming pregnant, and although she had been doing well at school and was expected to go on to higher education, Alys lost interest in her studies and began truanting; she left school without completing her final year. Alys smoked and occasionally drank alcohol but had never experimented with 'recreational' drugs. Her boyfriend Dave (19 years) lived in rented accommodation 20 miles away, close to the factory where he worked full-time. The young couple spent weekends together and were saving to buy their own home. Angharad assisted her daughter with childcare, especially at weekends; Alys wanted to become a physiotherapist and intended to resume her studies as soon as Aled started nursery. Alys and Angharad contributed two joint interviews to the study: one prior to birth and another when the baby was two years old.

April

April was aged 17 at recruitment when she was 10 weeks pregnant with her second baby; her daughter was nine months old. April was adopted at birth by grandparents; her grandfather, to whom she was very attached, died a few weeks before the research interview. She had intermittent contact with her mother, who lived locally but with whom she frequently argued; her mother did not participate in the study. April lived with her daughter and dog in council-rented accommodation which was in poor condition; many of the windows were boarded up and damp-related mould was visible on the living room walls. Household income was benefit derived, supplemented by occasional sex work. April smoked heavily, and prior to the birth of her first child she also consumed large volumes of alcohol; she had never taken 'recreational' drugs. She was estranged from her boyfriend (who had fathered both babies) on account of a violent incident during which he broke her nose. April contributed a one-off interview which followed on from my observations of her home-based 'booking' visit with a community midwife; labour and birth details are unknown.

Beca

Beca was 17 years old and 14 weeks pregnant with her first baby at recruitment; she had terminated a previous pregnancy. Beca was the youngest of three children; she lived at home in owner-occupied accommodation with both parents and an older brother; they were a close-knit family and were all bilingual (Welsh–English). She enjoyed a warm and affectionate relationship with her mother (Glenys); her boyfriend (Andrew) was ten years her senior and her former boss. Both Beca and Andrew smoked heavily. A serious car crash in her early teens, which had killed a younger sister, left Beca with constant lower back pain from spinal injuries; medical staff had advised that a caesarean section might be required to deliver her baby. Beca contributed a one-off interview which followed on from my observation of her hospital-based booking consultation with a midwife; labour and birth details are unknown.

Bronwyn

Aged 16 when she conceived, Bronwyn was the only teenager who stated her pregnancy was planned. She and her boyfriend (Michael) lived together in privately rented accommodation owned by Bronwyn's father; they had initiated a 'pre-booking' consultation with a community midwife when Bronwyn was seven weeks pregnant to discuss possible lifestyle changes they could make to optimise pregnancy outcomes. Bronwyn and Michael left school after passing their GCSEs (school-leaving exams); both were in full-time employment. The young couple contributed a one-off joint interview which followed my observation of their 'pre-booking' consultation with a community midwife; labour and birth details are unknown.

Catrin

Catrin was 18 years old and 16 weeks pregnant at recruitment. A political refugee who had been living in the UK for ten years, Catrin had recently been discharged from the 'care' system and was living in a single-person, supported-housing complex at the time of interview. Apart from her younger sister, also a refugee living locally with foster parents, Catrin had no contact with other family members. Catrin's parents had separated following her birth; she last saw her alcoholic mother when she was eight years old. She had not revisited her country of origin since leaving, although she hoped to return when her baby was old enough to travel; English was her second language. Catrin made contact with me after reading an information sheet about the study; she contributed a one-off interview when she was 16 weeks pregnant. Labour and birth details are unknown.

Elenor

Elenor was 16 years old and 23 weeks pregnant when she joined the study, having been referred by another participant; she had previously miscarried a baby from a different partner. She had no contact with the father of this baby as he 'took off' after she disclosed her pregnancy and refused to have the abortion he had apparently demanded. The youngest of seven girls, Elenor lived at home in owner-occupied accommodation with her parents and two older sisters. She left school at 15 with no qualifications and at the time of my study was working full-time in a local fast-food outlet. She contributed a one-off interview when she was 23 weeks pregnant. Labour and birth details are unknown.

Lowri

Aged 15 at conception, Lowri was the youngest of four children all of whom were of mixed-race parentage. Her parents divorced shortly after her birth and she had no further contact with her biological father. Lowri had a 'steady' boyfriend with whom she lived in privately rented accommodation; both were in full-time employment, Lowri as a trainee chef in a local hotel. Dilys, Lowri's mother, was pregnant at the same time as her daughter; she was 20 weeks pregnant at the time of the research interview which took place a few weeks following the sudden and unexpected intrauterine death of Lowri's baby daughter at 33 weeks gestation. Lowri and Dilys self-referred themselves to the study after hearing about it through a community midwife; they contributed a joint, one-off interview.

Luci

Aged 16 when she conceived, Luci was the younger of two children. An early ultrasound scan revealed a twin pregnancy; a subsequent scan at 14 weeks of pregnancy revealed that one baby had died. Luci's parents had divorced many years previously; she had no contact with her biological father. She lived in owner-occupied accommodation with her mother (Elain), her boyfriend Gavin, aged 19, and her mother's fiancé (who was Gavin's father). Luci attained four GCSEs (school-leaving exams) before she left school. Her plans to start a hairdressing apprenticeship at her local college were put on hold when she realised she was pregnant; Gavin was in full-time employment as an apprentice engine fitter. Elain, a nurse, worked full time. Luci, Elain and Gavin contributed a one-off interview to the study when Luci was 15 weeks pregnant. This followed on from my observation of her home-based 'booking' interview with a community midwife. Labour and birth details are unknown.

Megan

Aged 14 at conception, Megan was the oldest of three children. She was attending school when pregnancy was confirmed and she continued with her schooling until the baby was due. She lived in owner-occupied accommodation with her parents and siblings. Her relationship with John, her boyfriend and father of her baby, preceded pregnancy by 18 months; they had both attended the same school. Megan and her mother, Anwen, were referred to the study by a community midwife; they contributed a one-off, joint interview when Megan was 36 weeks pregnant. Labour and birth details are unknown.

Nia

Aged 17 at conception, Nia was living in privately rented accommodation with her student boyfriend, Tim (aged 20), in a town some distance from her home town and her parents. Nia was in her first term at university when she realised she was pregnant; she subsequently underwent an elective caesarean section for a breech presentation. Nia self-referred to the study after receiving information from a health visitor. She contributed a one-off interview six weeks following the birth of her son.

Rhian

Aged 15 at conception and attending school when she conceived, Rhian passed ten GCSEs (school-leaving exams) in late pregnancy. She continued to live in the council-rented family home with her parents and four younger siblings. Rhian and her boyfriend, Lewis, had been 'going steady' for two years prior to pregnancy. Lewis lived with his family 20 miles away and visited frequently, often staying overnight; the young couple shared the same bed in Rhian's house but in Lewis's home they were required to sleep separately. Rhian contributed a one-off interview to the study when she was 37 weeks pregnant. This followed on from my observation of a 'birth plan' visit in her home with a community midwife. Labour and birth details are unknown.

The South Yorkshire cohort

Clare and Chris, her mother

Clare was 14 years of age and 38 weeks pregnant at recruitment; she was the only 'late booker' in the study. Her daughter Chloe weighed 8lb 3oz (3.71kg) at birth; she was breastfed for the first ten days then formula-fed. Clare was living at home and preparing for her mock school-leaving exams when she became pregnant. She was the middle daughter and shared the all-female family home with her mother (Chris) and her two sisters, the oldest of whom, Laura, also became a teenage mother during the course of my study. Clare did not smoke nor 'do' drugs; she rarely consumed alcohol and had never been drunk. During pregnancy Clare had no contact with Carl, aged 16 and the father of her baby, but she started seeing him again after Chloe's birth; Carl and Clare had attended the same school. He lived with his grandmother and had little contact with either of his parents or his siblings. Despite having a part-time job Carl did not contribute financially to Chloe's upkeep and neither did he provide childcare; Chris disliked him.

Chris, aged 39, had not been in a relationship since she divorced her alcoholic husband eight years previously. He lived locally and visited regularly but made no financial contribution to the household; Chris periodically banned him from the family home because of his alcohol-induced violence. Both maternal and paternal grandparents lived locally and maintained regular contact with the family; the households took it in turn to cook and eat a traditional Sunday lunch together. Her only two brothers had died six months after her divorce and within six months of each other: one from suicide and the other from a brain tumour. Chris, who had her first child at age 20, had not been in paid employment since a brief period of work experience following school; the household income was benefit derived. Chris had debts of around £5K (approx. US$7580) and was in arrears with her mortgage repayments.

At the close of the study, Clare, who continued to live at home, had gained seven GCSEs (school-leaving exams) and was in full-time secretarial work with a local firm who had agreed to pay her one-day/week release for college study (business and administration skills). She paid rent and childcare to her mother and had £160 (approx. US$242) in savings. Clare and Carl were saving to buy a home although Carl's life was in disarray. He had failed his plasterer's apprenticeship exams, he owed £700 (approx. US$1000), had been drinking excessively and was smoking more heavily. He was pressuring Clare to give up work which he considered 'demeaning'; Clare thought he was 'depressed'. Chris continued to dislike him.

Clare's older sister Laura followed the female pattern of teenage childbearing and had a child with an extremely violent and abusive young man. Chris had threatened to involve social services with a view to having her grandson removed from Laura's care and adopting him herself.

Clare joined my study when she was 38 weeks pregnant; her daughter was almost two years old when it concluded. Throughout the study period I made a total of 34 contact visits, which included a mixture of observation sessions, telephone calls, text messages, social outings and formal interviews.

Jade and Bev, her 'dream' mother

Jade was 16 years old and 16 weeks pregnant with her first child when she joined my study. Her first daughter, Janey, weighed 6lb 12oz (3.06kg) and was breastfed for the first 12 days; her second daughter, Gemma, weighed 8lb 14oz (4.03kg) and was bottle-fed from birth. Jade was the younger of two girls; her older sister, Josie, had become a teenage mother three years earlier at age 15. The close relationship she had previously enjoyed with her sister ended when Josie started an affair with Jade's (then) boyfriend, Tom.

Jade was made homeless by her mother early in her first pregnancy – just before her GCSE (school-leaving) exams. She was rehoused in 'temporary' hostel accommodation and remained there until after the birth of her second child. Both Jade's children were fathered by different older men: Janey by 25-year-old Jack, whom she had known for six months, and Gemma by Tom, a 32-year-old co-resident in the hostel who had previously fathered seven children in three different relationships. Jade suffered physical and sexual abuse from the father of her first baby and began self-harming (cutting and burning and restrictive eating) when this relationship ended. She was a heavy smoker but did not 'do' recreational drugs. Prior to motherhood she had engaged in regular binge-drinking episodes, especially at weekends when she drank to get 'plastered'.

Jade's parents lived together; her father was 20 years older than her mother (who was aged 55). Jade had no contact with her mother throughout both pregnancies and only intermittent contact with her father. Following Jade's request, I did not invite her mother to participate. Bev, the owner of the hostel, assumed a surrogate parental role in relation to Jade, who initially referred to her as her 'dream' mother. Bev was one of five daughters but had no children of her own. She supported Jade through the labours and births of both her daughters; these were Bev's first experiences of childbirth.

At the close of the study Jade was living with her older daughter in squalid (council) rented accommodation; she was in arrears with her rent and had outstanding debts of £600 (approx. US$900). Her younger daughter, Gemma, was living with her sister and Tom (her ex-boyfriend and Gemma's father). Household income was benefit derived and at my final visit the electricity and phone had been disconnected because of payment arrears. The previous day Jade had been visited by an officer from the Child Support Agency who had threatened to deduct 40 per cent from her benefits if she continued to withhold details about the father of her first child.

Jade's elder daughter, Janey, was 18 months old, and her younger daughter, Gemma, was four months old, when my study concluded. Throughout the study period I made a total of 48 contact visits, which included a mixture of observation sessions, telephone calls, text messages, social outings and formal interviews.

Lou and Pete, her boyfriend

Lou was aged 16 and living at home with Pete, her mother, one of her mother's (violent) partners and two younger siblings when she became pregnant. She had miscarried an earlier pregnancy (also to Pete) at the age of 14. Lou was one of a large family including four siblings and five step-siblings; she frequently mentioned the existence of other siblings whom she had never met. Lou's mother was registered mentally disabled and had been hospitalised for extended periods; she had also served time in a secure unit for the attempted murder of Lou's youngest sister. From an early age Lou had endured physical and sexual abuse from a number of male perpetrators, including her mother's numerous boyfriends; at Lou's request I did not invite her mother to participate in the study. As a result of regular interventions by social services, Lou had lived with foster-parents and in care homes for extended periods of her life; she had regular contact with her biological father who lived locally.

Lou and Pete had been in a relationship for five years prior to pregnancy. Both were heavy smokers (30/day each) and although Lou reduced her intake during pregnancy, she continued to smoke throughout. Lou was on medication for depression, asthma, back pain and recurrent chest infections. She had a history of self-harming (overdoses and cutting) and she had suffered sexual and physical abuse from Pete on a number of occasions. Pete, who had three younger brothers, had also spent time in foster care because of parental violence. His parents lived locally and the young couple moved in with them when they had no alternative accommodation. Lou experienced Pete's mother as domineering and manipulative but she was also reliant on her for companionship and childcare.

Both Lou and Pete had left school without completing their final year; both had missed considerable amounts of schooling through truanting. At the conclusion of the study period, Lou and Pete were living in poor-quality, council-rented accommodation next door to Pete's parents. Although Pete had signed up for a number of government-funded, back-to-work schemes, he had yet to complete a training course. The family income was mostly benefit derived, supplemented by occasional cash payments, including some resulting from petty thefts and small-scale burglaries; the young couple were £200 (approx. US$300) in debt.

Lou was 12 weeks pregnant when she was recruited to the study; her daughter was 16 months old when the study concluded. Throughout the study period I made a total of 52 contact visits, which included a mixture of observation sessions, telephone calls, text messages, social outings and formal interviews.

Michelle and Polly, her mother

The youngest of four children, Michelle lived at home and was preparing for her GCSEs (school-leaving exams) when she became pregnant. Michelle continued her education during pregnancy, obtaining nine GCSEs, plus certificates in business studies and IT. She had intended to undertake a nursing degree but put this aside after she was 'talent spotted' by a local modelling agency and subsequently signed up to work as a fashion model doing European tours and earning upwards of £200/day (approx. US$300) plus expenses. Immediately prior to recruitment, Michelle's beloved horse had been put down after being savaged by another horse. Michelle, who was riding the horse at the time, narrowly escaped serious injury. She had stopped riding and was still recovering from the shock when she discovered she was pregnant. Six months after her son Daniel's birth, her maternal grandmother, to whom she was very close, died suddenly.

Polly was the only mother in the South Yorkshire cohort who had continued to live with her husband, the same man who had fathered all four of her children. In addition to Michelle's son, she also often looked after her eldest daughter's two young girls. Although life had been very difficult since her husband had been declared bankrupt the previous year, Polly was a gritty and determined woman; it was only on account of her canny manoeuvring that the family home had not been sold to pay off outstanding debts. Polly had suffered with depression since the birth of her first child and periodically visited her GP to request further medication. She had never been engaged in paid work outside the home although she had cared for her mother prior to her recent death. Polly was someone I thought of as a homemaker: she took enormous pride in having things 'just so'. Whenever I called there were usually home-made biscuits in the tin and often fresh flowers on the table; the house was always extremely clean and tidy. Although all her children had now left home, they lived locally and every Sunday returned home with their partners and children to enjoy the Sunday dinner which Polly continued to cook. Towards the end of the study Polly's husband found another job and she was looking forward to feeling less stressed and being less financially cautious than she had been in the recent past.

At the close of the study Michelle and her boyfriend Ryan were living in owner-occupied accommodation close to her mother's house. Ryan, aged 19, worked locally in a warehouse. One of eight children (fathered by three different men), Ryan was prone to violent outbursts and on a number of occasions had attacked Michelle, causing injuries which warranted hospital admission and/or surgery. Michelle initially refused to press charges against him but eventually changed her mind after she was badly beaten while on honeymoon. Ryan was subsequently convicted of grievous bodily harm and received a custodial sentence.

Michelle was 17 weeks pregnant when she was recruited to the study; her son Daniel was 16 months old when the study concluded. Throughout the study period I made a total of 35 contact visits, which included a mixture of observation sessions, telephone calls, text messages, social outings and formal interviews.

Susan and Marg, her mother

Susan, aged 15, was living at home with her mother and stepfather (whom she disliked) and attending school when she conceived. Although she managed to pass nine GCSEs (school-leaving exams), she was forced to delay starting her hairdressing course because the local college crèche did not admit children under two years old and she had no alternative childcare as her mother was in full-time employment.

The younger of two girls, Susan also had a stepsister the same age whom she described as 'my best friend'. Her older (by nine years) married sister, who had also been a teenage mother, lived locally and visited daily. Susan had been closely involved with caring for her two nieces since their births and expressed few worries about her ability to cope with the practical aspects of caring for her own newborn infant. Susan's maternal and paternal grandparents and her biological father also lived locally; she had regular contact with her grandparents and occasional contact with her father.

Marg, who had also been a teenage mother, differed from the other mothers in the study in that she had been in paid employment most of her adult life; she often succumbed to pressures to resolve debts for other family members. Although her current post – managing a local nursing home – was reasonably well paid and fairly secure, Marg worked long and unsocial hours; the demands of her job, and her refusal to take holidays, were a constant source of friction between her and her partner. She was the most financially solvent of all the mothers and hence enjoyed a reasonably comfortable lifestyle.

Susan's boyfriend, Joe, was in full-time employment in a local garage. The second oldest of four boys, he lived at home with his parents and brothers. He and Susan had been dating for eight months prior to pregnancy and moved into rented accommodation together shortly after the birth of their son, Jed.

At the close of the study Susan and Joe had purchased their own house, on the same street as Susan's parents. The mortgage (just under £300/month = approx. US$450) was considerably less than the rent (just over £400/month = approx. US$600) they had been paying.

Susan was 16 weeks pregnant when she was recruited to the study; her son Jed was 11 months old when the study concluded. Throughout the study period I made a total of 33 contact visits, which included a mixture of observation sessions, telephone calls, text messages, social outings and formal interviews.

Tracey and Jasmine, her mother

When she became pregnant with her first son at the age of 14, Tracey was in her GCSE (leaving) year at school and had been going out with Luke, her boyfriend (age 17), for eight months. A midwife confided that Tracey's pregnancy was initially thought to have resulted from rape by one of her mother's many boyfriends, although DNA testing subsequently confirmed Luke's paternity. Tracey lived in the family, council-rented, two-bedroom home with her mother (Jasmine) and two younger step-siblings for whom she was primarily responsible. Following the violent death of a younger sibling in suspicious circumstances Tracey was removed from home and registered with social services; she subsequently transited a number of care/foster homes where she was exposed to significant emotional and physical abuse. She had been hospitalised on a number of occasions for vague symptoms including 'abdominal pain' and 'headaches'; however, with the exception of positive results for a number of sexually transmitted infections, all other investigations proved negative.

Jasmine, also a teen mother and one of 12 children, was abandoned by her alcoholic mother shortly after she was born. Throughout her formative years she lived in a series of foster and care homes where she was periodically subjected to sexual abuse and emotional cruelty. Her first child, born when she was just 17, was removed by social services and placed for adoption. Jasmine subsequently had four more children by three different fathers. Her oldest daughter was addicted to crack cocaine and lived on the streets, surviving by prostitution, petty crime and drug dealing. Jasmine had finally banned her from the house after she discovered that she was servicing clients in her bedroom. Over the course of my research Jasmine had a number of boyfriends who not infrequently moved into the family home. Sometimes they brought their own children with them and this created considerable tensions, not least because it resulted in severe overcrowding and additional pressures on scarce resources. Jasmine displayed a somewhat ambivalent attitude towards her children and regularly left the younger ones in Tracey's care – a practice which had started when Tracey herself was still a relatively young child. Towards the end of my study Jasmine secured a part-time job which had followed on from voluntary work; she was in considerable debt and lived in terror of having her home repossessed and the family being made homeless.

Luke was registered disabled on account of long-standing mental health problems for which three possible scenarios had been advanced: that he was born with severe foetal alcohol syndrome; that as a small child he accidentally overdosed on 'recreational' drugs left on a bench in his mother's house; that he became heroin addicted himself and started having seizures following an accidental overdose. Luke, one of three siblings and an unknown number of step-siblings, was a 'cared-for' child until the age of ten when he was reunited with his drug-rehabilitated birth mother who now lived locally. She offered tremendous support to the young couple and greatly assisted their adjustment to parenthood. Tracey declared that she had never taken drugs and neither did she drink or smoke; she frequently stated that she 'hated' her sister for the 'bad name' she had bequeathed the family. Tracey was recruited to my study when she was nine weeks pregnant with her first son, Josh. Her second son, Ricky, was six days old when I completed data collection. Throughout the study period I made a total of 61 contact visits, which included a mixture of observation sessions, telephone calls, text messages, social outings and formal interviews.

The following chapters (Chapters 3–8) draw on my empirical research and include text in the form of verbatim, but anonymised, quotations derived from interview transcripts and field notes. Where text has been removed for the purpose of condensing a quotation, this is indicated: [...]. Throughout the text, participants from Wales are indicated (W); those from South Yorkshire (SY).

In Chapter 3 I describe the teenagers' accounts of the events which preceded pregnancy, who they selected to tell and what responses they received. In so doing I make reference to mother–daughter/family relationships, male partners and kinship networks, sexual health knowledge and sources of information, and interactions with maternity staff. Teenagers' and their mothers' views on, and knowledge about, abortion are also discussed. I conclude the chapter with a brief discussion on family dynamics, with a particular focus on interactions with, and between, the teenagers' families.

3
How it Happened: Pregnancy Realisation and Disclosure

With the exceptions of Catrin and Elenor, all the teenagers had boyfriends with whom they sometimes had sex; most claimed to be in a 'love relationship' at the time of conception. Although the duration of relationships varied, the majority reported they were 'courting' or 'going steady' for only a few months prior to conceiving. Lou and Pete were the exception, having been in a relationship for almost six years and living together for most of that period. Bronwyn was alone in stating from the outset that her pregnancy was planned, but she nonetheless reported being surprised when she 'fell' during the menstrual cycle after she ceased using oral contraception.

Doing sex, becoming pregnant: teenage girls, eroticism and romance

> [Falling in love was] an extraordinary self-awakening, especially if you have a romantic temperament [...] [Teenage sex] was so exciting, and without any of the baggage that comes later. It was connected with animal desire, which girls lose quickly. They're just as likely to want sex for its own sake but get tricked out of it. (Winterson, 2004)

Teenager's self-reported references to being 'on the pill' were often a euphemism for engaging in sexual intercourse although, as Rhian explains, this was usually within an established relationship:

> I was on the pill for about a year before I got pregnant. It wasn't like, oh, I just had sex for the first time and then I got pregnant. I had sex for quite a long time before I fell. (Rhian, 15 years old; 37 weeks pregnant. W)

Although I did not explicitly ask the teenagers to describe their sexual experiences in any depth, we did talk about first sexual encounters and the sex which had immediately preceded pregnancy: the story of 'how it happened'. With some of the teenagers I was able to engage in 'sex talk' more easily than with others, perhaps because I am too easily embarrassed. Discussing this issue with Alys and her mother was exceptional, in that the conversation felt relaxed and unconstrained, which seemed to mirror the relationship between them. Unlike the other teenagers, Alys was a confident communicator who initiated conversation on a range of sensitive topics which others avoided, especially in front of their mothers.

HS: What was that [first experience of intercourse] like?
Alys: Mmm. It wasn't very nice at all. I was petrified.
Mother: Oh, she said it was awful. She came crying to me the first time. [...] We sat here in the kitchen next day and she cried it out all over me. We laugh about it now though don't we? *Both laugh.*
HS: Can you remember what you were expecting?
Alys: I think I expected it to hurt [...] Everybody said that for girls it hurts. But really it was crap. I mean it was really really crap. *Laughs.*
HS: In what way?
Alys: Oh he just wanted to get straight inside me. It was all over in two seconds. I was like, Oh, is that it then? I didn't feel anything. It didn't even really hurt. Now looking back I don't know why I was so upset about it.
HS: Did the sex get any better with that boyfriend?
Alys: No. No not with him it didn't. [...] But it was much better with [current boyfriend]. Not giving him a big head or anything, but it was really a lot better. I was more best friends with him. [...] I was going out with him for three months before I'd even thought about sleeping with him.
HS: And he didn't pressure you?
Alys: No, he didn't. Not like the other one. (Alys, now 17 years old; son aged two years. W)

That teenage girls experience sex, especially for the first time, as 'crap' is not altogether unexpected; that Alys anticipated it would also be painful suggests a need for further research.

Considerable tensions were evident in some mother–daughter relationships particularly regarding whether, and how, girls negotiated a sexual identity within the family setting, and the (un)suitability of boyfriends. Individual capacity to 'weather' the associated pressures significantly influenced the degree to which daughters trusted, and confided in, their mothers:

> Since I hit my teens I haven't really gotten on with my mum. I don't sit down and talk to her if I've got a problem anymore. (Susan, 15 years old; 30 weeks pregnant. SY)

> Some things I just wouldn't ever tell my mum. Like with this new boyfriend [father of her baby] I knew she wouldn't like him so there were no point in asking her opinion. She hasn't liked any of my boyfriends. Not really. That was when we stopped being so close. When I started going out with boys. (Clare, 14 years old; 30 weeks pregnant. SY)

In my conversations with mothers, it seemed that daughters' attempts to lay claim to a sexual identity were often problematic for all family members, especially for males. This is perhaps not surprising, as overt expressions of female sexuality, especially in early adolescence, are often denied the legitimacy afforded to adolescent boys, and this creates particular difficulties for girls wishing to 'do' sex. For a more in-depth discussion of adolescent female desire, see Michelle Fine (1988) and Deborah Tolman (1994). Accounts of Sex and Relationships Education (SRE) in the schools attended by the teenagers revealed that these sessions – 'about boring biology' – had failed to equip them with the necessary skills to negotiate the timing of, and the location for, sex, and many had not acquired the assertiveness they needed to discuss contraception. The ongoing inadequacies and inequities of UK school-based and school-linked SRE are described in a recent systematic review of service provision in this area (Owen et al., 2010).

The 'technologies' (Stewart, 1999: 375) governing the reputations of teenage girls are intricate and complex but it seemed to me that those participating in this study positioned themselves, and were positioned by others, as (hetero)sexual subjects in oppositional ways: as defiant and confrontational characters who earned themselves reputations as 'slags', 'sluts', or 'girls who'll go with anyone', or in Wales, as 'sad mongs' (mongols) because their sexual explorations were mostly conducted furtively and secretively (if at all). None of these identities helped the teenagers to discover what pleasured them, before they were expected to be proficient in pleasuring others.

Almost all the teenagers were living at home and/or attending school when they first started their sexual explorations, and most reported that their sex lives were constrained by pressures which reflected the spatial and temporal characteristics of domestic spaces:

HS: Before you actually fell pregnant had you been having a lot of sex with Carl or was it just like now and again?
Clare: It were quite a bit I'd say. *Laughs.* Yeah, a fair bit, weekends mainly. That were only time we could get by ourselves. (Clare, 14 years old; daughter aged nine days. SY)

Most of the teenagers lived in crowded homes where any degree of privacy was rarely possible. Shared bedrooms were the norm and a few shared beds with younger siblings; one young woman rotated between the floor and a sofa when bed space was unavailable. Sex, then, was perforce often in haste, with little time for romantic prelude; it is possible that time pressures were such that persuading (inexperienced) young men to don a condom reduced the already restricted opportunities for erotic pleasure. It is also understandable that even if they possessed the necessary negotiation skills, adolescents (like many adults?) might nonetheless choose immediate sexual gratification rather than spend precious time apportioning responsibility for contraception use.

That's life, accidents happen: sex, pregnancy and contraception

Most teenagers initially reported that pregnancy was 'an accident', that it 'just happened' and was unplanned and unexpected. This was in contrast to the attitudes they perceived midwives to hold:

I think they [midwives] just think I've gone out and done it on purpose [...] I didn't do it on purpose. It was an accident. Just like anyone can have an accident and not mean to get pregnant. (Lowri, 16 years old; three weeks after the stillbirth of her daughter. W)

Although pregnant teenagers are no longer punished 'in the old and cruel sense of the word' (Arney and Bergen, 1984: 17), for example by being dispatched to homes for unwed mothers or forced to relinquish their babies for adoption, they are nonetheless disciplined. The moral discourses within which teenage pregnancy is framed in Western societies identify female sexual desire that is acted on 'inappropriately' as transgressive and in need of correction. Health professionals play important roles in shaping these discourses and, indeed, many of the teenagers reported that interactions with maternity staff left them feeling humiliated and infantilised, and occasionally sexually harassed. Such attitudes are detrimental, and indeed potentially harmful, to adolescent females because they reinforce the perception of 'error in the *proper* timing and location of (their) sexual desire' (Arney and Bergen, 1984: 17; emphasis added). Assumptions that pregnancy necessarily results from consensual sex may also prevent midwives from exploring other possible scenarios, including rape, incest and prostitution, which arguably impact rather more negatively on the health and well-being of teenage girls.

Official explanations for teen pregnancy suggest it results from failure to use contraception (effectively) or failure of a chosen contraceptive method. One feminist academic, however, interpreted her personal experience of teenage pregnancy in terms of 'body betrayal [...] the body that began this whole nonsense by conceiving without consent' (Pietsch, 2002: 5). Literary accounts of 'clever' girls who nonetheless become pregnant confirm that teenagers are not necessarily protected by superior intellect. Sex happens and when it happens the experience may be uncontrollable and uncontainable, as the late Lorna Sage – formerly Professor of English at the University of East Anglia – attested when describing her first experience of teenage sex (which resulted in pregnancy):

> It's a hot, bright afternoon summer [...] we are trying to get inside each other's skins, but without taking our clothes off, and the parts that touch are swaddled in stringy rucked-up shirts, jeans, pants. There are no leisurely caresses, no long looks, it's a bruising kind of bliss mostly made of aches. [...] we're dissolving, eyes half shut, holding each other's hands at arm's length, crucified on each other, butting and squirming. Our kisses are like mouth-to-mouth resuscitation – you'd think we were dying it's so urgent, this childish mathematics of two into one won't go. (Sage, 2001: 234–5)

Accounts of the erotic, and sometimes humorous, nature of teenage sexuality are uncommon in scholarly writings and academic publications. Conventional narratives tend to locate teenage pregnancy as a matter of individual choice, although, in reality, when certain choices are acted upon they tend to be (re)constructed as personal pathologies. Hence, 'failure' to comply with the dominant (middle-class) paradigm – which emphasises industriousness, discretion and prudence – tends to cast working-class teenagers as deviant and in need of correctional strategies (Wilson and Huntington, 2006). Reiterating existing research (Tripp and Viner, 2005) on adolescent patterns of contraceptive knowledge and use, all the teenagers were aware that contraception was available and most reported using it, albeit not always consistently or appropriately:

> We'd been together for nearly a year. [...] Mostly we used condoms but sometimes we didn't. [...] We knew it were a bit risky but you think, Oh we'll be all right. *Laughs.* (Clare, 14 years old; daughter aged nine days. SY)

Many of the teenagers admitted taking some sexual risks. Corporeal risk-taking is normal behaviour during adolescence, however, as this is a time when physiological changes transform, and re-transform, the body into a site of unpredictable 'otherness'; this is a period in the lifespan when desires are intensely felt and appetites least resistant to restraint and moderation. Using the body as a vehicle for risk-taking is not uncommon during this time and, indeed, drug and alcohol experimentation, and the induction of extreme physical states through a variety of sport and 'leisure' activities, have been documented (Bloustein, 2003). With specific regard to teenage pregnancy, sexual risk-taking has been noted as more prevalent in areas of social deprivation (SEU, 1999). Sexual risk-taking – as suggested by non-, or irregular, use of contraception – should not necessarily be regarded as actively seeking pregnancy, however, as various factors militated against teenagers in this study accessing reliable information and suitable contraception. In this respect, my research confirmed earlier findings (Free et al., 2002; SEU, 1999), namely: inaccessible family planning facilities which were not open 'after hours'; negative attitudes from health professionals; fear of parental disapproval; lack of confidentiality; a belief in personal or a partner's infertility; and a reduced sense of personal vulnerability.

In keeping with previous research (Dudgeon and Inhorn, 2004), the teenage girls in this study tended to assume responsibility for providing contraception, for ensuring its continued use and for deciding 'how far you go'. This reaffirms the widely held belief that pregnancy is 'a risk that boys were not responsible for' (Chambers et al., 2004: 401). Teenagers using contraception cited burst condoms and oral contraceptive failure as the most common reasons for pregnancy; delayed withdrawal and not using contraception '*properly*' were additional factors. As Clare reports in the following quotation, however, teenagers were not necessarily aware when mishaps with contraception occurred and were therefore not well positioned to take remedial action, even when they knew emergency birth control (EBC) was available:

HS: Did you think about getting emergency contraception?

Clare: Yeah well I would have done but I didn't know it [condom] burst, did I?

HS: How did you figure out it had burst?

Clare: Well 'cos [boyfriend] told me about six days later. [...] It were too late to do owt then.

HS: Why do you think he didn't tell you at the time?

Clare: I dunno. [...] He were scared as well 'cos I were only 14, like.

HS: And when he told you six days later, what did you do then?

Clare: I didn't really think nowt about it to be honest. I didn't think, Oh my God, I could be pregnant. It sounds stupid now, but at time I weren't really thinking about it. I were just blanking it out, I think. (Clare, 14 years old; 38 weeks pregnant. SY)

Clare was not alone in volunteering that she was somewhat preoccupied when she first realised she might be pregnant. While 'blanking' may be interpreted as a psychological defence, or disassociative, mechanism, it appeared to serve Clare as an effective coping mechanism, protecting her from attempting to engage in rational discourse at a time when she felt very mentally and emotionally confused.

With the exceptions of Jade and April, all the teenagers agreed that intercourse resulting in conception had been consensual. However, as the research proceeded, conception stories were sometimes re-presented in such a way as to suggest that events leading up to pregnancy were rather different than had originally been described. For example, Michelle was initially adamant that she and her boyfriend Ryan 'always' used condoms and that pregnancy had resulted from a burst condom. When her baby was six months old, however, she confided that 'Well, sometimes he were [wearing a condom] but that time he wouldn't and it were just that one time but one time's enough isn't it?' Alys also offered an alternative explanation to that which she had originally proposed: that she forgot to take her oral contraceptive pill when she went away on a school trip where, in fact, she had run out of supplies and had left it too late to obtain a repeat prescription. And Susan later confided that she had planned the pregnancy and had 'tricked' her boyfriend into believing she was taking her oral contraception as prescribed.

The midwives I observed and/or interviewed mostly concurred with the premise that adolescents, especially those at the lower end of the age range, do not generally deliberately engineer pregnancy. That said, some midwives were acutely aware of the harrowing home circumstances endured by selected clients and empathised with their attempts to use motherhood as a means to create better lives for themselves:

> The practice nurse was telling me she had a youngster in the surgery recently who said she was planning to get pregnant so she could leave her dreadful home conditions and get her own flat. It's very sad. She's only 13. I know the family and to be honest I can't blame her for wanting to get as far away from them as possible. (Community midwife Lisbert. SY)

Manipulating the system to improve one's personal circumstances is not new, especially in Western societies where dependency is viewed as anathema and the relationship between poverty and inequality is very evident, so the negative association between welfare and dependency has similarly become more pronounced. Indeed, both issues tend to be conflated in current discourses such that – at least in the public imagination – the notion of dependency appears to be singularly applied to lone mothers who, if only they applied themselves, could also better themselves.

Welfare dependency is widely seen as a social problem because it is understood to undermine the drive to self-sufficiency, is corrosive of self-esteem, is stigmatising, isolating and generative of an underclass group of marginalised citizens. Most of all, dependency is portrayed as a problem of *individuals*. In their genealogical analysis of dependency, however, Nancy Fraser and Linda Gordon (1994) have argued that the assumptions and connotations currently applied simply privilege dominant social groups at the expense of those who are subordinate, and that it is the *relentlessness* of such conditions which renders people disenfranchised and feeling useless.

Disclosure stories: responses from significant others

Many of the teenagers reported having rehearsed disclosure scenarios a number of times before they enacted them, but, despite rehearsals, some failed in their first attempt. The time between pregnancy confirmation and disclosure varied, although the majority of teenagers waited only a few days, or at most a few weeks, before confiding in someone, usually a boyfriend or mother. In addition to recognising that pregnancy was something of a calamity, the 'WOW' factor was also clearly evident in some accounts; for these teenagers the absence of a congratulatory response from significant others was lamented. Health professionals were identified as the group least likely to recognise pregnancy as a positive, exciting and life-affirming event:

> I felt stupid but I also felt, like, Wow, this big thing had happened and I was pregnant. That part was really exciting but they [health professionals] didn't want to know that. But I had my mam and [boyfriend] for that. I was lucky I had them for that. (Alys, 15 years old; 30 weeks pregnant. W)

Positive feelings towards being pregnant may, at least in part, be accounted for by the teenagers' relative lack of personal agency and their restricted opportunities for engaging in occupations other than motherhood: 'the less social status women have in public in terms of work, the more likely they are to feel that pregnancy confers status' (Coward, 1992: 49).

Teenagers' mothers frequently assumed the role of envoy in transmitting news of the pregnancy to others. Most intimated that this was a delicate and difficult task which required considerable skill in managing the conflicting, and often volatile, feelings from immediate family members and close relatives. The majority of the teenagers admitted to pregnancy during the first trimester of pregnancy (that is, the first 12–14 weeks); however, Clare was entering the third trimester when she finally agreed with her mother's assessment that her changed body shape reflected advanced pregnancy. Bianca, a community midwife, claimed that Clare had deliberately 'concealed' her pregnancy and that this was unfortunate because it reduced midwifery contact time and, hence, 'educational' opportunities:

HS: That word 'concealed' – I know it's a word midwives use when they're talking about women who don't reveal that they're pregnant – but what's it mean to you? Can you unpick it a bit for me?

CM: Oh well a lot of the young girls conceal. You see it all the time. It's mostly with them that you *do* see it. The problem is when they do conceal you don't get much time with them, which is a shame really because there's so much they need to learn and then it's all crammed in. [...] Like with Clare, because she concealed [the midwife drops her voice to a whisper on the word 'concealed'], so I didn't have all that much time with her. It all had to be squeezed into just a few weeks right at the end, so it wasn't ideal. (Community midwife Bianca. SY)

Later in the interview Bianca reflected on her relationship with her own children and framed Clare's relationship with her mother as aberrant by comparison:

Another thing I can't understand is when a mother does not realise that her daughter's pregnant. I cannot understand how it took so long for Clare's mother to realise. I think it's because I've got such a good relationship with my own daughter. Maybe that's why I find it so difficult. I think when you want to conceal, you can. If you want people not to know you're pregnant, they'll not know you're pregnant. But when you live at home, under your mum's roof, that's when I can't understand why they don't know. (Interview with community midwife Bianca, following a booking consultation with Clare (aged 14) when she was 28 weeks pregnant. SY)

Of note is Bianca's failure to take due account of Clare's reasons for keeping such sensitive information private until such time as she had identified a trustworthy person in whom to confide. In failing to recognise that while it may be advantageous to talk to a parent or another adult, some young people simply do not have this option. The ability to contain information, until the time for enlightening others feels individually appropriate, may be indicative of a mature, rather than an immature, personality and in this respect both disclosure and concealment may be regarded as communicative 'performances' which are context bound. Clare's persistent denial of her pregnant status, however, caused her mother to wonder whether there was something 'seriously wrong' with her physical health:

It were a case of wringing it outta her. [...] She'd not tell me straight. I did ask her. I asked her several times. [...] 'You don't think you could be pregnant do you?' She said, 'Don't be stupid, what d'ya think I am?' [...] So then I started thinking, 'Oh God, what's wrong with her then? There's something wrong with her. She must be sick, like.' I thought there might have been something seriously wrong with her. It does goes through your mind. (Chris (Clare's mother). SY)

Clare's account differed from explanations offered by her midwife and her mother. Rather than offering a single rationale for her silence, in the following quotation Clare justifies her decision by invoking multiple factors, and hence keeps the discursive space wide open for alternative interpretations, including those which are self-, and other, generated. On the one hand she agrees that she has indeed 'concealed' her pregnancy, but she disagrees with the construction of this decision as 'bad'. Rather, she considers herself 'lucky' because, by continuing to wear the same clothing, she avoids 'showing' and thus inviting unwanted questions; by not 'thinking', she is able to continue inhabiting her 'dream' world and thus resists pressure to consider an abortion which, like most of the teenagers, she 'doesn't believe in':

HS: When the midwife was here the other day she said you concealed your pregnancy – that you hid it. Was that a fair comment? Did you hide it?

Clare: Yeah, I did hide it. [...] I were lucky I didn't show much. *Laughs.* My jeans were really close fitting so you couldn't really tell. Not early on you couldn't 'n that's how I could keep it from my mum as well. *Smiles.* I were lucky in that way. [...] She [midwife] made out it were really bad that I hid it but I don't see what difference it makes. [...] I weren't going to have an abortion anyway.

HS: What was it like in those early months when you first realised you were pregnant?

Clare: I weren't really thinking about it. It were like I were in a dream or something. [...] I just blanked it. (Clare, 14 years old; 38 weeks pregnant. SY)

'Concealment' may be considered a normal aspect of adolescent development, in that young people generally do hide (parts of) their bodies and their activities from others, especially from authoritative elders. Teenage girls 'do' adolescence in ways which are often strange, irritating and/or offensive, especially to parents and other adults. Adolescents commandeer domestic spaces, especially bathrooms; take refuge in sleeping; communicate in grunts and monosyllables; and engage in a variety of behaviours designed to protect the spaces and places they consider private. All this is normal behaviour.

Parents' responses to daughters' sexual development and pregnancy disclosures

Some mothers reported that they had responded to pregnancy disclosures with outbursts of anger and that this effectively deterred daughters from elaborating further. As mothers were generally the first sources of comfort in times of trouble, their lack of availability reinforced daughters' feelings of distress and isolation.

> When I first got pregnant, I really wanted to tell her [mother]. But I couldn't ... I were too frightened of what she'd do. Then when I did tell her, it were so bad I had to stay out of the house for two days. She's so angry I can't tell her things. There's no one to talk to about pregnancy. There's no one I can really pour my heart out to. I were crying last week 'cos there were so much pressure. (Susan, 15 years old; 16 weeks pregnant. SY)

My own interactions with mothers during early interviews confirmed that some were indeed very angry with their daughters, especially when news of the pregnancy had been withheld from them until it was too late to consider abortion. While displays of maternal anger heightened daughters' sensations of fear and loneliness, this was mostly a temporary phase. When trust between mother and daughter was well established, and pre-existed pregnancy, it did not jeopardise long-term relationships.

Some mothers volunteered that they 'instinctively' recognised that something was amiss with their daughters, often before the news of pregnancy was divulged.

> On the Sunday night I came home and she was in bed. She called out, 'Mum'. I said, 'What's the matter?' but I just knew. I don't know how, I suppose it's instinct. I knew what she was going to say. (Anwen (mother of Megan, aged 14). W)

Mothers occasionally mistook changes in their daughters' general demeanour and behaviour as indicative of 'growing pains', while others considered that increased weight and changing body shape reflected the accumulation of 'puppy fat'. Mothers' everyday performances of housekeeping roles, and daughters' departures from normal dress codes, however, eventually signalled that 'something was up':

> I do all the shopping and the washing and I empty the bins so you do notice things. [...] I knew there were something up with her. I mean, you could tell. Especially over the last few weeks when she were just wearing her tracksuit bottoms all the time. (Chris (Clare's mother). SY)

As pregnancy progressed, maternal support was generally forthcoming and enduring – which is not to understate the period of intense turmoil which enveloped all the study families following pregnancy disclosure. Even the teenagers who had been accustomed to warm and loving relationships with their mothers reported that the announcement of pregnancy 'was like a brick wall coming between us'; many volunteered words to the effect that their mothers would generally have preferred to see them 'married and a bit older' before they embarked on motherhood.

Some of the teenagers refrained from early disclosure of pregnancy because they sought to avoid becoming the focus of parental, especially paternal, disappointment. Many parents had hoped that their children would enjoy the career opportunities they themselves had been denied and early pregnancy was perceived as jeopardising these aspirations. Girls tended to assume disclosure responsibility on behalf of boyfriends and to position themselves as morally culpable for interrupting their educational and career progression:

> He [boyfriend] didn't tell his family till five months. He was scared his parents would go mad. [...] He's like in his second year of university. (Nia, 18 years old; son aged six weeks. W)

Interestingly, Nia was also in her first year of university studies and did not tell her own parents until she was around six months pregnant. Alys also expressed concern about her boyfriend's future but initially failed to mention her own future career plans:

> They're fine with me now. [...] But in the beginning it was terrible. [...] like we've done all this for him, given him good schools and he's got all his exams and now this. [...] it's all for nothing now. (Alys, now 17 years old; son aged two years. W)

Negative reactions from fathers (and stepfathers) were widely anticipated by female family members. Irate, sometimes violent, outbursts were usually followed by indefinite periods of cold and aloof behaviour as fathers struggled to come to terms with their daughters as sexual beings:

> My husband can't look at her, doesn't want her in the house. (Anwen (mother of Megan, aged 14). W)

He [Michelle's father] took it very badly. [...] He was gutted really. He wanted the best for his girls. He wanted them all to have the best education. He wouldn't speak to her for weeks after she told him. [...] My brother's a bit the same. He's been very hard on me about Michelle's pregnancy. He told me I'm soft in the head to let her get away with it. He's got a 12-year-old daughter himself and he told me that if she ever gets pregnant as a teenager, she'll be out on her ear. [...] He said I'd never support her the way you've done with Stacey [Michelle's older sister who was also a teenage mother] and Michelle. (Polly (mother of Michelle, aged 16). SY)

As I have mentioned, with the possible exception of Jade's mother, men tended to be the more hostile recipients of pregnancy announcements and many teenagers looked to their mothers to intercede with respect to the actual timing and presentation of disclosure stories. As intermediaries, mothers tended to adopt a placatory and pragmatic role, soothing tensions between fathers and daughters. Although some fathers were considered 'very open-minded', and were liked and admired by daughters, none enjoyed the intimacy and ease of communication which characterised relationships between mother–daughter dyads. Within the home, intimate talk was gendered and spatially specific. When it occurred, it was in rooms which afforded a high degree of privacy: bedrooms and bathrooms – where a locked door restricted entry – were the most frequently mentioned locations. Fathers were excluded from these domains:

I would never have talked about sex and boyfriends and stuff like that with my dad [...] Like my dad wouldn't come in [to the bathroom] on me and my brother wouldn't either, but my mum would. And my dad wouldn't go in on my brother and my brother wouldn't go in on my dad. [...] My dad's very open minded as well though, and if I needed to speak to him I would, but my mum's way more easy to talk to than my dad is. Especially about things like my periods and contraception and what I do with my boyfriend. (Beca, 17 years old; 32 weeks pregnant. W)

For a few of the teenagers, pregnancy and motherhood provided the impetus to develop new relations with previously estranged family members, especially fathers, and this provided an additional, and much-needed, resource.

Boyfriends' responses to the news of pregnancy varied. Most were not only shocked but also alarmed, especially if their female partners were under the legal age of consent. Half of the teenagers (n=8) were underage when they conceived, although there was no suggestion that they, or their parents, intended to pursue criminal proceedings. For their part, it seemed that young men's cognisance of the seriousness of their actions initially deterred some from maintaining contact with their female partners, and with the young woman's mother:

Mother: Well, he's breaking the law for starters isn't he?

HS: Was that an issue for you, the fact that your daughter was underage? Was the legal side of it an issue?

Mother: Not really. Not with us it wasn't. With him it was so because he was afraid to come here and see her. [...] They've been seeing each other for about 18 months and I know it sounds bizarre because they're so young, but when I look at some of the girls her age and the way they are and what they're up to, obviously it's not the immaculate conception and she's done the deed, but it takes two to tango and all that doesn't it? So even though Megan's only 14 I can't only blame him. (Anwen (mother of Megan, aged 14). W)

Her boyfriend was too scared to come here and then later I found out he'd been on the phone to the Samaritans. I said, 'What did you do that for?' He said he could go to jail. I said, 'Yes you could but then again you've got to be sensible, you didn't jump out of the bushes and rape her did you?' (Marg (mother of Susan, aged 15). SY)

Although mothers in particular were disinclined to apportion blame, some couples nonetheless stayed away from the young woman's family home in order to avoid inflaming an already difficult situation. This was particularly the case where the young woman's mother had previously expressed disapproval of her daughter's choice of boyfriend, whose baby she was now carrying:

We haven't been here [at home] much because I don't know if she [mother] wants us to be here, 'cos obviously wherever I am he's [boyfriend] coming as well and well, she's not rude to him or anything, but you can tell she doesn't like him. [...] She's never liked him. She don't like the family either. (Clare, 14 years old; 16 weeks pregnant. SY)

Teenagers themselves tended to describe intimate relationships with their boyfriends on the basis of whether they thought it was likely to be 'cas'(ual) or whether it constituted a 'friendship' with potential for future development. When intimate relationships were sustained throughout the upheaval effected by pregnancy, girls generally referred to their boyfriends in affectionate terms, which suggested deepening attachment and an intention to parent co-operatively. Announcements of pregnancy were more positive when boyfriends were already regular, and welcome, visitors to the family home:

HS: So your mum's been OK about you getting pregnant?
Beca: Yeah, she's been fine about it. She would have been upset if me and [boyfriend] hadn't been together. Like if it had been a one-night stand or somebody who I'd already split up with, then she would've been upset. (Beca, 17 years old; 22 weeks pregnant. W)

Mothers were often quite forthright in voicing their expectations that young men would act with integrity and become involved in childbearing and rearing activities. Although such matters might be presented in a humorous light, the threat that action would follow if paternal responsibilities were avoided, was clearly evident in responses:

HS: So [boyfriend's] sticking by Alys then?
Mother: He's got no choice, he's not going anywhere now! *Laughs.* I told him, I've got a shot-gun upstairs if he tries to get away now! No, he's not going anywhere! [...] No, he's going to stick with her if I have anything to say about it. *Laughs.* [...] He's been very good though. (Angharad (mother of Alys, aged 15). W)

In fact, the majority of young men did 'stick with' their female partners and most assumed some level of parental responsibility.

Many teenagers drew on abortion narratives from within their immediate social networks to illustrate male decision-making power in this regard. Indeed, a few reported having delayed disclosure until it was 'too late' for fear their boyfriends would leave them, or coerce them into having an abortion:

His [boyfriend's] best mate's girlfriend, she fell pregnant and she got rid of it and then he says to me if you ever fell pregnant I'd make you have an abortion. I mean he were only joking when he said it, but how do I know that? [...] So then he says, 'Oh, I wouldn't make you do anything you didn't want to.' [...] He says to me other day, 'Oh, I don't hate you for not telling me or anything.' 'n I says, 'Well that's good, 'cos it's too late now.' *Laughs.* (Susan, now 16 years old; son aged six months. SY)

Two of the teenagers reported being 'dumped' by the fathers of their babies and three experienced relationship difficulties and/or break-down at a later date. Some, including Clare, whose relationship had already ended before she realised she was pregnant (but which she later resumed), were unsure about whether to disclose to ex-boyfriends:

I'd like, I'd already finished off wi' [boyfriend]. [...] I mean [boy-friend] says to me now, 'If you'd have told me I wouldn't have left you,' and obviously he's still here now, but you don't know that at time do you? You don't know what they're gonna do. [...] (Clare, now 15 years old; daughter aged three months. SY)

Some mothers intimated that although pregnancy in a teenage daughter was an unwelcome event, it was also something of a biological inevitability; that it was simply a matter of time before early childbearing manifested as an actual, rather than as a potential, event:

When you have daughters I think you're always preparing yourself for them to come home one day and say 'Mum I'm pregnant.' [...] It's always going to be a shock, but with girls, well it's always there in the back of your mind isn't it? [...] Girls you worry about more I think than boys. (Polly (mother of Michelle, aged 16). SY)

The bond between some mothers and daughters was especially strong and this enabled them to resist male pressures (especially from the teenagers' fathers) to conform to a (masculine) modelling of 'appropriate' feminin-ity. Mothers occasionally reported colluding with their daughter's need to 'go out and have some fun', although such conspiratorial behaviour was potentially very threatening to parental harmony and hence was only risked when relationships between mother and daughter were strong and steadfast. The following quotation attests to an unusually high degree of mutuality and trust in Angharad's relationship with her daughter, to the extent she was willing to collude with her in deceiving her father.

Mother: Oh, it was nothing to go upstairs and fluff a pillow up and make it look as if she were in bed, so she could go out with her friends and have some fun. *Laughs.*

HS: And would you do that for her?

Mother: Oh, yes, I'd do that for her. I had to. I couldn't stand the misery of it. Her locked in and all her friends out having fun. It didn't seem right. It wasn't as if she weren't sensible. She had a good head on her, even then. Even when she were quite young. And my husband would put his head through her door and say, 'Oh good, she's not gone out, she's asleep!' He'd look in and see the hump in the bed and think she's in bed, she's all right ... So then he'd go to bed ... If he'd have gone in and shook her, Oh then, there would have been hell. *Laughs.* [...] He wouldn't think twice about the boys going off mind. First time she went away with the school, before she could go, he wanted phone numbers and a list of who she was with and would the teachers be there all the time. (Angharad (mother of Alys, aged 15). W)

Limitations on freedom of movement, and hence on an individual's social life and the on-going project of self-construction, have been described in relation to pregnancy (Longhurst, 1996), childbirth (Sharpe, 1999) and the transition to parenthood (Aitken, 1999). Parents in this study employed different strategies to protect their teenagers from what they understood to be unsuitable company and/or dangerous environments, and the first line of defence typically involved setting (different) restrictions for sons and daughters. Girls were generally required to be more explicit about where they were going and with whom; unlike their brothers they could not just go where they liked, when they liked. Girls were less able to negotiate going out alone after dark and, hence, night-time worlds were less accessible to them. Restricting activities also limited girls' interactions with others, although this is perhaps of less significance than for previous generations, when the demarcation between behaviours considered 'girlish' and 'boyish' was more rigid. Nonetheless, girls were more likely to be restricted in their social contacts because parents preferred their daughters to associate with 'nice girls' rather than with 'slags'; such restrictions were understood to protect daughters' reputations from being corrupted.

Regret

Extant research suggests that many teenage girls express subsequent regret for early and unplanned intercourse, particularly when this results in an unwanted pregnancy (Dickson et al., 1998; Wight et al., 2000) and/or the imposition of penalties. Only a small number of teenagers in this study anticipated the isolation and restrictions which followed on as an automatic consequence of (early) parenting; they especially lamented the speedy decline in opportunities for socialising with their peer group:

> I'm still gutted really. When I first found out, I was, like, oh no, I can't do anything now. My life is finished. I can't go out any more. Things like that. I used to go out with my friends all the time. We were a big gang. [...] I can't go out to pubs any more. I can't drink any more. I mean I can go out and socialise, but it's not the same seeing everyone else having a good time and you're just sitting there with a coke. It's not my idea of fun. [...] I get depressed thinking about it. I think, oh, I hate this. I think my life's finished. I've got 20 years of this. (Alys, 15 years old; 30 weeks pregnant. W)

Two years later, Alys confirmed her prediction that the quality of some aspects of her life had indeed diminished as a result of motherhood:

> HS: How would you describe your life now?
> Alys: To be honest, if I could go back, I would have waited to have him. I would have, because my life is not my own now. I don't get to do the things I want to do, like before I used to go out all the time, you wouldn't see me for hours on end. I'd go out with my friends and have a laugh. But now I've got to work around him. [...] Like if I want to go out, I have to ask my mam to watch him or get somebody else to watch him or take him with me. I haven't got the option of just putting my coat on and going out any more. (Alys, now 17 years old; son aged two years. W)

Only very rarely, however, and usually only in response to particularly stressful events, did any of the teenagers voice regrets about being a mother to their particular child:

> She's been a right pain in arse. Yeah, she has. [...] I told her I don't want to be 'er mum if she carries on like that. *Laughs.* (Lou, now 17 years old; daughter aged nine months. SY)

I told [ex-boyfriend] he'd have to take her [younger daughter] 'cos I can't look after her. I have to get m'self sorted. I can't look after both of 'em. Not now I can't. (Jade, now 18 years old; daughters aged 16 months and two months respectively. SY)

Jade and Lou were among the poorest, most isolated, and most marginalised of the young mothers; they had few friends and little access to the sources of support which might have alleviated the hardships they faced in their respective transitions to motherhood.

Disclosure and help-seeking: responses from maternity staff

Girls who were not using contraception generally recognised that they might be pregnant immediately they failed to 'come on' with their monthly period. Contraception failure was very likely to delay help-seeking behaviour because, believing they were protected, teenagers generally failed to notice, or take seriously, the early signs of pregnancy, including a missed period. Lack of knowledge about the circumstances in which conception is possible, however, was evident from the girls' accounts of events preceding pregnancy. The belief that being 'due on' was protective against pregnancy, for example, was widespread:

At first I wasn't sure 'cos well, I had my period a few days after we had sex [using a condom, which burst] so it's like, oh well I thought, I won't be pregnant then [...] so I thought, well, there's no need to worry, but like obviously you can still get pregnant if you're due on [a period] can't you? (Clare, 14 years old; 38 weeks pregnant. SY)

Recent research in this area suggests that misconceptions and confusion about the type of sex acts which may result in pregnancy are common among adolescents; the perception that menstruation is protective against pregnancy, for example, is widely believed (Wynn et al., 2009). Delayed help-seeking tended to reinforce negative stereotypes of pregnant teenagers, and had negative consequences for antenatal screening and termination options.

I was on the pill. Then my periods started going a bit funny. I was bleeding at the wrong time, between my periods. I asked my mum and she said I should go to the GP. [...] I did a pregnancy test and it was positive. [...] Two weeks later the midwife feels my tummy and she says, 'No you're not ten or 12 weeks, I think you're 24 weeks. [...]

You're too late now for any of the tests.' (Lowri, 16 years old; three weeks after the stillbirth of her daughter. W)

Confirmation of pregnancy was generally sought through established channels, including GP and family planning clinics; those who could afford to do so purchased over-the-counter kits for self-testing. Making an appointment with a GP required teenagers to exercise considerable initiative as most were not in the habit of arranging their own diaries and nor did they usually instigate meetings with adults. Although most teenagers acknowledged the gravity of their situation, many reported they were nonetheless censured by health professionals and were made to feel 'stupid' when consulting them:

> At the doctors it was all, 'Oh dear, you're pregnant. You stupid girl.' That's how they made you feel. (Lowri, 16 years old; three weeks after the stillbirth of her daughter. W)

Dilys, Lowri's mother, was pregnant at the same time as her daughter. In the following excerpt she articulates her more positive experience of conferring with maternity staff and suggests the differences were age-related:

> The midwife sat down with me. She explained everything. She obviously felt she needed to explain and then I asked questions afterwards. I was given an opportunity to discuss anything that I wanted to discuss so there were no problems there at all. It was a very, very different experience from [Lowri]. It couldn't have been more different. It was a different midwife but I don't think that was the reason. I think it's because she's a teenager and I'm obviously older. (Dilys (Lowri's mother), 20 weeks pregnant. W)

Teenagers' mothers were ideally positioned to evaluate the maternity care their daughters received as their own maternity experiences were relatively recent and hence their knowledge about, and understandings of, childbearing norms provided accurate reflections of local service provision. Interactions between maternity staff and teenagers were mostly described in negative terms, leaving the latter feeling belittled and upset – sentiments which persisted throughout their childbearing trajectories. The quality of communication in clinical settings has been shown to be related to (positive) health outcomes (Di Blasi et al., 2001) and, in a changing healthcare environment, patients (now more commonly referred to in market-speak as 'clients/customers') are increasingly encouraged to air their views and to participate in decision-making processes. This level of engagement is only possible, however, when relationships between all parties are based on mutual respect and egalitarian principles. Indeed, a defining characteristic of 'successful' professional–patient relationships is the high degree of patient autonomy and lack of medical paternalism; the professional regards the patient as the 'expert' in their condition (Coulter, 2002; Department of Health, 2001).

Although both the teenagers and their mothers were of the opinion that (young) age was very likely to trigger discriminatory treatment from maternity staff, surprises were occasionally reported:

> So I took her to the surgery and she saw the GP. She wasn't chastised in any way because of her age. *Laughs.* I thought it would be an issue, but it's like if you're 25 these days you seem old. (Anwen (mother of Megan, aged 14). W)

If all childbearing women were subjected to less rigid categorising by maternity professionals (for example on the basis of 'risk' factors, especially age, and clinicians' perceptions of prospective 'good'/ 'bad' maternal capacity), the process of deconstructing adolescent motherhood as problematic might be made easier. It might also enable the circumstances (the 'how', 'why' and 'for whom' questions) surrounding an individual's pregnancy to be disentangled and taken-for-granted associations unpacked. For example, is young motherhood problematic because of premature childbearing, low educational attainment, intellectual impairment or unmarried status? Or declining family values or individual female sexual transgression? Furthermore, is the 'problem' located with the teen mother herself, her child/ren, her family and kinship group, or the wider society in which she lives? And are these issues of relevance only when the teenager is still attending school, or when she is deemed irresponsible and incapable by virtue of her class, race and/or social standing?

Teenagers' narratives suggested that midwives were often dismissive of their relationships with their male partners. Indeed, a small number were reported as refusing to include boyfriends' details in maternity records, and occasionally making inaccurate and unwarranted predictions about their clients' romantic relationships:

> What really got to me was that she [midwife] wouldn't put down that he was my boyfriend. She wouldn't put it down that I had a steady

boyfriend. She told me it wasn't worth it 'cos I'd be split up with him before baby was born. She said, 'Oh they all do it, you'll be no different.' [...] Well [two years on] we're not split up. He's still my boyfriend. [...] We're engaged and we're going to get married. (Alys, now 17 years old; son aged two years. W)

Midwives' projections concerning the longevity of adolescents' relationships were more transparent when they disapproved of partner choice, although the quasi-parental role many adopted may equally be regarded as inappropriate. In this regard midwives helped, however unintentionally, to shape stereotypes of young parents-to-be as feckless and fickle.

Teenagers, decision-making and personal agency: to keep, or terminate, the pregnancy?

A study of UK teenage conceptions (Lee et al., 2004) revealed that more than 40 per cent end in abortion, but that these statistics disguise wide variations among local populations, with very young teenagers and those from affluent backgrounds most likely to access this option. As might be expected, abortion rates tend to be lower in disadvantaged areas, even though they have the highest rates of teenage conception; they are higher in areas where there is more extensive family planning provision, where the proportion of female GPs is higher and where there is easy access to independent abortion services.

A number of teenagers had friends and acquaintances who had undergone a termination, either voluntarily (and sometimes secretively) or in response to external, often parental, pressure. Few studies have examined the long-term effects of abortion on teenagers, although the results of an early study suggested that coercive decision-making may engender subsequent guilt and regret (Sharpe, 1987), while more recent research suggests an association with a 'rebound' repeat pregnancy at a later date (Seamark, 2001). Additional research in this area proposes that termination of pregnancy in adolescence has a stigmatising effect (Lee et al., 2004) and may be linked to depressive illness in married adolescent females (Reardon and Cougle, 2002). The majority of teenagers in this study, and their close kin, indicated that they were averse not only to abortion, but also to adoption:

You've got to have balls of steel to give up a baby up for adoption, or have an abortion. [...] You know that keeping the baby is a really,

really hard thing to do, and you know your life is going to change completely, but to have an abortion, or to have to give the baby away to be adopted ... Oh I couldn't. (Alys, 15 years old; 30 weeks pregnant. W)

Although most teenagers initially denied that they would ever contemplate a termination, some did later imply that they might reconsider this option in the event of the baby being identified as having a problem for which there was no known medical cure:

HS: So you think if the baby was affected by Down's syndrome or spina bifida you might have considered a termination?

Alys: Yes, I would have had to, 'cos it wouldn't be fair on the baby if I kept it.

Mother: Mmm. It's like, well, you can't carry this baby now, but, you know, she's young enough to have more, isn't it Alys? (Alys and Angharad (her mother). W)

Moral responsibility is thus repositioned to take account of the baby's future and anticipated (poor) quality of life, alongside the teenager's youthfulness and the ease with which a (healthy) replacement baby might be conceived. References to potential fertility status were well received when they came from teenagers themselves or their close kin; when health professionals made such comments, they were generally considered hurtful and/or offensive. Perhaps because of widespread antipathy to abortion, teenagers expressed disappointment when this was the first, and sometimes the only, option suggested by GPs:

I went to the GP for a pregnancy test. [...] She just said, 'It's positive.' That's all she said. There were no congratulations or anything. There was nothing. It was just, 'Well, do you want an abortion?' (Beca, 17 years old; 22 weeks pregnant. W)

It appeared that teenagers' low expectations of health professionals were a significant factor influencing their (un)willingness to seek help early in pregnancy. Although existing research does not specifically link an individual's reluctance to seek help with pressures to abort, as Elenor intimates in the following excerpt, negative attitudes may hinder some adolescents from hearing, and/or heeding, medical advice. It also makes it more difficult for them to decide the most appropriate course of individual action and to proceed confidently.

> The GP was horrible. [...] She told me straightaway I should have a termination. She said I was too young to be a mother. She said I'd ruin my life if I kept the baby. Then she said I'd be better having it adopted. [...] She put more on not having the baby than she did about actually keeping the baby. She was really terrible. [...] I know it's stupid but when they're like that with you it just makes you want to do the opposite. *Laughs.* (Elenor, 18 years old; 23 weeks pregnant. W)

A significant number of teenagers received incorrect information from health professionals about abortion. Some were misinformed about the upper legal time limit (24 weeks), some were told they were too young, while others were told they required parental consent. Research in this area suggests that clinicians particularly dislike requests for abortion beyond the first trimester of pregnancy (Lee et al., 2004), but this is problematic for adolescents who may be unaware of, or unable to admit to, the possibility of pregnancy at this early stage. Some teenagers reported difficulties with doctors whose religious beliefs prohibited them from providing the information they needed to make an informed decision:

> I didn't like the GP. She said she can't discuss abortions because she's Catholic. I thought that wasn't very professional of her. It's her job isn't it? (Rhian, 15 years old; 37 weeks pregnant. W)

It appeared that teenagers accessing general practitioners who objected to abortion on religious/moral grounds were rarely offered a referral to another practitioner.

Some teenagers were unwilling to consider abortion because of concerns that such interventions 'muck with your brain', and are potentially spoiling of sexual identity. As Alys indicates in the following quotation, the spectre of the post-abortion teenage 'tart' may pose a significant threat to the integrity of a young woman's future sexual reputation:

> They tell you to have an abortion like it's the easiest thing to do. It's like, 'Oh you made a mistake, you can get rid of it. You can have another one'. They don't tell you that it's going to muck with your brain. My mother's friend, her daughter's 14. She got pregnant and she had a termination. And now she's a right tart. [...] Anything in trousers she'll sleep with. (Alys, now 17 years old; son aged two years. W)

Most of the teenagers knew someone in their immediate peer/friendship group who had been 'forced' to have a termination, or relinquish their baby for adoption, when they would have preferred to keep it. Narratives suggested that some individuals were unable to 'move on' from their experiences, retaining an imaginative link with the aborted foetus (or adopted baby) and continuing to seek information about its developmental milestones. As previously mentioned, rebound pregnancy following abortion was not uncommon:

A girl I was at school with she had a termination. Her parents made her. [...] She's not moved on from it. It's sad really. All the time she says things like, 'If I'd have kept it now, it would be, how old would it be now? It would be about so many months old, it would be 12 months old by now ...' She says that sort of thing all the time. (Susan, 15 years old; six months pregnant. SY)

You see them on the telly, 20 years later and they're still upset about it and they want to find their children and things like that. It's something you can't let go of. [...] They give up the baby for adoption and then you find they've had four more kids, and then you think, but she let that kid go for adoption but then she had another four. You think why did she do that? Why didn't she just keep the first one? (Alys, now 17 years old; son aged two years. W)

While teenagers' mothers were influential in their daughters' pregnancy-related decisions, most supported their preferences. Regarding abortion, both parties expressed concern for their future relationship in the event of a mother acting coercively:

I told her she had options. I'm against abortion but that isn't my choice to make. [...] I think I could have put her off having an abortion because she will listen to me and be influenced by me, but I don't think that's fair. I think in years down the line she would have blamed me. [...] So it had to be her decision. (Polly (mother of Michelle, aged 16). SY)

You would never forgive your parents for forcing you to do it [have an abortion] would you? There's a rift then between you that's always going to be there. (Nia, 18 years old; son aged six weeks. W)

Luci was alone in volunteering that she initially intended to have a termination. When an ultrasound scan at ten weeks revealed she was carrying twins, however, she changed her mind and decided to go ahead with the pregnancy:

> It was a helluva shock when we found it was twins I was carrying, but then we thought we just couldn't not keep them. (Luci, 16 years old; 15 weeks pregnant. W)

Family dynamics: interactions with, and between, adolescents' families

While both sets of the teenagers' parents generally played a central role in the young couple's transition to parenthood, prior to the baby's birth the parents of young men tended to be background figures, uninvolved in day-to-day decision-making and other events, with the exception of festive occasions associated with the exchange of gifts, such as birthdays and Christmas. It may be that the absence of the young men's families reflects the orientation of my study, which did not seek their direct involvement (although individual family members occasionally contributed to data generation), or it may indicate an area for future research. Although parents of the young couples were sometimes familiar with one another by name or reputation, the majority had not met prior to the announcement of pregnancy. Some were unaware that their sons and daughters were in a relationship; indeed, one young couple had become formally engaged but withheld this information from the young man's parents for some months:

> Me, and [boyfriend], we've been engaged since Christmas Day and he didn't tell her [mother] about that at all, but then she found out last month and she wasn't happy at all. (Alys, 15 years old; 30 weeks pregnant. W)

Mothers displayed a range of responses to the young men with whom their daughters consorted. Some welcomed them, regarded them as 'family' and encouraged them to take a full and active role in the life of the household. Sometimes, however, the young man's family was firmly regarded as 'other'; differences were attributed to disparities in class, income and (higher) parental expectations regarding the young man's future:

He's the only boy. [...] His father's a headmaster. [...] But they're not better than us. They're not. You know what I mean. You see [boyfriend] and you see his parents and you wouldn't think they were from the same family. You wouldn't think he was from that family ... [boyfriend] is more ordinary. They're a bit ... They're a bit stuck up. (Alys, 15 years old; 30 weeks pregnant. W)

They've just got different ideas haven't they? They've got different ways, different opinions like. They're a different lot from us. (Glenys (mother of Beca, aged 17). W)

Differences in family social status were most remarked upon by mothers in the Wales cohort, although unless the teenagers pointed them out, any such differences were subtle and were generally invisible to me as an outsider, with the exception of language (Welsh speaking signalling both status and belonging). For reasons I cannot fully explain, mothers living in Wales seemed more inclined to make unfavourable comparisons between themselves and the mother of their daughter's boyfriend, and indeed between both families more generally. Interestingly, exposure to the young woman's family was seen to have a maturing effect on young male partners:

Mother: He [Alys's boyfriend] hasn't got the sort of relationship with his mother that she's got with me ...

Alys: His mother's of the old school. From what I know she babies him. [...] She won't let him grow up. [...] I think she likes keeping him a baby. He's very quiet. [...] He's a bit more rugged now mind, after being round us ... *Both laugh.* (Angharad (Alys's mother. Both were Welsh speakers). W)

During pregnancy, male partners generally spent more time in the young woman's home than the reverse. Once the baby was born, however, the newly constituted family spent increasing periods of time in the young man's household. The majority of young men's parents showed an interest in their grandchild's development and some became very involved indeed, providing childcare and supporting the young family in other ways.

Kinship networks, especially among female relatives, played a pivotal role in the lives of most teenagers, providing them with on-going practical, financial, social, and emotional, support. For those without access to this resource, life was grim indeed. The absence of female kin during pregnancy and the early years of children's lives worked against teenagers' early assumption of a competent maternal identity. The historical significance of mother–daughter bonds, and the support provided by these connections, has been well documented, as has the importance of extended kinship networks, and their 'ordinariness' in the lives of previous generations of working-class people (Young and Wilmot, 1957). Research within areas of the UK with traditionally high rates of teenage pregnancy contradicts the stereotype of single, socially isolated schoolgirl mothers, concluding instead that young mothers are generally well supported within these (working-class) communities (Ibbotson, 1993; MacLeod and Weaver, 2003). Where such support is not available from family networks, 'the main conclusion to be drawn […] is that offering socially disadvantaged "at risk" mothers additional support during pregnancy has a positive impact on measures of children's health status and family well-being seven years later' (Oakley et al., 1996: 20). Hence, reliable and individually acceptable social support throughout the transition to motherhood has long been associated with a reduction in many of the more negative outcomes associated with early childbearing. As the narratives from the young mothers in this study confirm, maternal discourses were grounded in class, gender and locality-based relationships and kinship networks, which, in turn, promoted mostly affirmative, and adaptive, responses to unexpected pregnancy and early motherhood.

In the next chapter I describe how the teenagers responded to the physical aspects of pregnancy, including food cravings and weight gain, and how these events impacted on, and shaped, their emergent maternal identities. I also discuss decision-making opportunities and processes, including those relating to antenatal screening and attendance at antenatal 'education' classes. I make passing reference to teenagers pre-existing health status and the lifestyle changes adopted by some in response to pregnancy (modelling 'healthy' behaviours to children was emphasised as an important aspect of the future parental role). The teenagers' narratives demonstrate how their pregnancy-related experiences affected their access to public and institutional spaces, and their relationships with significant others, especially their mothers. Their (mostly negative) views of midwives reiterated teenagers' perceptions of staff as unhelpful and critical; in this sense midwives were cast as the 'bogey (wo)men'. Finally, I briefly discuss intergenerational transmissions of childbearing and rearing knowledges and practices, a theme I return to periodically throughout the remaining chapters.

4
Through Pregnancy

Adolescent status afforded little protection from the physical discomforts of pregnancy, particularly morning sickness and tiredness. Although physical indicators were generally accepted with the pragmatism I came to associate with teenagers, many were nonetheless surprised by the intensity of symptoms:

> I had it [morning sickness] quite bad [...] it was terrible. I'd be going down the street but then I'd have to come back home and lay down. I felt sick all the time. I couldn't eat anything. I couldn't bear the smell of food. It was terrible. (Elenor, 18 years old; 23 weeks pregnant. W)

> I was just feeling tired and whatever all the time and it just got worse really. I was feeling more and more tired. Eventually I stopped going to work because I couldn't get up to go to work. (Lowri, 16 years old; three weeks after the stillbirth of her daughter. W)

One sign of pregnancy, which all the teenagers viewed with a mixture of irritation and amusement, was that of food cravings. Jade referred to herself as 'mad keen on pickled onions' while Alys 'couldn't stop eating liquorice allsorts'.

The physicality of pregnancy: daughters' and mothers' interconnected experiences

Some mothers reported feeling physically connected with their daughters through the pregnancy-related sensations that they experienced.

These feelings were unexpected and did not necessarily reflect their previous childbearing experiences:

> I feel like I'm having this baby as well. *Laughs.* It's like every little niggle she [daughter] has she tells me and I know what she's feeling. It's like I feel it *with* her. [...] It's really weird. When I had mine I didn't feel like this. [...] When you're pregnant yourself, you're pregnant and that's that. [...] But this baby [...] It's really weird. It's a really nice feeling. *Laughs.* (Anwen (mother of Megan, aged 14). W)

> Chris: Every time she says, I'm feeling this or that, I think well, yes, I've been feeling that as well. *Laughs.*
>
> HS: Would you say it's the same sort of feeling as when you were pregnant yourself?
>
> Chris: No. No not at all. I think when I were pregnant I knew I were pregnant, so I were sort of expecting to feel things. But with her, it's like I know it's her that's pregnant but then I'm feeing it like I were. *Laughs.* It's more like, it's like it's an all-over thing. I can't explain it any better than that. *Laughs.* (Chris (mother of Clare, aged 14). SY)

The embodied sensations mothers reported seemed different from the more commonly described masculine experiences known as 'couvade' (from the French *couver*, to 'brood' or 'hatch'). Albert Doja (2005), quoting the early works of Edward Tylor (1889: 254), describes the couvade thus: 'the father, on the birth of his child, makes a ceremonial pretence of being the mother, being nursed and taken care of, and performing other rites such as fasting and abstaining from certain kinds of food or occupation, lest the newborn should suffer thereby' (Doja, 2005: 918–19). While couvade has a long anthropological history, only recently has it been considered a stress response manifested by men exposed to the events of maternity (Thomas and Upton, 2000); more recent research proposes a physiological basis (Bartlett, 2004). Couvade, or 'sympathetic pregnancy syndrome', is a relatively common, but poorly understood, phenomenon whereby the expectant father experiences somatic symptoms during his partner's pregnancy, which typically resolve once the baby is born. Unlike expectant fathers, however, teenagers' mothers in this study did not report similarities with their daughters' pregnancy-related symptoms, but, rather, a more global feeling of interconnectedness which anticipated the baby's future 'becoming' and presence within the family.

Observing their daughters' progression through pregnancy often prompted many mothers to reflect on their own childbearing experiences and relationships with their own mothers, a generation for whom reproductive talk was generally proscribed. As Angharad explains in the following excerpt, her uninhibited relationship with her daughter bore no comparison to what she had experienced with her mother:

HS: What kind of relationship did you have with your mum, Angharad? Would you've been talking to her like you do with Alys, you know, sharing stories about sex, having babies and stuff like that?

Angharad: My God no. Oh no ... *Laughs.* You couldn't talk with her about sex. You didn't even talk then about having babies. You just had them and that was that. [...] The sex word I never ever heard mentioned in our house. It was forbidden. You didn't talk like that. [...] I remember when I first started my period. I was about 12 and a half. I was at the comprehensive school. I couldn't go to my mother. I was terrified. I went to my sister-in-law but she just laughed at me and then she marched me straight to my mother. I'm cryin' like and sayin' to my mother, 'I'm sorry, I'm sorry ...' I didn't know what for like. Stupid now, isn't it ... But I didn't know ... It wasn't told to you then. [...] Not like with Alys. *Laughs.* Oh, she knew all about it [menstruation]. All excited she was when it happened, wasn't it Alys? *Laughs.* (Angharad (mother of Alys, aged 15). W)

As I have already explained, prevailing attitudes to illegitimacy, combined with ignorance about sex and reproduction, and communication taboos, made it difficult for women in previous generations to access appropriate help and support when they suspected pregnancy. In the following excerpt, Michelle's mother describes attitudes prevalent in her adolescent years, when the chaperoning of daughters by fathers was common practice, and sex outside marriage was unthinkable:

I were scared to death. We all were 'cos it were all illegal then. Only married people had sex then. [...] And if you ever got pregnant – look out! You'd end up in workhouse. That were the end of you. *Laughs.* [...] If you went anywhere your dad went with you just to be sure like. *Laughs.* (Polly (mother of Michelle, aged 16). SY)

Liberated from the etiquette and norms of their forebears, many mothers in my study relived their childbearing and rearing experiences through their daughters' emergent maternal identities.

Teenagers and maternity staff 'doing' antenatal care

At the time I carried out my research, none of the maternity units attended by the teenagers offered special provision for this client group. Substantial changes have since been introduced, however, with teen-specific maternity care now a common feature of UK service provision. Most teenagers encountered a different professional at each antenatal consultation; during labour the majority were attended by unfamiliar midwives. Later, a consultant midwife with a specific remit for teenage pregnancy was appointed in one of the research areas and anecdotal information suggested that her presence rapidly became a much valued and sought-after resource. Indeed, two teenagers, whose older sisters became pregnant after they themselves had become mothers, spoke enviously about the 'better deal' their sisters received. This generated considerable tension because older sisters were perceived to have less need of additional support.

Fragmented maternity care was problematic for the most marginalised teenagers because they tended not to be consulted about changes to arrangements in care provision.

> HS: So it wasn't your choice to switch to Bettina [another community midwife]?
>
> Tracey: No. I didn't have nowt to say about it. I'd have rather stayed with [community midwife with whom Tracey had originally booked] but she said she were too busy. […] She told me she were changing me to other midwife. She just crossed her name off my folder and wrote in other lady's name. I didn't like it. I didn't think she could do that but she did. She didn't even say sorry or nowt – like it weren't nothing to her. (Tracey, 14 years old; 29 weeks pregnant. SY)

During my follow-up interview with Bettina, it became apparent that she had not been consulted about managerial decisions to rearrange her caseload and was unaware that Tracey would have preferred to stay in her care. This mirrored how midwives themselves were made vulnerable by practices within their employing organisations. Reflecting the (low) status of their client group, midwives' opinions were rarely sought, or were largely discounted by more powerful others and this reinforced their relative insignificance in the institutional hierarchy. Meanwhile Tracey, who had hitherto not missed one antenatal consultation, started to skip appointments and by late pregnancy was referred to as a 'non-attender'.

Although the frequency of antenatal consultations has gradually declined, this fails to take account of the increased volume of information to be disseminated and the complexity of decision-making processes. The 'Informed Choice' study (Kirkham and Stapleton, 2001) I referred to in the introduction to this book indicated that the more pronounced the hierarchical distance between staff and client, as measured by variables including age, ethnicity and social class, the greater the tendency for staff to withhold information and to talk 'over' clients as if they were non-existent. Looking back, I think I was particularly sensitised to these types of behaviours when they occurred between childbearing women and midwives because of my expectation that women-to-women encounters would be less influenced by traditional class and gendered power relations and, hence, would be qualitatively different. When mothers accompanied their daughters to clinic appointments I observed midwives directing conversation exclusively towards the older women. When teenagers' mothers were unable to attend appointments with their daughters, midwives tended to direct their questions to me. This was despite lengthy explanations about the purpose of my study, including my observer role. The following excerpt from my field notes typifies these interactions:

CM: Oh dear, she's got her hands full hasn't she? [The midwife looks in my direction and addresses her comments to me.] With two to look after now it's not going to be easy for her is it? [...] Has a social worker been allocated do you know?

HS: I don't know. You could try asking Jade herself. *Laughs.*

CM: Do you have a social worker then, petal?

Jade: Mmm. Yeah. It's same one I had before.

CM: Good, 'cos I just need to get a referral off to health visitor as well. Do you know where she'll be living after she's had the baby? [Once again, the midwife looks in my direction and addresses her question to me.] (Community midwife Joan interacting with Jade, now 17 years old and 38 weeks pregnant with her second baby. SY)

Midwives were not alone in their tendency to usurp teenagers' agency and hence limit their potential contribution to maternity care proceedings. With the possible exception of social workers, with whom some teenagers had a previously established relationship, many health professionals were observed, or were reported as, acting in a punitive and/or judgemental manner. While they may not have intended to cause offence, their behaviour nonetheless upset many of the teenagers, their families and friends. Repeated experiences of being ignored also diminished their willingness to actively engage in decision-making processes, with a potentially negative impact on short-term maternity outcomes and, indeed, on health outcomes over the life course.

Aneez Esmail (2004), quoting from Vikram Seth's ([1993] 2004) novel *A Suitable Boy*, makes the point that it is not so much the prejudices of 'bad' people that are problematic in the health services but rather the intolerances shown by individuals deemed to be 'good' on account of their education, accent and other such markers of elevated social status: 'what [such] people *think* is not what matters – what they *do* is what matters, and in that respect the [medical profession] in the United Kingdom has a long way to go' (Esmail, 2004: 1449; emphasis added). I would extend this commentary to include midwives, whose negative treatment of women in their care, including 'bullying' behaviours (Dietsch et al., forthcoming), has been attributed to working conditions where they are 'ruthlessly manipulated' (Mason, 2000: 247) by the demands of general management. While all NHS staff might argue that they suffer the incursions of management into their respective spheres of practice, doctors are arguably better protected than all other professional groups because, at the point of entry into the NHS, they negotiated contractual arrangements which have continued to ensure their professional autonomy and protect their elevated and privileged status.

Mothers were widely appreciated as important sources of embodied childbearing knowledge. For their part, daughters were valued translators of technical knowledge:

HS: And did you read any of this information, Polly?
Polly: Oh yes. *Laughs*. I had to. I was told to read it, by miss here! *Laughs*. I didn't have an option. She told me I had to. *All laugh*.
HS: So why is it important for your mum to read it, Michelle?
Michelle: Umm ... So she can understand. I know lots of things have changed from when she had us. Like scans and machines, things she never had when she were having

us. I know it's all different now, but I just want her to understand what's going on now and how things are different, so she can help me. So she knows what to expect. (Polly and her daughter, Michelle, 16 years old. SY)

There's still a lot that's the same as when I had mine. They use some different words now but soon as she [Alys] explains it to me, I can say 'Oh, but that happened to me, too.' [...] She takes the logic out for me. I can understand it if it's put in common sense. (Angharad (mother of Alys, aged 15). W)

Rephrasing technical concepts in the language of 'common sense' enabled some mothers to reinterpret their own childbearing experiences in the light of current practices. For daughters, dismantling and re-presenting the 'logic' of maternity events in response to their unfolding experiences allowed them to breach the discursive space of rational thought and conventional childbearing wisdoms. To that end I observed a few teenagers contravening communication conventions, for example by initiating conversation, actively soliciting information and/or questioning a health professional's viewpoint. Such 'infringements', although relatively rare, tended to be negatively interpreted by staff:

I think with your first baby, with health professionals, you do tend to feel intimidated. If they tell you something, you're not supposed to turn round and say, 'Well I disagree with you.' Especially when you're young, that's not an easy thing to say, not really. (Lowri, 16 years old; three weeks after the stillbirth of her daughter. W)

You're not a baby any more but that's how they [midwives] make you feel. They should just be telling us, look, this is what we think you should be doing, but it's up to you if you do it. If you don't want to do it, well, that's your problem. But they don't. They make you feel like you're a baby. Like you're not a grown up at 16. (Susan, 15 years old; 36 weeks pregnant. SY)

Despite lack of previous exposure to medical environments, most teenagers were very sensitive to the unspoken rules of conversation etiquette governing institutional exchanges. Rather than risk possible censure, teenagers tended not to question staff but turned to their mothers for advice and information. When mothers were unable to provide answers, the more literate and confident teenagers consulted alternative sources, including other females, books and the media. Staff occasionally confused mother–daughter identities, with detrimental consequences for their adolescent clientele:

> Some of them you can see they think. Oh, who's that old woman with her then? Must be her gran she's brought along with her! *Laughs*. And they're probably saying the same about her [Susan]. You know, 'Look at her now, don't she look young!' Stupid isn't it that they can't just treat you as normal. (Marg (mother of Susan, aged 15). SY)

The concept of 'normal' is a relatively recent invention, which assumes that a person has a basic repertoire of 'cognitive, psychological, emotional, and social skills' (Wong, 1997: 278). To be read as 'normal' requires the individual to subscribe to normative values, at least on a superficial level, because this protects them from being mistaken for deviant or atypical. Situating the concept as a 'faithful retainer, a voice from the past [...] one of the most powerful ideological tools of the twentieth century' (Hacking, 1990: 161–9), it thus serves as a yardstick against which all previous experience may be compared. To be 'normal', then, is to be 'good' (Wong, 1997: 278), although the term tends to obfuscate the 'fact/value distinction' (Hacking, 1990: 161) and hence to effectively mask power relations.

Although teenagers often appeared uncritical of the stereotyping behaviours of maternity care providers, they were not unaffected by them. Subjectively, to be labelled in ways which diminish one's sense of agency is to be personally discounted; it is as if one's history and experience have no value. While such experiences are not peculiar to adolescents, lack of previous exposure across a range of environments may mean they have acquired fewer coping strategies. At different times throughout this study I asked the teenagers what it felt like to be young and pregnant, and to be accessing maternity services. The following responses are typical and emphasise that it was the relational, rather than the physical, aspects of childbearing which most teenagers experienced as problematic:

> Yeah. Well ... It wasn't very friendly at all. It wasn't a very good experience really. Pregnancy was easy. I found that part really easy. [...] It was the midwives and the doctors that made it not a very good experience. They looked at me like I wasn't old enough to have sex. They

were like 'Oh, you shouldn't be having sex anyway! You shouldn't be pregnant!' It's all your own fault sort of thing. (Alys, now 17 years old; son aged two years. W)

They [staff] look down on you. You can see 'em thinking, 'Oh, she's just a slut. She's a right slapper she is.' (Tracey, 14 years old; 30 weeks pregnant. SY)

The accents of maternity staff and the technical language they used were also problematic, especially for the younger teenagers. Doctors' accents were described as particularly challenging and the problems some teenagers experienced were compounded by their low educational attainment, and, in the case of one teenager, mild hearing loss. Although I observed at first hand the difficulties teenagers experienced trying to understand and communicate with doctors who spoke heavily accented English, and indeed I experienced similar difficulties myself, it was not easy to engage the teenagers in discussions on this issue. It was Megan who alerted me to concerns about such talk being (mis)construed as racist:

I couldn't understand anything 'cos he, like, mumbled all the time and then he had this awful accent. I mean, don't get me wrong, I'm not racist or anything, but he was so hard to understand. I was trying to listen really hard but I still couldn't understand him. (Megan, 14 years old; 36 weeks pregnant. W)

Asking staff to repeat themselves was not a favoured tactic, not least because teenagers wished to avoid being constructed as 'rude' or 'stupid', with perhaps further erosion of an already fragile identity:

HS: Some of the other teenagers said they've had problems with not understanding maternity staff 'cos of their accents. Has that been a problem for you?

Clare: Yeah I'll say it has, big time. *Laughs*. The doctor I saw last time, her accent was so strong I couldn't understand a word she were saying. I kept saying, 'Pardon, pardon ...' [...] You think afterwards, 'Well I didn't get half of that,' but then you don't like to ask them to repeat themselves all the time 'cos then it sounds like you're being rude, or you're just stupid or something. (Clare, 14 years old; daughter aged three weeks. SY)

Additionally, some teenagers were concerned about the implications of failing to grasp information considered to be essential in 'knowing what's going off':

> I felt a bit cheeky saying all the time, 'What? Sorry I can't understand you, could you repeat that please?' I think you can only say it once, then you feel a bit ignorant, like they'll think, 'Oh she's not paying attention.' […] It's really hard, 'cos when you can't understand then you don't know what's going off, do you? (Rhian, 15 years old; 37 weeks pregnant. W)

I assessed the majority of interactions I observed between teenagers and midwives to be of mediocre or poor quality – an assessment which was repeatedly confirmed by the teenagers themselves and their mothers/ significant others. Occasional exceptions were noted. Exceptional staff did not judge their clients on the basis of age or appearance, but focused on pregnancy-related matters. They assumed teenagers might feel nervous and perhaps frightened to be facing both an unplanned pregnancy and an unknown health professional, and attempted to put them at their ease by keeping to scheduled appointment times; making eye, and sometimes physical, contact; offering a drink where facilities permitted; asking whether, rather than assuming, that the teenagers would want their mothers and/or boyfriends present at consultations; directing questions at teenagers themselves rather than at others; providing good-quality information and following this up by asking questions and actively soliciting responses; and exercising restraint when requesting sensitive information. I observed one such midwife undertaking a booking consultation with a young couple; the following excerpt is taken from my field notes:

> The community midwife greets the young couple by name, shows them into the consultation room, invites them to sit down and then asks if they'd like a coffee(!). They accept her invitation. As I am familiar with the layout of the building I offer to make the drinks. The midwife suggests that I also fetch the tin of biscuits she keeps for 'special occasions'. When I return, the midwife has started the consultation. She is very focused on the young couple and barely acknowledges my re-entry. I distribute the drinks, leave the biscuit tin open in front of the threesome and retire to my chair in the far corner of the room. The midwife has moved her chair round from behind the desk and sits alongside her clients; she makes a lot of

eye contact with them, smiles frequently and encourages them to participate in discussions by making openings for them and waiting for them to speak. She leans back in her chair and acts as if she has all the time in the world (although I know she is extremely busy and has a large caseload of women in her care). Each time she makes an entry in the maternity record she explains what she is doing and uses the opportunity to translate medical terminology – for example *'primigravida'*. She frequently reminds the young couple to tell her if there are words they don't understand. Towards the end of the consultation both young people are spontaneously asking questions: the young man asks what *foetal* means; his partner asks about *mongol* babies and this leads into a discussion about the pros and cons of antenatal screening. The midwife reiterates the need to 'read everything we write in your notes and if you don't understand it, or if you think we've got it wrong, then you must tell us'. She introduces the topic of blood tests by explaining that the majority are 'what we call routine, for things like your blood group, iron count, to see if you're immune to German measles and to see if you've ever had illnesses like hepatitis'. She adds that 'most pregnant women have all of them but that doesn't mean you *have* to have them'. Before the midwife delivers each package of information, she invites the young couple to tell her what they already know about the subject. The midwife closes the consultation by congratulating the young couple, telling them how 'good' they look together and what 'marvellous parents' she thinks they will make. Later that evening, as I am writing up my field notes, I regret having not told this midwife how marvellous I thought *she* was and that if I were pregnant, I would want her as my midwife. (Field notes. Observation with community midwife Teresa. W)

The 'booking consultation' generally takes place between ten and 12 weeks of pregnancy, after the vulnerable period when miscarriage rates are highest. In addition to taking a medical and reproductive history, the location of this visit, usually within the private sphere of women's homes, provides opportunities for midwives to make moral judgements about their clients' domestic circumstances and hence their 'fitness' for motherhood. The time required to complete this consultation is significantly greater than for subsequent consultations due to the (ever-increasing) amount of information midwives are required to collect from, and disseminate to, pregnant women.

I accompanied Teresa for two days and observed her interacting in a similar manner with other clients, championing their rights and encouraging them to articulate their needs, irrespective of class or other markers of social status. Unlike other midwives, Teresa confronted obstetricians and powerful others on the occasions she considered their actions or decisions were unreasonable, their practice was not based on credible evidence or their policies were detrimental to her clients' best interests. Many of her colleagues behaved rather differently. Some prided themselves on having 'protected' clients by avoiding truth-telling, or indeed by lying outright to block their preferred choices. For example, I observed midwives recording higher than measured temperatures and blood pressures, overstating cervical dilatation to forestall requests for epidural anaesthesia, and advising clients that it was 'illegal' not to comply with management directives, for example to leave the bath for routine vaginal examinations, or to refuse the administration of routine antibiotics. Colluding with management against clients' interests most commonly occurred when midwives anticipated they might be required to practise outside their clinical 'comfort' zones (for example, when clients made requests to birth at home, or in water). Change in clinical practice was thus more likely to be resisted than embraced, although some midwives defended their actions by explaining that competing agendas and/or fears of litigation required that they increasingly resort to 'stealth tactics' (Stapleton et al., 1998). This rather contradicts extant literature which emphasises the unique quality of midwife–client interactions; indeed, the formation of a 'partnership' between women and their (female) midwives is a cornerstone of contemporary New Zealand midwifery (Freeman et al., 2003), a country where practice is acknowledged as extremely progressive.

My observations confirmed that pregnant women's (male) partners occupied a very marginal position and status throughout the maternity care episode, and then only in relationship to female partners, rather than midwives. The community midwife Teresa, whom I described in the previous excerpt, was unusual in that she welcomed male partners by name and actively encouraged their participation. She did not permit them to dominate proceedings, but rather acted as if she *expected* to form a relationship with them and that this would be reciprocated. Although the profile of young fathers has increased in recent years, they remain largely invisible in statistics on teenage pregnancy, indeed, 'there are no population-based data on the age at which fatherhood starts, compared with the voluminous statistics on motherhood and female fertility' (Quinton et al., 2001: 2). With respect to maternity care, while the concerns of (authoritative) middle-class men are taken seriously, the opposite is true for working-class men, particularly adolescents, and those from black and ethnic minority groups. For these groups, the maternity environment is generally experienced as unwelcoming, with staff perceived as unreceptive to non-mainstream views.

Technological imperatives: antenatal screening and estimating the expected date of birth

Routine antenatal screening for all pregnant women had only recently been introduced in some study areas. As a result many service users, and indeed occasionally service providers, were unfamiliar with important procedural aspects, including the timing of tests in relation to gestational age. Suggestions that a foetus might be 'damaged', for example from genetic malformation, and therefore be considered (by staff) as appropriate for termination, generated significant anxiety among the teenagers and their significant others, not least because termination was negatively regarded across the sample. As no baby was diagnosed *in utero* with a congenital or other life-threatening/limiting abnormality, however, it is difficult to predict whether attitudes to abortion might have changed in direct response to such a diagnosis. Attitude to abortion is anyway not necessarily related to screening uptake and, with the exception of two teenagers, all consented to routine antenatal screening procedures.

Teenagers' mothers commented that they were only able to relax when their daughters' pregnancy proceeded beyond the 'worry stage'; when screening for foetal abnormalities had returned a 'low risk' result and an ultrasound scan revealed a healthy and viable foetus:

> I'm just glad she's got past the worry stage now ... We can both settle down. [...] I'm enjoying it now. *Laughs.* The first four months were a real worry for me. She was coming to me all the time asking me things. She hadn't felt it wiggle so she says to me, 'When did you feel yours move ma ...?' [...] And then there were all these tests they do now to see if the baby's all right. They didn't do them when I were having mine, so that's all new isn't it? (Angharad (mother of Alys, aged 15). W)

Indeed, it was through talking to mothers that I realised the degree to which worry and fearfulness have become embodied aspects of how women in contemporary societies 'do' childbearing:

> I think I had two scans and four babies. But I didn't have the worry. That was the good thing. I carried those babies without the worry. [...] You didn't have a clue in those days what they [maternity staff] were talking about. No one told you anything and if they did it went right

over your head. *Laughs*. I think it were more relaxin' in my time. [...] With her [Alys] she's supposed to be understanding it all, and I think it's quite a strain on them, especially when they're young. (Angharad (mother of Alys, aged 15). W)

Participating in screening programmes generated unwanted, and unsolicited, doubts about the baby's well-being and viability, often before teenagers and/or their mothers had such thoughts themselves. More importantly, perhaps, it introduced medically derived conceptualisations of risk. In the following excerpt, Alys draws attention to a change in the midwife's attitude after her screening results assigned her a 'low risk' status:

It's like you're a guinea pig. You *could* be carrying one of these babies but in their eyes, you *are* carrying one until they find out you aren't, but until then, until they tell you that you aren't, they treat you like you are carrying one. After they told me I was a low risk, they changed then. The midwives started to tell me about other things then, but before it was just all about whether my baby might have Down's syndrome or spina bifida. (Alys, 15 years old; 30 weeks pregnant. W)

In the event that concerns were raised about the baby's viability and/or health, sometimes to the degree that pregnancy was temporarily recategorised as 'high risk', teenagers tended to remain in a state of heightened anxiety for the remainder of pregnancy. Even when such concerns were subsequently found to be spurious, doubts about the infant's well-being persisted well into the postnatal period, echoing research findings from almost three decades ago (Fearn et al., 1982). The current litigious climate, however, encourages (indeed, insists) maternity staff to practise defensively, regardless of the consequences for childbearing women. For example, it is no longer acceptable practice to convey information to pregnant women without also conveying an approximation of the attendant risks, but as there is no standard definition by which maternity-related risk is assessed, and because childbearing women are vulnerable to suggestions that they might be exposing their babies to risk, it is perhaps unsurprising that *any* discussion about antenatal screening is likely to provoke maternal anxiety. This issue is further complicated by research (Teixeira et al., 1999) which suggests a negative association between maternal anxiety and foetal outcome, and this adds to earlier work in the field (Statham et al., 1997) which revealed that anxiety about something being wrong with the baby is very common among pregnant women. Inviting pregnant women to consider additional notions of risk might, therefore, reasonably be expected to accelerate the spiral of maternal worry.

As something of an antidote to the anxiety generated by screening procedures, undergoing an ultrasound scan was generally regarded as a pleasurable, and positive, experience. This was especially the case for young men who, perforce, relied on 'second-hand' impressions to compensate for the lack of embodied knowledge afforded their female partners. The ultrasound scan generated 'visual knowledge' (Draper, 2002: 771) in the form of real-time, and photographic, images which seemed to help young men absorb the physical actuality of pregnancy and to better locate themselves on the father-to-be trajectory.

Most teenagers and their boyfriends and families regarded ultrasound scans as social, rather than medical, events. The air of excitement which accompanied the 'first viewing', together with the purchase of the ultrasound photo – printed and later framed and with the baby's chosen name – confirmed this as a significant aspect of the contemporary antenatal care package:

> The first time we saw it, it was amazing. To see it on the screen like that. Ooh, it's so exciting the first time you see it. *Laughs.* I thought Oh my God, God, look at it ...! Look at my baby ...! Brilliant! It was brilliant. After it was finished she asked us if we wanted a photo. Which of course we did. *Laughs.* (Alys, 15 years old; 20 weeks pregnant. W)

The emphasis on the social aspect of scanning has implications for staff undertaking screening procedures because, unlike pregnant women and their families, they regard these occasions as diagnostic opportunities. This contrasts with service users and their families who regard scans as benign and routine interventions; as opportunities to see the baby and confirm its health and well-being, rather than to identify potential problems.

Estimating the expected date of birth

Although most of the teenagers were able to cite the first day of their last menstrual period – information which identifies the date of conception with reasonable accuracy – this tends to be discounted by maternity staff, who perceive ultrasound results to be more accurate. The greatly increased reliance on ultrasonography for ascertaining information about women's childbearing bodies has resulted in a gradual erosion of other ways of knowing; women's experiential knowledge has thus been largely superseded by the authoritative knowledge derived from reproductive technologies. Teenagers and their loved ones were frustrated when staff changed the expected 'due date' (of birth) without apparent reason and in the absence of consultation with those affected:

> They kept giving me different dates. First of all it was the 17th and then it was the 19th [of May] when it was going to be born and then it was the 21st and then it went straight to sixth [of June]. They told me different dates, every person I've seen. [...] I've had three different scans and they still don't know. [...] I still think I'm going to have it at the end of May. (Beca, 17 years old; 14 weeks pregnant. W)

> Luci: Yeah, and then they gave me a different date.
> Gavin: Yeah, but there was a month's difference. A whole month! I thought that was quite a lot seeing as the whole pregnancy is only nine and a bit months.
> Luci: Yeah, fifth of January I was given and now I've been given December the fifth.
> HS: And what did you make of that?
> Gavin: Stupid, that's what I think.
> Luci: What they did finally was, they said 'Well, it's in-between the two.'
> Gavin: It doesn't seem like they know a lot really. If you ask me, it's like the left hand doesn't know what the right hand's doing. (Luci, 16 years old; 15 weeks pregnant, talking with Gavin, her boyfriend. W)

While early ultrasound scanning for pregnancy screening and dating purposes is now not only widely accepted but also acknowledged as good practice, it cannot take account of the (wide) variation in women's menstrual dates and hence 'actual gestational age tends to be over-estimated' (Shennan and Bewley, 2006: 939). Indeed, earlier research suggests that as many as 25 per cent of babies diagnosed as already pre-term are found to be an additional week younger at birth than their scan-based gestational age (Gardosi and Francis, 1999). In other words, despite the supposedly 'hard' evidence of maturity provided by ultrasound scanning, approximately a quarter of babies are identified, at birth, as being at least a week less mature than their predicted age (by ultrasound). Besides health and related implications for the infants concerned – many of whom are already classed as 'vulnerable' – this has serious resource implications for health service providers.

Resisting norms and conventions: antenatal 'education'

During pregnancy, many women attend NHS/private-sector antenatal education ('parentcraft') classes, which typically provide information about labour and care of the newborn infant. Such classes play an important role in the construction of (certain kinds of) mothers. Adolescent women, particularly those who are single and unmarried, are generally under-represented at these events. Mirroring the findings of earlier research (Howie and Carlisle, 2005; Rozette et al., 2002), most of the teenagers in this study expressed negative views about parentcraft classes, and those who attended on one occasion generally failed to repeat the experience. Some teenagers demonstrated considerable skill at resisting midwives' attempts to include them.

Classes were dismissed as an irrelevance, not least because many teenagers had sisters or friends who had recently experienced childbirth and from whom they sought 'no bullshit' information. Mothers and aunts who had given birth were additional sources of advice which was generally considered more appropriate and responsive to individual needs than that provided by midwives and other maternity professionals. Finally, many teenagers had been very involved with bringing up younger siblings and/or other kin, and, hence, were well versed in the practical skills of childcare:

> I think they're [education classes] a waste of time to be honest. [...] I've looked after both my younger brothers and I've fed my sister's baby right from the start. I've winded him, changed his nappies and everything, so I know all that. (Elenor, 18 years old; 23 weeks pregnant. W)

One midwife was observed colluding with April's prediction that classes would not benefit her because she was already a mother:

> Well, as your baby's only nine months old, I'd say the classes would be a waste of your time, really. You'll know it all. It'll all be still pretty fresh in your mind, so I'd say it's not worth your while. (Community midwife Katy. W)

Although the community midwife's stance could be interpreted as giving credence to April's embodied and experiential maternal knowledge, her response undermines the value of classes as a potential vehicle for social networking, which might support vulnerable teenagers in the longer term. Classes were often further discounted because they focused on the forthcoming labour, an event from which many teenagers were more concerned to distance themselves:

HS: Tell me more about what you think goes on at parentcraft classes.

Alys: Parentcraft class is … Well, you go there 'n you drink tea and you talk about labour and things. But I didn't want to go and talk about it. Uggh … No way. I didn't want to think about it happening. Yuck! I knew it was going to happen. That was enough. *Laughs.* (Alys, 15 years old; 30 weeks pregnant. W)

Teenagers identified breathing techniques, emphasised by staff as an appropriate method for managing labour pains, as particularly irrelevant, because such practices emphasised the corporeal aspects of child-bearing, which teenagers were seeking to avoid:

It's just the vision of how stupid you look. […] like you're lying there on floor and you're doing all this breathing and looking really stupid 'n stuff like that. […] It were nothing for me. It were just stupid things. *Laughs.* (Jade, 16 years old; 38 weeks pregnant. SY)

The focus on physiological aspects of childbirth also detracted from the emotional and psychological support central to the teenagers' needs; those with unreliable support networks emphasised the importance of humour and the significance of social context in their lives:

I just wanted a laugh. There was one woman, she only had a day to go and I was just thinking, 'Oooh what if she dropped the baby here. That would be a laugh wouldn't it?' *Laughs.* (April, 17 years old; ten weeks pregnant with her second baby. W)

HS: If there'd been classes for younger girls might you have gone?

Jade: Yeah, that would've been different. […] If it were all young-sters you could have a laugh. (Jade, now 17 years old; first daughter aged five months. SY)

Many teenagers complained that staff attitudes made them *feel* 'stupid', although they themselves strove to avoid *looking* stupid. Maintaining a 'cool' appearance, an essential aspect of comportment in contemporary adolescent culture, was an important consideration for participants, hence activities which focused explicitly on the physicality of pregnancy, and which emphasised physical limitations, were not well received. Stigmatising, threatening or coercive staff attitudes were identified as particularly problematic; they also acted as a barrier to future participation:

> She [midwife] said, 'Well I think 15- and 16-year-olds shouldn't be having children' and then she just sort of looked at me. I thought, well I'm not going to say anything in the middle of a class but if that's what she thinks I'm not coming back. (Lowri, 16 years old; three weeks after the stillbirth of her daughter. W)

> Susan: She [midwife] tried loads of times to get me to go. [...] She were on and on about the classes this and the classes that. I said I didn't want to go but then she said she'd come and get me. [...] She said, 'If you don't come I'll come and get you.'
>
> Mother: Yes and she was right scared after that. *Laughs.* She'd not answer the door or the phone or nowt for ages after that. *Laughs.* (Marg (mother of Susan, aged 15). SY)

Subtle forms of peer pressure also acted as significant deterrents:

> I don't know anybody my age that's been to them. I don't think anybody ever said 'don't go', so I don't really know why I didn't go. Nobody I knew had ever been. (Elenor, 18 years old; 23 weeks pregnant. W)

Appreciating that antenatal classes suffered from an 'image' problem, a small group of midwives in one area created a teenage-friendly alternative. In the following excerpt, Nia's praise may be read as a eulogy to their success:

> The antenatal classes were brilliant, I was really impressed. I thought they'd be a bit old fashioned [...] [but] they were really interesting. They did games and stuff, they made them good fun. You could ask as many questions as you wanted, you could talk about anything. (Nia, 18 years old; son aged six weeks. W)

The publication of the Teenage Pregnancy Strategy (SEU, 1999) was instrumental in highlighting the need to create responsive, and appropriate, maternity services for pregnant teenagers. To that end, a national

(UK) Teenage Pregnancy Midwifery Network was established in 2001 by two teenage-pregnancy specialist midwives with the aim of providing a teen-focused maternity agenda for all childbearing adolescents in the UK. With funding through the Teenage Pregnancy Unit as part of the National Teenage Pregnancy Strategy, and support from the Royal College of Midwives, the network supports midwives working with young parents and facilitates the sharing of good practice and innovative ideas (see The UK Royal College of Midwives Standards and Practice website).

Aquanatal classes

In some areas, aquanatal, or water-based, exercises were available as an additional resource for pregnant women. While such classes are generally highly regarded, and tend to be in great demand, the corporeal emphasis once again created difficulties for teenagers because such classes were only available in late pregnancy, at a time when their self-esteem was fragile and body image in flux:

> There were something she [midwife] said I could do at the swimming pool – 'aka' something. *Laughs.* Oooh, but then she said you had to wear your swimsuit. [...] No way am I going. Not looking like this. I'm so fat. *Laughs.* (Alys, 15 years old; 30 weeks pregnant. W)

Given the significance of the body and its potential for (re)presentation during adolescence, self-image was of prime concern. Most of the teenagers resented their inability to control their weight gain and the changes in body shape induced by pregnancy, and looked forward to birth as an opportunity to regain a sense of self. Being read as 'fat', rather than pregnant, was a particular worry; fears about gaining excessive weight which would then 'hang around' were widespread. Unlike research undertaken with older pregnant women (Stapleton, 2006), the teenagers in this study did not report a sense of relaxation over the monitoring of their shape, weight and body image during pregnancy, but neither did they appear to engage in disordered eating practices, nor strenuous exercise regimes, to control their size. Although most of the teenagers considered female fatness to be generally abhorrent, a range of understandings about size and body image were advanced by individuals, both for themselves and for other young mothers. For example, a considerable number of the teenagers had figures which I would call 'solidly built' or 'well endowed', although this was not necessarily how they perceived themselves, as I realised when I was walking through a supermarket car park with Susan, 20 weeks pregnant and just beginning to 'show'. Susan stopped for a brief exchange with an average-sized ex-schoolfriend who was leaving the supermarket with bags of shopping and a toddler in tow. As we walked away, Susan shuddered and commented that she'd 'rather die' than end up looking like her friend whom she denounced as having 'gone to fat' following childbirth. Susan added that if she hadn't known her friend was definitely *not* pregnant she might think, from her figure (which looked within normal parameters to me), that she was. Like many of her contemporaries, Susan wore crop tops and low-cut jeans which exposed both her pregnant belly and the 'handles' of flesh around her hips and midriff. Regardless of the weather or the time of the year, teenagers in both localities dressed in this way, changing only for antenatal consultations or late in pregnancy, when a degree of relaxation over the project of self-management permitted the wearing of tracksuit bottoms ('trackies') and loose jumpers ('baggies').

Concerns about weight gain were most commonly articulated in relation to the side effects of hormone-based contraception, and during the early postnatal period when body shape and 'texture' could be mistaken for pregnancy. These issues are discussed in more depth in the following chapter.

Corporeal events in pregnancy: threatened miscarriage, ill health and self-harming behaviours

Concerns about threatened miscarriage were associated with episodes of vaginal bleeding or abdominal pain, or when maternity staff initially failed to locate the foetal heart. Teenagers' mothers sometimes intuited when things were 'not quite right' before health professionals suspected anything was amiss; teenagers living at home who experienced a pregnancy 'scare', such as unexpected pain or bleeding, were far more likely to seek and act on their mothers' advice in the first instance than consult with a maternity professional:

> I started bleeding at half three in the morning and I phoned her [mother] straight up and she said to me, 'Don't worry about it, I did the same thing when I was having you. Don't worry about it, we'll get you to the doctor's tomorrow morning.' (Beca, 17 years old; 30 weeks pregnant. W)

Mothers viewed vaginal bleeding, which was generally considered 'out of place' in pregnancy, as a particularly ominous sign, and indicative of imminent miscarriage:

> I know it's a long time ago, but when I was pregnant they always used to say, the sight of blood you must take seriously. They said you should always go straightaway to be checked. But then here, with her [Rhian], they're not bothering with her at all. Why aren't they bothering? That's what I want to know. (Gwyneth (mother of Rhian, aged 15). W)

> My mum was really freaking out because I started having like a period. I went to the doctors but they weren't that bothered so then my mum rang up the hospital. (Michelle, 15 years old; 17 weeks pregnant. SY)

Blood loss was especially worrying for Michelle who, prior to the onset of menarche, experienced an episode of heavy vaginal bleeding. Tests subsequently confirmed that she, and other female members in her family, were carriers for Patau syndrome, otherwise known as Trisomy 13. After Down's syndrome, this is one of the most common of the autosomal trisomies (where an individual has three of a particular chromosome instead of the normal pair). Staff attitudes to threatened pregnancy loss did not necessarily reassure teenagers who, anyway, tended to be perceived as individuals with unlimited future reproductive potential:

> Every time I were bleeding I were panicking, thinking something's wrong and nobody's telling me. [...] We were all worried sick, in case I were going to lose it. I think the doctors didn't care if I did. They probably thought, 'Oh well, she's young anyway, she probably didn't mean to get pregnant so it doesn't matter if she loses it. She can have another one,' sort of thing. (Michelle, 16 years old; 37 weeks pregnant. SY)

Fears about the baby's well-being were also sometimes inadvertently generated through technical incompetence or technological failure:

> They couldn't hear the heartbeat and they were all standing there looking at each other, but then the nurse said the machine wasn't turned on. Then they were all smiling at me, all cheesy like, when

they got the scanner working. They found it, but for a while I thought, oh, it's dead. (Michelle, 16 years old; son aged three months. SY)

As I have already explained, once concerns had been raised about foetal well-being, teenagers and their loved ones found it hard to cope with the resultant anxiety.

Daughters' experiences of pregnancy-related events often prompted mothers to articulate their own traumatic experiences of childbirth, and some reported this was the first time they had reflected on these events in any detail. Mothers who had themselves experienced pregnancy-related problems worried that their daughters might suffer similar experiences. To that end, some reported that they attempted to shield themselves from further distress by encouraging their daughters to ask others to accompany them on visits to the antenatal clinic and to seek other sources of labour support. Maternal absences at these key maternity episodes tended to be misinterpreted by staff and they invariably upset daughters. However, in the event of labour starting, all mothers who had previously voiced reservations changed their minds and most reported being overwhelmed with relief and happiness that they had been able to put aside unpleasant personal memories and support their daughters.

When problems did arise during pregnancy, some of the teenagers reported being 'palmed off' or made to feel 'stupid' by staff who refused to answer questions. This was particularly difficult when information was required about illnesses which threatened the continuation of pregnancy, for example acute cystitis:

I was in hospital [because of acute cystitis] and I was waiting for a scan and this didn't happen for three days. I was being wound up with people not telling me anything. [...] I don't think the Sister liked me. I think she thought I was just another stupid teenager that doesn't know which end of the packet the pill comes out. They never treat you like you're going to be a mother, just like a stupid teenager. (Rhian, 15 years old; 37 weeks pregnant. W)

Being excluded from discussions about their own health and well-being was particularly difficult for unsupported teenagers because they had no one to intercede for them and hence were generally unable to fully appreciate the implications of decisions which were made on their behalf, but without their involvement.

Differentiating symptoms of ill health from those associated with pregnancy

Staff tended to dismiss the concerns mothers raised about their daughters' health as the inevitable, and inconsequential, results of pregnancy rather than as possible indicators of general ill health:

HS: So you suspected there was something wrong?

Dilys: Yes I did. It wasn't anything I could put my finger on. I just knew something wasn't quite right. In fact I was convinced something was wrong even though she'd [Lowri] just come out of hospital and they'd [maternity staff] said there was nothing wrong.

Lowri: She [Dilys] kept telling me that I needed to go to the doctors again. I went to the surgery quite a few times, but then one doctor he said, 'Well you must just be having a bad pregnancy,' so after that I didn't go back. [...] In the end I started thinking as well, oh well it [the vague feeling of unwellness] must be because I was pregnant. [...] In the hospital the doctors [...] they told me it was because I was pregnant. But then she [Dilys] kept saying, 'No, something's not right.'

Dilys: If she hadn't been pregnant and she'd just gone to the doctor's with those symptoms something would have been done about it. It would have been investigated. It was just assumed that it was pregnancy [but] you know when your own child is ill. [...] It's that instinct, being a mother I suppose. [...] I'm a woman and to me what she was having was an illness. It wasn't pregnancy. (Lowri, 16 years old, talking with her mother Dilys (who is currently pregnant). W)

The results of an autopsy following the birth of her stillborn baby confirmed Dilys's suspicions: her daughter had contracted cytomegalovirus, a viral illness which her baby had also contracted, resulting in its death.

Teenage pregnancy is associated with a number of adverse medical outcomes, but research is lacking about the possible consequences of staff failing to take seriously the health concerns raised by pregnant teenagers and their significant others. It is quite possible that reproductive outcomes for this vulnerable group might be improved if service providers could be persuaded to listen more attentively, and respond more rapidly, to their complaints of ill health during pregnancy.

Changing habits: smoking, drinking, disordered eating and self-harming

In contemporary Western societies the responsibility for maintaining a healthy pregnancy, and for ensuring a positive pregnancy outcome, is increasingly understood to be the sole responsibility of the mother. Maternal liability for reproductive outcomes has become more pronounced following research linking the intrauterine environment with health in adult life, and one obvious consequence is the shift of focus ever further back in the life course, encapsulating the mother–foetus dyad. The duty to abstain from harmful activities and to prioritise the health and well-being of the foetus at all times and, indeed, over their own needs, is a taken-for-granted responsibility for pregnant women. Hence, they must strive to achieve optimal health status not only for themselves but also for those conceived, though as yet unborn. The bodies of pregnant women are thus 'acted upon', which is in keeping with their medicalised 'condition', and their perceived role as mere containers or vessels for the foetus.

Smoking in pregnancy is known to be associated with poverty-related indicators, including an early exit from full-time education, unemployment, single or divorced status and living in rented accommodation. A number of the teenagers were heavy smokers and, prior to pregnancy, were also regular and/or binge drinkers, although most abstained from drinking alcohol throughout the maternity episode. Few knew anything about the link between alcohol consumption in pregnancy and foetal alcohol syndrome.

Efforts to stop smoking were largely unsuccessful, although most teenagers were aware of the deleterious affects, including increased risk of prematurity, low birth weight and stillbirth. Despite UK government targets for reducing smoking among disadvantaged pregnant women, there is a dearth of qualitative research on the smoking-related behaviours of *young* pregnant women. This evidence gap raises questions about the basis for current policies, especially smoking-cessation interventions. The teenagers who had commenced smoking in childhood (sometimes with parental encouragement) experienced greatest difficulty in reducing their intake and/or ceasing altogether.

April: I don't drink much now anyway. Not now I have her [first baby]. [...] Before I had her I just used to sit in my room and drink and drink and smoke and smoke. [...] [If] I had the money I'd go down the pub with my mates and get as drunk as an idiot [...] we used to hold each other up like a pair of crutches. I used to drink eight double rums and about three pints of cider. If I could afford it I'd drink Malibu as well. [...] I'd be totally legless by end of an evening. [...] We'd all just get totalled.

HS: And when you realised you were pregnant did you just go off alcohol or did you have to make a real effort to stop drinking?

April: Oh no I had to make a really big effort. It was really hard. I love the drink. It's the thing that keeps me going. It's the same with smoking. I try and forget them but wherever I go there's an ashtray or a lighter or there's someone smoking outside and I'm away. I'm always craving one. I was 11 when I started smoking. It was my father's fault. He said, 'Go on have a puff of this. If you don't like it that's all right.' He said, 'Go on I won't tell your mother.' So I had a puff on his cig. Ever since then I've smoked. [...] Other people have the willpower, but I haven't got that. Drinking, that's not a problem, I can stop that. But stop smoking? I don't think I could do that. I haven't got the willpower.

HS: When it's really hard to give something up like smoking, how does it make you feel when the midwives and doctors go on and on at you to give it up?

April: It depends on my mood. *Laughs.* [...] Sometimes I lie just to get them off my back. Before I got pregnant I was on like over 40 a day, now it's like 30 a day. He [doctor] said, 'You could give up.' I said to him, 'Do you smoke?' He said no, and I said, 'Well you don't know what I'm going through.' He said, 'Well other people haven't got a problem giving up.' I said, 'Well I have, I can't give up.' I gave up for ten hours once [...] at the end of it I was, I was like ... *Growls.* (April, 17 years old; ten weeks pregnant with her second baby. W)

April was not alone in admitting she lied to maternity staff, usually to 'get them off my back' – a strategy which was generally adopted when an individual teenager anticipated being rebuked or humiliated for the 'bad' habits which they were aware of, but which they were unable to forego. For example, the teenagers who smoked were generally well aware of the link between smoking and the negative consequences for their own health and that of their children, but, as Hilary Graham concluded from research almost two decades ago, 'it was how women lived rather than what they knew which was the stronger predictor of their smoking status' (Graham, 1993b: 101).

Teenagers who smoked heavily experienced considerable distress on the occasions that they were hospitalised. The period immediately following delivery was often a critical time for nicotine-addicted teenagers, when their desire for a cigarette was overwhelming, especially following a long and physically gruelling labour. In the following excerpt, Lou attempts to persuade staff that a 'drag' is quantitatively different from a 'fag', and, when this ruse fails, she expresses an intention to resort to more devious tactics:

HS: How're you doing with the stress of not having had a fag for nearly 24 hours?

Lou: That's killin' me that is! *Laughs*. All I want is like, two drags ... But, like, when doctor come in, he said no fags. He didn't say I couldn't have three drags though. *Laughs*. He said a fag, 'cos you know with some people, you know a fag means different things, dunnitt? You could say, oh three drags ain't done nowt to you, but with t'other person it would be same as having whole fag ... So I asked midwife if I could go for three drags and she says, no, you can't smoke at all. Your lungs are too bad. So I says to her, why can't I just go to smokers' room for three drags ...? I think I'll go and hope she's not lookin'. I can't wait no more. It's killin' me ...

Pete: I wouldn't. I don't think you should risk it. Not from what doctor said.

HS: What would you be risking?

Lou: He says ... Doctor says if I have a fag I'm gonna be in intensive care by tomorrow morning. It's me asthma that's got so bad with me smokin 'n all. It's getting worse all the time ... He says, I'm like, I'm 16 years old and I've got lungs like I'm 80 years old. (Lou, 16 years old; first day following the birth of her baby daughter by caesarean section. SY)

When I interviewed maternity staff providing in-patient care for teenagers who smoked, I asked if they had ever considered whether the 'disruptive' behaviour some reported might be linked to nicotine withdrawal. I also enquired whether therapeutic initiatives, including nicotine patches, had been considered, at least for the duration of hospitalisation. Although some staff appeared interested in my proposal, none of those interviewed had previously considered this issue.

I did not make comprehensive enquiries about the prevalence of smoking by the teenagers' male partners, although my own observations, and anecdotal reportage, suggest that the majority were also moderate to heavy smokers. Although there is now substantial, and well-established, evidence linking passive infant smoking with poor health outcomes (Blair et al., 1996; Cook and Strachan, 1999) and is positively, and incontrovertibly, associated with sudden infant death syndrome (Mitchell, 1995), expectant fathers are not generally targeted for smoking-cessation interventions. This is despite the fact that parturition is widely viewed as a time 'when discontinuities in everyday life associated with the transition to fatherhood and the presence of a new baby provide opportunities for establishing new routines' (Bottorff et al., 2006: 3096). The gendered nature of smoking-cessation programmes may thus be interpreted as an attempt to regulate and sanitise the pregnant female body, as much as public health initiatives to promote infant well-being. By characterising the consumption of alcohol and cigarettes as activities unsuited to 'responsible' childbearing, pregnant women are pressured to conform to a moral understanding of motherhood which privileges the child's future health and well-being over the mother's, but not the father's, continued indulgence in sensual and pleasurable activities.

Some boyfriends, and family members on both sides, regularly engaged in drug-related activities and, indeed, a number had criminal convictions for dealing. There was no evidence, however, that the teenagers who participated in my study were involved in the 'dark play' (Schechner, 1993: 36) which might have posed serious threats to their social status, and/or their health and well-being. Indeed, most voiced strong disapproval of such behaviours, and those with drug-dependent family members spoke passionately about the damaging effects of drugs on the lives of individual family members and on family cohesion.

Tracey and Jade described self-harming behaviours of a more serious nature. Tracey had been hospitalised on numerous occasions, each time undergoing examinations and intrusive interventions for which no cause had ever been identified. Prior to pregnancy she had made two attempts at suicide by overdosing on paracetamol. On two occasions during pregnancy she threatened to 'top' herself.

In times of stress, Jade severely restricted her food intake and had begun self-harming (cutting) when her abusive relationship with the father of her first baby ended abruptly, after he began an affair with another young woman. Following pregnancy disclosure, Jade was made homeless by her mother and at this point her disordered eating and self-harming behaviours worsened significantly. Improvement occurred only when she was rehoused and was able to access support from her landlady and landlord, and when she realised the potential consequences of her behaviour for her future relationship with her child:

Jade: When I first come here I hardly ate anything 'n I was hurting [self-harming] myself all the time but now [landlady and landlord] helped me talk about things. [...] They said it's not good for bubba if I don't eat 'n if I keep hurting myself, 'cos the social [services] can take bubba off me. [...] They just keep sayin' you have to think of bubba now. So that's what I'm tryin' to do.

HS: Is that hard for you?

Jade: Yeah. It is. There's so many things going off round ya, but what I try and do is just think about bubba. Yeah. That's helpin' me. (Jade, 16 years old; 26 weeks pregnant with her first baby. SY)

Social services were invested with significant power in the minds of the most vulnerable teenagers. Jade, April, Tracey and Lou all volunteered repeated anxieties about their babies being removed from their care. The teenagers' concerns about this potential-for-action were independently verified by maternity staff.

For the most marginalised young women such as Jade and Tracey, distress arising from situations over which they had little or no control (eviction from home, abuse, inadequate/inappropriate housing, insufficient money, etc.) provoked self-harming behaviours. Their stories support the claim that 'anger directed against the self or others is always a central problem in the life of people who have been violated [although] "acting out" is seldom understood by either victims or clinicians as being a repetitive re-enactment of real events from the past' (van der Kolk, 1989: 391). There appeared to be few resources available within local communities to assist young women to manage the aftermath of the psychologically damaging experiences they had endured, sometimes over a period of many years. For example, two teenagers were referred to mental health services for psychological assessment and were subsequently identified as needing on-going therapeutic help. The support they so desperately needed, however, could only be accessed on a short-term basis, and at an institution which provided neither transport nor childcare facilities.

Socio-spatial exclusion and maternity environments

Boundaries, as represented by the location and timing of consultations, for example, reinforce divisions between service users and providers. Within hospital settings, especially within labour wards, such divisions operate along spatial, class and hierarchical lines. That certain places are freely accessible only to certain categories of people, and that identities are spatialised and politicised through the operations of power and 'territorialisation' techniques (Skeggs, 1999: 228), suggests that maternity environments, and the populations passing through these locations, may be similarly regarded. David Sibley's (1995) research examined shopping malls (including Meadowhall, a highly regarded and much visited haunt by the South Yorkshire teenagers), and the ways in which space is ambiguously presented as 'public' although organised as 'private', through the presence of security guards and surveillance cameras restricting 'undesirables'. Hence, adolescents hanging about in shopping malls 'doing nothing', or at least nothing which costs money, come to be viewed as 'trouble', as 'matter out of place' (Douglas, 1999: 109), because they do not conform to the normative model of the urban shopper. Non-consumption, and 'hanging out', are construed as forms of deviance because these 'activities' are undertaken in spaces designed for other purposes and for other people. Shopping malls are for shopping; for purchasing; for consuming. Above all they are family spaces, and the presence of nonconforming 'others' in such spaces is discrepant and threatening.

Narratives frequently suggested that many maternity care professionals similarly viewed the institutional spaces in which they worked as 'adult' spaces which properly belonged to 'respectable' people who, by definition, are not youngsters and not working class. Young women were admitted to these 'adult' spaces only because they had transgressed social norms. Hence they could justifiably be classed as 'other' and undeserving of civil treatment:

Angharad: Some of them, you see 'em thinking, 'Why am I bothering? Why am I wasting my time with ones like you? Why am I bothering with you? You shouldn't be in this condition anyway ...'

Alys: Yes. It's like, instead of it just being well, all sorts of people get pregnant and I'm just one of those sorts, you can see they're thinking, 'Oh you shouldn't be havin' sex at your age. You shouldn't be goin' out with boys at your age.' *Laughs*. (Alys and her mother, Angharad. W)

Shopping malls and maternity environments may appear to have little in common, but they are both locations in which certain individuals, especially those who are young and working class, are likely to be regarded as outsiders:

> It's her [midwife] disapproval is the worst thing isn't it? [...] If she [Michelle] were older and she were married it would help her. [...] They're more polite to older ones aren't they, but because she's just a slip of a kid ... That's what they think ... You're only a teenager ... You shouldn't be here ... You're far too young to be here. (Polly (mother of Michelle, aged 16). SY)

Health professionals' stereotyping practices and attitudes had an alienating and/or muting effect on the teenagers. Their own observations confirmed what most suspected: that they were indeed treated very differently from their older counterparts; most of the teenagers reported feeling generally unwelcome and unwanted in maternity settings.

The presentation of self in the antenatal clinic: dressing up for the midwife

During observation sessions, I often heard midwives commenting on the dress sense and bodily adornments worn by their young clients. Such comments were occasionally made during the consultation and hence were available for interpretation by the teenagers concerned; more disparaging remarks were generally withheld until the consultation concluded and the young woman had left the room. Although I had expected that teenagers would be well versed in contemporary fashion trends as personal identity statements, I had not anticipated midwives would show much interest in this aspect of their clients' personal management. That they did so reflects early research which suggested that circulating discourses of both adolescence and femininity are often shaped by professionals and articulated through 'a hierarchy of authority' (Hudson, 1984: 33). In this instance, it was midwives who assumed an authoritative stance and whose opinions influenced how pregnant young women were portrayed and perceived. The attitudes of professional groups, especially those involved in the lives of vulnerable young people, play an important role in media constructions of adolescence; their opinions carry weight and are read as authoritative. As such, they may be purloined by the media and re-presented as stereotypical images for consumption in the public arena.

In order to deflect possible criticism by midwives, considerable numbers of young women reported changing from their normal clothing to clothes 'I'd not be seen dead in' prior to attending antenatal appointments. This midwife-induced pressure to dress differently caused some young women considerable distress, especially those who possessed very few clothes and who had no money to buy new outfits. While some young women were fortunate, in having accommodating mothers who allowed them to borrow clothes for clinic visits, most young women rarely shared the same size and taste in fashion as their mothers. Dressing for an antenatal appointment, then, provoked anxiety and assumed an inflated importance, as young women strove to adjust their embodied appearance to the 'appropriate' dress code. There is a considerable literature on the links between female corporeality and clothing, whether as a practice of female consumption (Colls, 2004), as an ingredient in identity construction (Green, 2001) and/or as fashionable lived experience (Entwistle, 2001). Discourses on dressing as a social practice in the context of pregnancy (Beale, 2002; Longhurst, 2000) have highlighted the importance of appearance for all women, including those previously considered to be removed from such concerns. The teenagers in this study suggested they were more likely to be governed by dress codes than were older pregnant women:

> When I went to antenatal I did dress tidily. [...] There were some [pregnant women] there in leggings and tee-shirts, but they were older so they could get away with it. *Laughs.* I wasn't comfy in half the clothes I was in, but you put up with it. Mmm, even if I was killing myself with the clothes being really uncomfortable, I still wore them. *Laughs.* It was hard, 'cos I didn't have many clothes that I could wear, but my mum let me borrow some of hers. *Laughs.* (Lowri, 16 years old; three weeks after the stillbirth of her daughter. W)

The efforts young women made to dress in accordance with perceived 'proper' norms of maternity attire were not necessarily successful. As Alys describes in the following excerpt, clothing must not only be deemed 'appropriate', it must also comply with an ideology which privileges foetal welfare:

> I bought some really good jeans and I wore them to the clinic. They were really really expensive and the midwife told me off. *Laughs.* She said, you're not supposed to wear jeans when you're pregnant. *Laughs.* [...] She told me I shouldn't wear them 'cos I'd crush the baby. I did wear them anyway, 'cos I felt like really comfy in them. They weren't tight around my stomach or anything, they were just really comfy. [...]

She said you shouldn't wear high heels either, because they're bad for your posture 'n everything. (Alys, 15 years old; 30 weeks pregnant. W)

Midwives responded similarly to teenagers with tattoos and pierced navels, claiming these were also potentially injurious to foetal well-being. Tattoos were potential sites of infection, and pierced navels, in particular, were thought to impede the expansion of the young woman's belly and hence to compromise foetal growth. A focus on the external surfaces of young women's bodies thus emphasised the power of the techno-medical gaze in mapping foeto-maternal corporeality. It also emphasised the pursuit of ever more precise parameters by which to measure foetal status and, if deemed necessary, introduce correctional strategies.

Young women's mothers described the efforts their daughters made to look 'presentable' before attending antenatal appointments. They hoped that such efforts would deflect attention away from staff perceptions of their 'inappropriate' youth and, with it, the negative connotations generated by being teenaged in maternity environments.

She [Beca] always dressed up and made herself really presentable. Rather than be comfy and go down there [to the clinic] in a little tee-shirt, or something she'd wear round the house, she always made sure she looked all right. She was really worried about looking tidy, so they wouldn't think badly of her because she was young. (Glenys (mother of Beca, aged 17). W)

Realigning dress codes in accordance with midwives' expectations may be understood as another aspect of the totalising processes of 'confinement' to which pregnant women are routinely subjected. As Robyn Longhust (2001) has noted, the word 'confinement' – meaning limit or boundary – is a recurring image and experience in women's lives. It is also one which comes early and forcefully in pregnancy, restricting access to public spaces, sometimes limiting indulgence in alcohol and tobacco, and curbing a range of other previously taken-for-granted pleasures and freedoms. Gillian Rose (1993), quoting an earlier piece of research (Frye, 1983), contextualises the notion of 'confinement' within a classed environment:

If I have to think of one word that can work as a motif for this experience [of being a white working-class woman], it is confinement – the shrinking of horizons, the confinements of space, of physical and assertive movements within institutions, the servility that masqueraded as civility, the subjugation of my body, emotions and psyche. (Rose, 1993: 27)

White working-class women, then, are increasingly 'marked as the national constitutive limit to propriety' (Skeggs, 2005: 968). This is even more so if they are teenaged and pregnant.

Pregnant adolescents were seldom read by maternity staff as 'normal' and, as a result, tended to be positioned as marginal, at least as far as their evolving maternal identities were concerned. Such positioning complicated an already difficult transitional period and reaffirmed the negative scripting and stereotypes of young motherhood. It is not unusual for adults to feel uncomfortable when faced with the physicality of adolescents' bodies, their distinctive dress codes and body modifications, and particular behaviours. In middle age, when our own bodies may be sagging into shapelessness, and years of pleasurable, but ultimately self-abusive, practices have taken their toll, the adolescent body may serve as the perfect *tabula rasa* upon which to project personal, but unacknowledged, envies and dissatisfactions. Thus, midwives, many of whom are middle-aged, may be unsettled when confronted with teenagers presenting (flaunting?) their maternal selves within institutional settings and may react by trying to suppress the adolescent's (sexual) self-expression.

The (re-)enactment of an assigned role, and the importance of maintaining a consistent, and appropriate, 'front' during individual role performance, was remarked upon by Erving Goffman ([1959] 1969), who employed the metaphor of the stage and the language of theatre to describe the 'dramaturgical' aspects of social encounters. It was Goffman's contention that if we can understand the archetypal interactions presented by actors working within the contrived and imperfect environment of theatre settings, then we may be better placed to recognise when these archetypes are at play in everyday social interactions. Goffman also appreciated the operations of social mobility within stratified societies and the pressures on individuals to maintain progress from lower to higher status. Such progression is not without costs, however, as 'upward mobility involves the presentation of proper performances and efforts to move upward and efforts to keep from moving downward are expressed in terms of sacrifices made for the maintenance of front' (Goffman, [1959] 1969: 31). Many young women in this study strove to present an acceptable 'front' within (maternity) environments which were, by and large, hostile to unconventional representations of maternity. Their efforts to create an acceptable identity were generally not appreciated by midwives, however, and, hence, could not work to advance the teenagers' status.

The next chapter describes individual teenagers' labour and birth trajectories, and their subsequent transitions to motherhood. The teenagers who were able to access reliable and up-to-date information, and reliable support networks, reported being better prepared; the experiences of mothers and close female relatives were important factors in this respect. The focus on power relations and the interplay between the teenagers, their mothers and their boyfriends, and maternity staff make for difficult, and depressing, reading. This is not least because the technologies of management associated with contemporary, and institutionalised, labour and birth practices all too vividly illustrated the disempowering nature of maternity encounters between the disenfranchised and powerful others. The testimonies from the two teenagers who suffered a foetal death in pregnancy are particularly revealing in this respect. Finally, I discuss a number of key issues confronting the teenagers during a period of major adjustment as they embraced the (sometimes harsh) realities of mothering a new baby.

5
Labour and Birth Narratives

Birth, whatever its origins and associations, is normally a celebratory event, which, in ideal circumstances, could serve to counterbalance critical responses to non-normative childbearing. That *young* motherhood is seldom understood as an event to celebrate has been noted (Baker, 1999); indeed, narratives of labour and birth suggest that, to the contrary, these appear troubling events for maternity staff. Once the charged family atmosphere which accompanied pregnancy disclosure had subsided, most of the teenagers looked forward to becoming mothers and stated an intention to do the best they could for their child's welfare. Their journeys through pregnancy, however, were made more difficult by the stigmatising attitudes they faced, not least from health professionals; many young women thus approached labour with a mounting sense of dread. Mothers were also anxious, especially those with painful memories of their own labours, and the cruel treatment they had received from maternity staff.

The majority of teenagers repeatedly mentioned fears about labour-associated pain. When I reiterated their concerns to midwives, a common response was that any such fears might have been reduced had the teenagers attended 'parentcraft' classes: 'learning for themselves that there's nothing to be frightened about. It's ignorance that's their main enemy.' In the minds of midwives then, it was education – in a very particular form – which they perceived as the route out of 'ignorance' to an easier labour. Relational elements, which would require midwives to consciously engage with their young clients, were not mentioned. This was in contrast to the teenagers' narratives which frequently highlighted negative staff attitudes such as refusing access to their boyfriends and loved ones at critical points and despite displays of obvious distress:

I were really frightened. [...] They wouldn't let Pete [boyfriend] stay with me 'cos they said I weren't in proper labour. Then they put me in a room all on my own 'cos they said I were making too much noise, 'cos I were getting loads of contractions and I was just falling off the bed I were in so much pain. [...] I were so tired 'n all I just cried and cried. (Lou, now 18 years old; daughter aged 18 months. SY)

You tend to forget the horrible bits if the people around you were nice. But I remember the nurses were not very nice with me. [...] *Labour was horrible because they were horrible.* (Alys, now 17 years old; son aged two years. W; emphasis added)

Evidence has been available for some time to suggest that although women may forget the physical pain of labour, they never forget things which were said and done at the time (Leap and Hunter, 1993; Simpkin, 1991). The routine, and numerous, abandonments, together with the persistent rejections and refusals which all the teenagers described – occasionally in heart-rending detail – seemed to somehow intensify memories of pain and, hence, to foreground the 'sensational' and corporeal elements of labour. The routine practices of maternity staff thus appeared to undermine, and further fragment, individual teenagers' already fragile sense of self.

Space and power in the birthing environment

All the young women laboured and gave birth in hospitals. This location emphasised the separation between the familiar and the unfamiliar, between kin and strangers. Although teenagers were adamant that hospital was the most appropriate place to labour and birth, some mothers expressed greater ambivalence, with one who had enjoyed a home birth and another who had considered this option offering alternative understandings, particularly with respect to privacy, risk and safety:

I said to her, 'Well you can always have it here at home.' She said, 'Oh no mum, I couldn't.' I said to her, 'Yes, you could, you could have it in your bedroom, it's private if that's what you're worried about,' but then she said, 'Oh no, all that mess, all that blood 'n stuff, imagine that.' *Laughs.* Then I said she could have it in the bath but she won't have anything like that. To her, it's like if you're having a baby it's the hospital is where you go. (Chris (mother of Clare, aged 14). SY)

Prior to labour, some mothers voiced their scepticism about the (poor) quality of maternity care they anticipated staff would provide for their daughters. Low expectations reinforced their opinion that labouring and birthing at home was the better option:

> Mmm, yes, everything's there but can you actually get it when you need it? Most of the time midwives are just sat there chatting and having cups of coffee at their desk. They're just sat there doing nothing for you. Part of me is thinking, they're there and they're not there. So I think well, what's the point of going to hospital. Why doesn't she just have it at home, like I had her at home. (Anwen (mother of Megan, aged 14). W)

Space affects our 'feelings about others' (Sibley, 1995: xiv); this became very apparent after Lou gave birth. The combination of her existing poor health status, and her prolonged labour and surgical delivery, required that Lou remain under medical observation, on the labour ward, for 24 hours following her caesarean section. During this time she was nursed in a pleasant single room to which her boyfriend, Pete, had unrestricted access. At the end of this period she was judged sufficiently recovered to transfer to the postnatal ward. Both Lou and Pete expressed reservations about the proposed move. Lou was worried that her appearance would make her an object of derision and pity, because she had no 'nice maternity clothes' to wear but only her (smelly) trainers, ill-fitting tracksuit bottoms and grubby tee-shirts. She also worried that her constant coughing and noisy expectoration (a result of chronic asthma exacerbated by heavy smoking from an early age) would annoy other mothers and generate anxiety about whether she was potentially 'infectious'. Pete was concerned that the combination of restrictive visiting hours and poor public transport meant that he would have little time with Lou and his baby daughter; the cost of transport was an additional worry. During labour, Pete had discovered that a number of single rooms were available on the maternity unit, and Lou asked a midwife she considered 'friendly' whether she might be transferred to such a facility. The following excerpt, taken from my field notes, graphically illustrates Lou's 'unworthiness' and her lack of bargaining power to access NHS spaces reserved for the exclusive use by privileged 'others'.

> The midwife who had apparently told Lou she would be transferring to the postnatal ward visits Lou just as I am about to leave.

She neither knocks at the door nor, on entering the room, does she wait for Pete to complete his sentence. The midwife takes up position at the foot of Lou's bed, glares at Lou and demands to know, 'If it's true what I've heard, that you're after a single room?' Lou hesitantly replies that yes, she had asked a midwife if that might be possible. The midwife then launches into a vitriolic tirade, which is delivered too rapidly and too furiously for me to make precise notes. She informs the young couple that, 'There are only two single rooms and they're reserved for special cases and anyway they're both occupied.' The midwife reiterates the details of the imminent transfer to the postnatal ward, and reminds Lou and Pete that, regarding visiting hours, 'Rules are rules, you'll have to stick to visiting hours and that's all there is to it. There's no exceptions.' She then leaves the room. I am shocked at this unprovoked attack on these two vulnerable young people; I also feel embarrassed and upset. Later I feel angry and my anger intensifies when I discover that both of the single rooms in question were, in fact, vacant and, indeed, had been for the past week, after the last 'special case' – an older mother, the wife of a hospital consultant who had given birth to twins as a result of IVF treatment – had been discharged. (Field notes. Observation of an interaction between a midwife and Lou, 16 years old; first day following the birth of her daughter by emergency caesarean section. SY)

Lou was so distressed by the midwife's attitude that, against medical advice, she discharged herself from hospital shortly afterwards. This excerpt demonstrates how individual 'worthiness' is evaluated and the ways in which individual identity may be 'mapped onto public space' (Jenkins, 2004: 168).

Labour and birth were perhaps the most obvious times in pregnancy when power relations between maternity professionals and their teenage clients were most visible. Initially I found myself stumbling over the application of the term 'abuse' within a midwifery environment. During readings of transcripts, I had to constantly remind myself that abusive acts are not concerned with the intentionality of the perpetrator but, rather, with how they are experienced. Conceptualised thus, the term fits the maternity context. Indeed, some scenarios described in this chapter suggest that, for some young women at least, the birthing environment must be considered a 'terrain of power' (Hagan and Smail, 1997: 260), in which oppressive, and abusive, acts are repeatedly visited upon defenceless women.

Anticipating labour: knowing signs

Although most of the teenagers expressed at least some anxiety about how they would cope with labour, they were generally pragmatic about its inevitability and about their capacity to endure it, although this is not to imply that they were fatalistic:

> HS: How're you feeling about labour – are you worrying about it?
> Clare: No. I haven't really thought about it. My mum's been on and on about it. *Laughs*. [...] [it] just goes in one ear and out other. *Laughs*. What's point in thinking about it? It's gonna happen anyway, nowt I can do is there? [...] I mean, if summat's gonna happen it's gonna happen, so no point worrying about it 'n getting m'self all stressed out. (Clare, 14 years old; 38 weeks pregnant. SY)

> HS: So ... labour could happen any day now. Are you ready for it?
> Jade: No. *Laughs*. But I'll be all right. It's only gonna be for a day, or two days, then it'll be over and I'll have a babba. (Jade, 16 years old; 39 weeks pregnant with her first baby. SY)

Perhaps the most dreaded scenario anticipated by the teenagers was that the amniotic fluid sac might suddenly burst in a public setting. Mothers reported on camouflage strategies devised by their daughters:

> She [Anwen] said to me, 'I'm going to take a bottle of water out with me from now on mum.' I said, 'Why?' She said, ''Cos all the girls have been telling me if my waters go in the street I can pretend I've tipped this [water bottle] down me.' I said, 'You'll look more stupid doing that, it's a natural thing it is when that happens.' *Laughs*. (Anwen (mother of Megan, aged 14). W)

Somatic concerns appeared to be more pronounced within maternity environments, perhaps because it was here that young women felt most constrained and self-conscious.

Although the majority of teenagers knew someone who had recently laboured and birthed, and their experiences carried significant influence, they nonetheless tended to seek their mothers' advice about the 'right' time to transfer to hospital. Teenagers often interpreted advice literally and disguised their anxieties with humour:

HS: And what about when labour starts. Do you think you'll know when it's time to go to hospital?

Clare: Mmm. My mum said you have to phone up when you go into labour, but then the midwife, she said you're not supposed to go into hospital until your contractions are coming about every three minutes, something like that. *Laughs.* [...] She said your womb has to be so much open inside, as well, or they send you back home. Six inches or something I think it were. *Laughs.* I don't know how you know it's six inches without a ruler stuck up inside you all time. *Laughs.* (Clare, 14 years old; 39 weeks pregnant. SY)

Mothers' own childbirthing histories also influenced young women's expectations:

HS: How long do you think your labour might last, Clare?

Clare: I dunno. *Laughs.* Haven't got a clue. Could be anything couldn't it? Midwife said for first baby it might be about nine hours. Something like that. [...] My mum said she were in nine hours with me. [...] She were ages with [younger sister]. She were about 36 hours with her, I think. (Clare, 14 years old; 38 weeks pregnant. SY)

In the event, Clare was induced, because of perceived postmaturity, although as she had first consulted her GP late in pregnancy and could not recall her last menstrual period with any degree of accuracy, estimating her 'due' date was always speculative. Her labour lasted a very typical 22 hours.

Labour and technologies of management

Within the paradigm of medicalised childbirth, labour is divided into discrete stages which reflect key physiological events. The first stage of labour includes descent of the baby in the birth canal and progressive cervical dilatation (0–10cm); the second stage, during which the baby is born, is confirmed by a fully dilated cervix (10cm) and descent and rotation of the baby's head (or bottom) through the birth canal; while the third stage is completed by the delivery of the placenta (afterbirth) and membranes. The addition of a fourth stage, which includes the first few hours following birth, is currently under consideration.

Most young women learned about labour from their mothers and female relatives, including how best to determine the onset and to manage pain. Concern about labour pain and the (in)ability to cope with it has been identified as a 'worrying trend [...] one of the indicators of a lack of confidence to cope with the forthcoming birth' (Green et al., 2003: 25). This same study reported significant increases in childbearing women, especially first-time mothers, stating that they felt 'very worried' about labour pain. Determining the 'quality' of contractions is considered an essential element of monitoring labour progress. Maternity staff generally regard 'effective' contractions to be those which dilate a woman's cervix at an approved rate while simultaneously exerting pressure on the presenting part of the baby, moving it progressively down the birth canal. Once the onset of labour has been confirmed, 'ineffective' contractions are not well tolerated by staff because they are associated with problematic labours:

I were getting contractions all day, but they said they weren't good ones 'cos they weren't making me open fast enough like, so then they said they'd have to give me something to make it open faster. (Clare, 14 years old; daughter aged nine days. SY)

Defining the constituents of 'good' contractions was an important consideration for maternity staff; towards the end of pregnancy it also became a topic of conversation which preoccupied teenagers and their mothers. 'Good' contractions meant admission to hospital and, if young women had been induced, 'good' contractions were an important criterion for admission to the labour ward and consideration for pain relief, particularly epidural anaesthesia. Not for these young women the glories of 'natural' childbirth; pain-free childbirth was what they sought, although this preference met with resistance from some maternity staff:

HS: So did you have anything for the pain in the end?
Clare: I were having gas and air for a while, then [...] later on, I think it were about half ten, 11, I had injection [...] then eventually I had an epidural. [...] I wanted the epidural right from the start, like, but she were like, Oh, no, you don't need that, you're fine. You'll have the baby soon. [...] It were ages before I had her. (Clare, 14 years old; daughter aged nine days. SY)

When contractions are considered 'ineffective', that is, deemed by the attending professional as insufficiently powerful to dilate the cervix according to a predetermined timeframe, it is routine practice to 'give something' to accelerate labour. Most often this 'something' takes the form of an internal examination, as a prelude to puncturing the amniotic sac, and/or inserting an intravenous infusion containing 'syntocinon' (a synthetic version of the naturally occurring hormone oxytocin) which stimulates the womb/uterus to contract. Prior to discussing medical interventions, however, midwives may advise women to try alternative measures such as an upright position or a warm bath; some maternity units provide purpose-designed birthing pools. Although the maternity unit accessed by the South Yorkshire teenagers had installed this facility, none of the young women were invited to use it. A manager in the unit confided that the majority of midwives working there lacked experience in caring for women labouring in water; an additional obstacle was the fee: women wanting to use the pool were required to book in advance and to pay £20 (approx. US$31) to cover the cost of a disposable liner. These issues deterred all but the most determined and affluent women.

Induction of labour

Of the 17 young women who participated in the study, labour and birth details are available for nine, including all six of the South Yorkshire teenagers, five of whom were induced. Jade was the only one in either cohort to experience a spontaneous onset of labour, which she managed with both her children. Tracey was induced at a little over 35 weeks with her first baby, because of premature rupture of membranes and concerns about foetal exposure to maternal genital infection (chlamydia and gonorrhoea). The remaining teenagers were induced at 41 weeks because of postmaturity.

Pregnancy is considered to have reached 'term' between 37 and 42 weeks. Babies born before the 37th week are considered premature, while babies born after the 42nd week are considered postmature. Seven days beyond the estimated date of birth is widely accepted as an upper limit; it was the maximum time permitted by the consultant obstetricians on the study sites. When I first discussed induction, most of the teenagers intimated they had willingly acceded to the advice of maternity staff and accepted this intervention. It was during the postnatal period, and sometimes long after the events of birth, that some teenagers reconsidered their decision-making processes. Others voiced discontent about the quality and the amount of information they had received from maternity staff. The lack of emphasis placed on the 'downside' of the induction process was especially criticised:

> They [maternity staff] don't put so much of the downside to you. [...] I don't think it's [induction] a good thing to do. Not when you know all the things that can go wrong. When you know all the side effects you think, well, why didn't I wait a bit longer then? (Michelle, 16 years old; son aged six months. SY)

> With the induction no one told me the side effects. No one followed the argument through. They just cut to the bit and say, 'It's for your benefit if you get him out. The quicker you get him out, it's for your benefit.' But they didn't tell me other side of it. (Alys, now 17 years old; son aged two years. W)

Research (Green et al., 1998) suggests that while most childbearing women perceive themselves to be well informed about induction of labour, many do not differentiate between a labour which is induced and one which is 'accelerated' with oxytocic (uterine-stimulating) drugs. When reflecting on the circumstances of their induction, a significant number of teenagers expressed a desire to avoid this intervention in a future pregnancy:

> HS: Is there anything you'd like to change [about labour or birth]?
> Clare: Erm, [...] I wouldn't ever want to be induced again.
> HS: Why is that?
> Clare: 'Cos it were awful, I hated it. [...] It were really really painful. I were screamin' in agony and then they wouldn't give me an epidural. [...] I weren't expecting that. [...] Nobody told me what they were doing or anything. I just went into hospital and then they woke me up about half five in morning to start me off. [...] If I ever have another one I'm never gonna let 'em near me. *Laughs.* (Clare, now 15 years old; daughter aged 12 months. SY)

All of the teenagers reported experiencing induction as extremely painful. It was also widely associated with a cascade of iatrogenic interventions, including the need for an epidural to control pain, and 'assistance' (forceps, ventouse and/or caesarean section) to deliver the baby.

Teenagers' accounts of induction were often conflated with the difficulties they experienced obtaining an epidural. As Clare describes in the previous excerpt, the pain from a labour which is artificially induced, and which rapidly increases in intensity without time to adjust, is usually felt as agonising. A number of teenagers in this study were in their early years of adolescence and had little previous experience of menstruation and the pain which can be a regular feature of this event. Hence, most were quite unprepared for the breathtakingly painful experience, and the gruelling work, of labour.

Although some degree of labour management is now widely regarded as routine by both users and providers of maternity services, the rapid escalation of technological intervention in all aspects of childbirth, but especially in labour, has led to the formation of a global counterculture. The central aim of the movement is to keep birth 'normal'; this involves re-educating childbearing women and professionals about, for example, the risks associated with routine induction and the value of pain in labour, stressing that pain which is intolerable may be constitutive of the abnormal and the pathological. That said, the values and beliefs of those advocating a return to less interventionist approaches have traditionally been those of the middle classes and, as such, are culturally derived; although their voices may be powerful, they are not representative. With a declining birth rate, especially among more affluent women, it is possible that the preferences of marginalised women – who, after all, are the more frequent users of maternity services – will take precedence. This might then result in greater, rather than less, intervention in reproductive healthcare.

Vaginal examinations in labour: a violation of selfhood?

During the postnatal period I explored the topic of labour pain in some depth both with midwives and with teenagers and their labour companions. It seemed that it was not just the physical sensation of pain accompanying contractions which were troublesome for the teenagers, it was also the excruciating embarrassment incurred through being subjected to regular vaginal examinations, often without due consideration to ensuring privacy. In the maternity units accessed by the teenagers in this study, four-hourly vaginal examinations throughout labour were routine practice; they were also a requirement prior to the administration of analgesia. This was rather different to practice in other maternity units where vaginal examinations are no longer performed routinely, perhaps because staff are sufficiently competent, and comfortable, with assessing labour progress within a 'whole body' or holistic framework which also takes account of a wider repertoire of women's behaviours and changing corporeal parameters. Despite the centrality of the vaginal examination in discussions about labour, it does not appear to merit much attention during the antenatal period, rarely being discussed in any detail. This may be one reason why some women, especially first-time mothers-to-be, enter labour unprepared for the (painful) reality of what these examinations entail. This state of 'unpreparedness' is of course exaggerated for teenagers who may never previously have endured such procedures in association with a smear (Pap) test.

The complexities involved in negotiating informed consent for intra-partum procedures, such as vaginal examinations, have been previously documented (Marshall, 2000), although I would suggest that consent processes may be more complicated when adolescents are involved. The difficulties midwives experience ensuring that clients are sufficiently well informed to provide consent in advance of a vaginal examination may also be exacerbated by training which stresses the importance of physiological markers such as cervical dilatation, rather than more subtle indicators of progress. A focus on physiology may encourage midwives to emotionally 'distance' themselves from their clients which, in turn, may shield them from acknowledging the unsettling effects of the penetrative acts they perform, and the raw physicality of women's seeping, fluid-filled (labouring) bodies.

Being required to present their 'private parts' for examination by strangers was a deeply unpleasant experience for all the teenagers. In the following excerpt, Clare provides a disturbing account of the every-day, taken-for-granted, violence embedded in contemporary midwifery practices, and which was frequently enacted by the midwives 'caring' for her in labour.

Clare: I had to have it [vaginal examination] again and I didn't want to have it done again. Not with that midwife 'cos she really hurt me. She were right horrible with me. Yeah she were just, I don't know, I think she had like a bad attitude [...] She got t'other midwife to hold me down so she could do it, so that put me off even more.

HS: How did she hold you down?

Clare: She got my legs and she made my mum hold one hand and she made me sit on other one, on other hand. Then she did it [vaginal exam]. [...] I were cryin out. I think I were screamin. It were so painful. [...] I did think if I were older they wouldn't have done it. It's because I were only young they did it. Silly girl, like, that's what they were thinking, silly girl, we'll teach her a lesson. (Clare, now 15 years old; daughter aged five months. SY)

Narratives from maternity professionals confirmed teenagers' accounts of the physical force sometimes applied when vaginal examinations were performed. Midwives tended to justify their actions as a reasonable response to restrain young women's 'hysterical' and 'tense' labouring bodies:

> Midwife: I couldn't do it [vaginal examination] because Lou was so tense [...] She became quite hysterical actually, which was a shame for her. [...] Especially when we had to do [vaginal] examinations on her. [...] She wouldn't let us do them. She became too tensed up and in the end I had to get another midwife in to help me.
>
> HS: How did the other midwife help you?
>
> Midwife: Oh, well one held Lou's hand and she talked to her. The other one, we had a leg each, we had to hold her open so I could do the internal. (Interview with Jocelyn, Labour ward midwife. SY)

The image of three midwives applying their collective physical strength to subdue a teenager's labouring body may be compared to the surgeons described by Joan Cassell (1996), and the pride they take in practising 'body contact sport' (ibid.: 41). Surgery not only involves patients' bodies, it also involves the surgeon's body in the practice of a 'uniquely physical, distinctively embodied medical specialism' (ibid.), and, in this respect, midwifery and surgery have much in common. Unfortunately, the fact that physical violence, including assault, were routine events in the lives of many of the teenagers participating in this study may have made it less likely that they would be identified as problematic when they occurred in the context of labour.

Epidural anaesthesia

During the antenatal period the teenagers were divided in their opinions about the pros and cons of epidurals; of those whose labour narratives were available, seven had an epidural during labour. Those desirous of a pain-free labour argued in favour of this intervention while those against expressed concerns about side effects, including headaches, paralysis and immobility during labour.

The association between the increased use of epidural anaesthesia and caesarean section rates has been widely reported, even in countries such as New Zealand, where midwives are arguably less pressured by a medicalised birthing agenda and are able to practise with a high degree of autonomy. Although strategies have been suggested for reducing rates, implementation is dependent upon 'the social and cultural milieu and on associated beliefs and practices' (Walker et al., 2002: 28). Enmeshed within these discourses are issues of control over the birthing agenda and over women's childbearing bodies. Rising rates of interventions expose tensions between those supporting 'technocratic' (Davis-Floyd and Mather, 2002) and 'normal' (Downe, 2006) approaches to childbirth. It may be useful in this context to consider childbirth as a 'performative' (Butler, 1990) act, in which birthing audiences have vested, but often opposing, interests. Hence, childbirth is no longer exclusively 'owned' by the mother herself, but rather becomes a collective and shared experience for all who are present in the labour room; increasingly the details are also available for public consumption by strangers viewing women's labouring and birthing performances on social networking sites such as MySpace or YouTube. Audience participation in the woman's labour may thus be used as a justification for epidural anaesthesia, because freedom from pain 'makes women nicer to be with [...] is akin to "sexual liberation" in placing women more squarely at men's disposal while in no way curing their estrangement from their bodies' (Oakley, [1979] 1986: 21–2). While relief from pain might be welcome, the sudden loss of bodily sensations and control is complex and confusing, all the more so for young women whose relationship to their rapidly changing bodies has been recently acquired and is therefore more likely to be experienced as both tentative and as a 'work in progress'.

When reflecting on their labours, many young women spoke about the difficulties they experienced when attempting to secure effective pain relief, particularly with respect to epidural anaesthesia. Midwives were identified as the group most likely to obstruct their wishes, either by denying requests outright or resorting to delaying tactics, for example failing to contact an anaesthetist, or falsely stating that labour was too far advanced and that birth was imminent. Predicting the baby's arrival is notoriously difficult, however, and teenagers not infrequently reported that they birthed considerably earlier, or later, than staff had predicted:

> As soon as I went in, I asked her [midwife], 'Can I have an epidural now?' She said, 'No, you're too far gone. You're 10 centimetres, that's

too far. You've gone too far. You can't have an epidural now.' (Alys, now 17 years old; son aged two years. W)

Even Lowri, whose baby was known to have died prior to the onset of labour, was initially refused an epidural, despite the fact that this had been previously agreed by her consultant obstetrician:

> I'd been promised I could have an epidural. My mum was going 'Do you want an epidural?', so I said, 'Yes', because the pain was really bad. My mother asked for an epidural and basically I didn't get one. (Lowri, 16 years old; three weeks after the stillbirth of her daughter. W)

Midwives generally seemed more willing to arrange the speedy insertion of an epidural when they encountered teenagers they perceived to be 'hysterical' or 'panicking'. The need to impose control, especially on those who are perceived to be out of control, may be particularly important for midwives, because their inferior positioning in the institutional hierarchy accentuates their own relative powerlessness. Because midwives played a very small role in data generation, however, and because those I interviewed did not necessarily contribute material of relevance to this particular discussion, it would be inappropriate for me to speculate about their reasons for obstructing requests for an epidural. It is also possible that at least some of the teenagers' recall of labour events was inaccurate, especially regarding the time lag between making a request for an epidural and it being actioned (or not). That said, the conclusion from a recent systematic review of the literature examining women's experiences of childbirth reiterates that: 'pain, pain relief, and intrapartum medical interventions on subsequent satisfaction are neither as obvious, as direct, nor as powerful as the influences of the attitudes and behaviors of the caregivers' (Hodnett, 2009: S160).

Most maternity units had insufficient staff to provide one-to-one care for women in labour, and the fragmented nature of antenatal care meant that very few of the teenagers had previously met midwives looking after them in labour. While there is no evidence to suggest that continuity of maternity *carer* is associated with an increase in negative outcomes, the need for consistency in *care* has nonetheless been emphasised (Green et al., 1999). Although it is important to differentiate between the organisational elements of maternity care and the content of that care, the characteristics and requirements of particular client groups must also be considered. Many teenagers encountered midwives during their labours who lacked knowledge about, and insight into, the (sometimes extremely challenging) circumstances of their lives. I suggest that lack of understanding seriously impinged upon their attempts to make informed assessments about the possible repertoire of responses the teenagers might make to the stresses of labour and hence the epidural became a mechanism for rendering 'hysterical' young women compliant and silent:

> She'd [Lou] become so hysterical after the [vaginal] examination, I decided she ought to have an epidural. She was totally panicking really. I suppose you could say I persuaded her to have one. *Laughs.* She had it done but she went absolutely hysterical while the anaesthetist was putting it in. We thought she'd react badly, but not that bad. *Laughs.* But the anaesthetist was very good with her, really. She was good for him as well. She did lie still eventually. (Interview with Jocelyn, Labour ward midwife. SY)

The insertion of an epidural not only requires labouring women to lie very still, it also requires them to assume, and maintain, the 'correct' (left lateral, foetal-like) posture for the duration of the procedure. Regardless of age and previous childbearing experience, labouring women generally find these requirements extremely difficult to accommodate. Midwives' narratives generally emphasised their collusion with anaesthetists, rather than a sense of empathy with those undergoing this intervention.

'Support' in labour

Midwives assume a central role in both supporting, and subverting, institutional arrangements for the care of childbearing women. Most young women experienced varying degrees of difficulty in having their chosen companions with them throughout what they perceived as labour. This became apparent when maternity staff refuted a teenager's claim that labour was 'properly' established and transferred her to the antenatal ward where visiting hours were rigidly observed. Maternity units enforced strict regulations on visitors, including labour supporters, with generally no more than two people permitted at each bedside; children were not allowed. While there were no facilities for partners and significant others to stay overnight, labour ward staff did not impose time limits on visitors, although labour supporters (including teenagers' mothers) were generally asked to leave the room for medical and midwifery procedures. Restricting the presence of loved ones caused teenagers considerable distress:

It was half past eight in evening. We wanted to stay [...] She [midwife] wouldn't let us stay. She told us we had to leave. I hated leaving her [Alys]. It broke my heart. She was only just turned 16. She'd never spent the night on her own. Not with strangers. She told us, 'You've got to go now, she'll be ages yet.' [*Angharad's voice distressed and high pitched*] I said to her, 'Please, can't we stay? We don't mind staying.' I told her we didn't have a car to get back in a hurry. [...] I could have left [boyfriend] there. He said he'd sit in the waiting room all night, he didn't care. He just didn't want to miss it. [...] He didn't want to not be there, if she was needing comfort like. But no, you can't do that she says, you've got to go. [Boyfriend] was cryin' his eyes out he were so upset. I thought, well, if I've got to miss it, but don't let him miss it, because he was so looking forward to it. If we'd had a car, we wouldn't have minded so much. It would've been hard leaving her there all alone with strangers, like, but we'd have been able to get back if we were needed in a hurry. We got the last bus home. Last bus goes at half eight. In the end, we had to call my friend out of work as soon as we got home to come straight back. (Angharad (mother of Alys, aged 15). W)

More than 25 years ago Sara Ruddick suggested 'that the most liberating change we can make in institutions of motherhood is to include men equally in every aspect of maternal care [...] to prevent or excuse men from maternal practice is to encourage them to separate public action from private affection' (Ruddick, 1980: 360). Although the presence of men is now customary in maternity settings, my research suggested that their presence is generally tolerated rather than welcomed, with marginalised men likely to suffer a similar range of indignities and injustices as their female partners.

Differences in working practices and staff attitudes between maternity and hospice settings may be relevant to this discussion. Although there have been significant changes with respect to humanising birth in recent years, I suggest that such changes have been less dramatic than those affecting the care of the terminally ill and dying. For instance, it is now widely considered normal practice for loved ones, including children, to remain at the bedside throughout the entire process, with staff providing rest and refreshment facilities, and including relatives in the care of the dying person. For a woman giving birth, however, similar 'freedoms' may only be possible if she remains at home.

Some young women spoke of being abandoned and/or ignored at crucial times during their labours, for example when birth was imminent.

As is suggested by the following excerpt, even the tragedy of giving birth to a dead baby did not shield teenagers from uncivil and callous treatment by maternity staff:

> It was half four when I got there and the midwife who took me over said, 'Oh there we are, gas and air, have that.' Then she left me. One midwife, I don't know who she was, she came in to take the chairs out of the room for somebody else. She didn't even look at me. She just said, 'Oh can I take these chairs?' Nobody else came in until just before I had her [baby]. Nobody came back in the room. [...] The only time the midwife came in was after somebody had gone and asked her to bring me something. [...] The midwife just left us, so then my mum took over. [...] She'd had babies as well as lost babies, so she knew what it's like from both sides. [...] I did think they'd pay me more attention, with me being so young, but I suppose they thought, 'Oh, well, the baby's already dead so nothing we can do.' (Lowri, 16 years old; three weeks after the stillbirth of her daughter. W)

That midwives often seemed unaware that their actions might be construed as transgressing the norms of professional conduct echoes an earlier observation: that while those who are marginalised and oppressed may be 'acutely aware of discrimination against them [...] exclusion is much less likely to impinge on the consciousness of conforming adults' (Sibley, 1995: xiii).

Jade, who was perhaps the most isolated and angry of the South Yorkshire cohort, was atypical in that she appeared unconcerned about who would accompany her to hospital in labour. That said, I found it difficult to assess whether the 'front' she presented was, in fact, a genuine lack of concern, or whether her anxieties were well disguised by the extravagant displays of bravado in which she regularly engaged. In any event, her labours were the most uncomplicated of both cohorts:

> HS: Have you thought that far ahead – to labour and who you'd like to have helping you?
>
> Jade: Nah, not really. I'm not bothered. *Laughs*. Bev [landlady and surrogate mother] says she'll come in with me, and then my sister's said she'll come if she can make it. I told her I'm going to ring her up and say, 'Get here! I'm in labour', so then she'll have to come. *Laughs*. (Jade, 16 years old; 36 weeks pregnant with her first baby. SY)

Pete, Lou's boyfriend, was alone among male partners in expressing ambivalence about providing labour support. Unlike other young men, Pete was generally at home when I called and he often stayed for the duration of my visits. Although he contributed a significant amount to our conversations, and his presence counterbalanced Lou's tendency to introspection, he had an aggressive disposition and tended to dominate proceedings. It was not until some months after her baby was born that Lou admitted that Pete physically (and sexually) abused her. Despite his belligerent stance, and his abuse of Lou, I eventually warmed to Pete. One day, shortly before the baby was due, I challenged him about his lack of commitment to accompanying Lou to hospital and supporting her in labour. I was unprepared for his reply:

> HS: Do you think you'll be able to be with Lou when she's in labour 'cos, you know, she's really scared of being by herself?

Pete pauses for a long time. Then looks me straight in the eye and says:

> Thing I'm most worried about is if I see her in pain and they're not doing nowt about it. I think if that happens I'll just flip out. That's what I'm worryin about. It's making an idiot of meself. Embarrassing meself. Faintin' 'n all. Or getting in fight with doctors when they're not doing nowt for her. I know I've got violence inside me. Everyone says sooner or later I'll be sent down for it big time. It'll be just my luck it'll happen on day the babba's born ... Just my luck I'll get done for smackin doctor or summat ... Better for Lou I'm out of it. She'll do all right by herself. Nurses'll see to her ... Nothin I can do they can't. (Pete (Lou's boyfriend). SY)

It is ironic that men such as Pete might dread being made to feel helpless and frightened by seeing their partners in pain, when they themselves are often perpetrators of another ordering of pain in the form of sexual and/or domestic abuse. Nonetheless, it is less than three decades ago since it was suggested that fathers who are unappreciated, who are poor or declassed or otherwise seen as 'failing', will 'know the pain of introducing their children to a world in which they do not figure. Sometimes their powerlessness is visited directly upon the mothers' (Ruddick, 1980: 363). In this sense, witnessing Lou in labour and in pain is indeed likely to be provocative for Pete because he might be forced (publicly) to confront his own violent self, with potential repercussions for Lou and their baby.

Giving birth

Of the nine young women whose birthing outcomes were known to me, one experienced a ventouse (suction cap) delivery and four underwent caesarean sections, of which two were undertaken as emergency procedures and two were planned in advance. Although the remaining five teenagers would be defined, for statistical purposes, as having experienced 'normal' births, most nonetheless experienced varying degrees of intervention, including artificial rupture of membranes, episiotomy, oxytocic drugs to hasten labour and/or deliver the placenta, and instructions regarding the consumption of food and drink, and physical movement during labour. Additionally, midwives frequently attempted to control the emergence of the baby by denying women's somatic messages that birth was imminent, and/or by issuing instructions about when, and how, to push.

Pushing in labour has been something of a debated issue in recent years, with discussions focusing on the pros and cons of directed (active or coached), versus non-directed (spontaneous or uncoached), maternal effort to birth the baby (Hansen et al., 2002; Schaffer et al., 2005; Simpson and James, 2005). Many teenagers in this study reported being instructed to push when they had no urge to do so, and as Jade and Michelle describe in the following excerpts, they were also requested to refrain from pushing when the urge was overpowering:

> With Gemma [Jade's second baby] they kept telling me, 'Don't push, don't push.' But I were just pushing anyway. Couldn't help it. I were in agony. You can't control it when it's like that. They kept saying, 'No, no, don't push yet!' I says, 'Why, why not? I can't help it, I have to push. I can't help it.' I were screamin at 'em. I were saying like, I'm not pushing, it's not me pushing. It's my body is! It's not me that's pushing. (Jade, now 17 years old; four months after the birth of her second daughter. SY)

> When I said, 'Baby's coming,' I were told, 'Shut up and close your legs'. [...] I said, 'I can feel baby coming.' She said, 'Don't be stupid, it's not coming, it's not.' I said, 'It is.' I could feel it. She said, 'Don't be so stupid, shut up and close your legs.' Well my legs didn't want to be closed. [...] I were going mad. [...] They were telling me it weren't

coming but I knew it were and then she said, 'Do you think I should have a look?', and the other one said, 'No, she's all right, she's all right.' Then the anaesthetist said, 'Well I think you should have a look.' Then the other midwife said, 'Oh, it's OK love, the baby's coming.' That were it then. (Michelle, 16 years old; son aged six months. SY)

A small number of the teenagers were unable to recall the physical experience of giving birth because of the effects of the pain-relieving drugs they had received in labour. In the following excerpt, April recalls her first labour and compares the experience with being 'smashed', with all the connotations of recreational drug use:

HS: You said earlier that when you went into labour that you didn't know what was going on?

April: Yeah. That's right. [...] I had two bottles of gas and air, and then I fell asleep about half 11. The baby was born at one minute past one. I woke up then, and she was on my stomach. [Boyfriend's] brother was standing by the side of me and there was this baby on me. I didn't know where it came from. I'd had way too much gas and air to remember anything. And they gave me an injection as well. I was well out of it. I hadn't been that smashed in a long time, and it wasn't my fault this time! *Laughs.* Next day I felt like I'd been on a real bender. I felt terrible. (April, 17 years old; ten weeks pregnant with her second baby. W)

Substantial numbers of teenagers reported that staff disagreed with their interpretations of embodied, labour-related, events. Even when teenagers reported sensations which suggested to them that birth was imminent, their appeals for help often failed. Not being listened to, or not having one's viewpoint regarded seriously, was a recurring theme in the narratives from women contributing to the 'Informed Choice' study (Kirkham and Stapleton, 2001). This same study also demonstrated that it was the voices of the most marginalised women which were most likely to be ignored by maternity care providers.

Culturally inscribed rituals: skin-to-skin contact

Unlike their middle-class counterparts, many young women expressed ambivalence about immediate (skin-to-skin) contact with their newborn babies.

HS: When Chloe was first born, what was she like?

Clare: She were just laid there on bed. She didn't do anything ...

HS: Did she cry?

Clare: No. She didn't cry for ages. She were just looking around. Midwife were telling me to pick her up, she were saying, 'Oh your baby's out now, your baby's born, you can pick her up now,' but I didn't want to. I were just looking at her.

HS: And did you pick her up?

Clare: No, midwife did. She gave her to my mum. I didn't want to hold her then. I were too tired. And anyway she were still all slimy. *Laughs.* (Clare, 14 years old; daughter aged nine days. SY)

Current expectations are that all mothers will respond immediately and positively to the birth of their baby; absent, or delayed, responses risk being interpreted by maternity staff as signs of incipient maternal pathology. Like other childbearing women, teenagers in this study were sometimes prevented by maternity staff from acting instinctively because the norms of the institution were the important arbiters in regulating individual performance. Insisting that mothers have immediate skin-to-skin contact with their newborns is now normative in Western birthing environments, because such contact is understood to facilitate maternal–infant bonding and to promote breastfeeding initiation.

The significance of positioning a *particular* child in relation to a *specific* mother – who exists not in a vacuum but in a social relationship to others, and within a geographical, age and class context – has been somewhat disregarded in academic accounts of motherhood. Intersections of class, race and age, and the specificity of the mother–child dyad, illuminate variations in childrearing and parenting practices and resonate with concepts such as 'good-enough' parenting, not least because they illustrate the futility of seeking universal standards for optimum childrearing. Theories about 'maternal bonding', as promoted by Klaus and Kennell (1976), and which continue to have contemporary saliency, may be seen in this light because they promote an essentialist scripting of femaleness and motherhood. Klaus and Kennell's work has, however, been subjected to substantial criticism (De Chateau and Wiberg, 1977; Chess and Thomas, 1983), and subsequent attempts to confirm the importance of rapid maternal–child bonding during an early 'sensitive period' have been inconclusive. Critiques by social scientists continue to unsettle established constructions of motherhood (and childhood) and question the parameters of 'normality': practices which might be considered harmful in one social setting may be judged rather differently in another. Indeed, anthropological accounts have long reiterated this point and decry the ethnocentric standards against which culturally specific concepts, for example childhood 'neglect' (LeVine et al., 1994), or maternal 'grief' (Scheper-Hughes, 1992), may be measured or understood.

That there is a 'right' (professionally defined) and a 'wrong' (teenager-defined) way of doing things was never in doubt for the teenagers and their significant others participating in my study. Throughout pregnancy and the postnatal period, pregnant teenagers were closely scrutinised by maternity professionals and were often identified as lacking in skills, judgement, or both. There was little encouragement for them to use their own initiative and even less recognition that 'mistakes' are an inevitable consequence of embarking on a parenting career, regardless of age.

Death and loss in pregnancy

Two of the teenagers suffered pregnancy losses during the research period. Luci, who was carrying twins, was informed in her 14th week of pregnancy that one baby had died. Lowri suffered a sudden, and unexpected, intrauterine death at 32 weeks gestation. The phrase 'pregnancy loss' is something of an anomalous term, but one which is usually taken to mean the unanticipated demise of the foetus at some point between conception and birth. Like other bodies, a foetus is 'always imbued with social significance, not the least when it is a dead body [...] what the body becomes – what it means – is tied up with one's way of approaching it' (Radley, 2000: 299). Loss of a baby, by any means and at any age, is now inextricably linked with bereavement rituals. But this was not always so. Historically, and indeed in contemporary non-Western cultures, the spontaneous loss of a baby in pregnancy, for example through miscarriage, is a routine event – a point made by Nancy Scheper-Hughes (1992) in her poignant account of the 'everyday' losses endured by impoverished women in childbirth. Infant death is also an event for which women may make pragmatic allowances, for example by anticipating stillbirth in advance (Stapleton, 1997) and having many children over the course of a childbearing career in order to replace babies 'born to die' (Cecil, 1996: 7). Scheper-Hughes has further suggested that the use of terminology such as 'investment' and 'strategy' in the context of contemporary childrearing reflects a Western mindset wherein the commodification of all experience (including those pertaining to reproduction) has become normative practice.

'New' reproductive technologies and significant changes to socio-economic patterns and structures in contemporary Western societies have resulted in women conceiving, and giving birth to, an ever-decreasing number of children. It has been suggested that 'these demographic changes, wherever they occur, affect perceptions of human life, personhood, life stages (including the modern "invention" of childhood and adolescence), and family roles and social sentiments (including mother love)'. They also alter perceptions about the relative value of the individual as measured against 'the collectivity, whether nuclear or extended family, lineage or community' (Scheper-Hughes, 1992: 401). One consequence of a reduced fertility rate (and greater access to material wealth), is the tendency to invest more heavily (materially and emotionally) in fewer children. Every child thus becomes an ever more 'precious' child, not least because there is neither the time, the inclination, nor indeed the financial resources in the case of privately funded fertility treatment, to replace it.

Reproductive technologies to confirm pregnancy are now available much earlier in the conception trajectory and this makes it possible to actively construct the sexed personhood of the child well in advance of its birth. And while every person confided in about the impending birth, every cigarette and alcoholic beverage abstained from, and every item purchased for the baby-to-be, increase its sense of 'realness', paradoxically it also magnifies 'the realness problem of pregnancy loss' (Layne, 2000: 323). When a baby dies, parents-in-the-making are confronted with social taboos and awkward questions about the baby that 'was', and when there is no baby to welcome, the support previously offered may be withdrawn and replaced by rejection and awkwardness. It has been suggested that the collective denial of pregnancy loss seriously 'challenges the validity of the cultural and biological work already undertaken in constructing that child and belittles the importance of the loss' (Layne, 2000: 323).

Losing a twin

Luci had first consulted her GP shortly after she had missed a period. She suspected she might be pregnant, as the last time she and her boyfriend had had sex she was mid-cycle and the condom had burst. Luci had initially considered a termination, but following an ultrasound scan which confirmed she was carrying twins she decided to proceed with the pregnancy. A further routine scan at 14 weeks revealed that one twin had died.

Luci's aunt had accompanied her to the hospital for the routine scan, to confirm the expected date of delivery. Neither Luci's boyfriend nor her mother had been able to attend the appointment, because neither employer would grant the necessary leave from work. The way in which Luci was informed about the death of one of her twins caused her, and her family, considerable distress:

Luci: When I had the scan, they just checked over the baby that was still there. [...] They weren't very nice. They just said, 'Well one of them's dead but the other one's still there.'

Gavin: She had no counselling. She had nothing. They should have tried to comfort her but she had nothing. [...] To her she's lost a child. To everybody else she's lost a child. It's part of us isn't it? It's not just a piece of bloody garbage you can chuck away. It's part of her body. It's the baby we both made. *Starts crying.*

Luci: When they told me one of the babies was dead, they took me into a room all by myself to tell me. They left my aunty outside and they took me in and they asked me if I still wanted to go ahead with the pregnancy, or if I wanted to have a termination.

Mother: She had no comfort at all. [...] They told her one baby was dead and then they left her aunty in the corridor and they took her into a room all by herself and one of them asked her if she wanted to continue with the pregnancy or, seeing as one was dead, did she just want to have a termination with the other one? She was all by herself and they took her inside this room and asked her that. [...] What right have they to do that, to take a young girl like her inside a room all by herself when she's just lost a baby without anyone to comfort her? (Luci, 16 years old; 15 weeks pregnant, talking with her mother and Gavin, her boyfriend. W)

The conflation of life and death in this narrative is heightened by the insinuation that, because one baby has died, Luci might want to reconsider her decision to proceed with the pregnancy. Although Luci told me she had not discussed her earlier deliberations regarding termination with maternity staff, they may have inferred this possibility. The absence of comfort in 'bad birth stories' (Murphy-Lawless, 1998: 246) highlights the lack of agency experienced by many recipients of maternity services, especially when they are poor, young or otherwise marginalised. By 'agency' here I mean the individual's capacity to actually command influence, as opposed to having any intention(s) in this regard.

Sudden death in late pregnancy

Lowri had decided from the outset she was keeping her baby. She had left school and had just been accepted for an apprenticeship, training as a chef, when she realised she was pregnant. Lowri had periodically complained about feeling unwell throughout pregnancy but staff repeatedly ascribed her symptoms to the fact she was pregnant, rather than poorly. However, a post-mortem on her baby revealed that Lowri had contracted cytomegalovirus, a type of herpes virus associated with miscarriage, congenital deafness, premature labour and/or stillbirth. The following narrative focuses on the events of labour and birth:

Lowri: I had my second pessary [to induce labour] and that was the only time anyone had looked at me down there. That was five hours and nobody had even looked at me. [...] My mother and [boyfriend's mother] were sent out of the room for me to have the epidural. After they put the injection in I said, 'No I can still feel it.' The midwife said to me, 'Oh, don't be so stupid.' Then the other one, she was like, 'No, no, don't take any nonsense with her.' [...] I mean all right, fair enough, they've got a job to do, but like I say, if I had something to look forward to at the end of it then maybe they'd have been different. But I didn't have anything to look forward to and after I delivered I was in a bit of a state, obviously. When I knew the baby was coming I was asking, 'Can my mum come back in with me?' 'Cos I was on my own. But the midwife said, 'No, no, you can do it on your own. You'll be all right love.' She said, 'You can do this on your own.' But in the end I told her to shut up and get my mum. [...]

HS: What happened after your baby was born. Did you see her?

Lowri: No, I didn't want to. It was offered. The midwives had been saying to me all day, 'We think it's best if you do [see the baby]' [...] I had my eyes shut and she [midwife] said, 'Do you want to see her' and I said, 'No'. So she took her away. She didn't say whether it was a girl or boy, she just said, 'Do you want to see the baby?' She came back in then, after she weighed her and everything, and told me everything. She asked me again, and then she kept on asking me all the time, but I kept on saying 'No'. [...] They did put a lot of pressure on me to see it.

Dilys: Yes they did, and they were asking her questions about what she wanted to do with the baby, and afterwards about the funeral and things, but she was just too shocked to think straight. If you asked her a question it was, 'I don't know, I don't know.' She didn't know anything. She was just so shocked. She didn't know herself. She didn't know what she wanted, but the hospital was trying to get her to make decisions all the time. She couldn't. She was just too shocked. I do think if it had been me going through that experience they'd have been more understanding, just on account of me being older. I do think the younger ones don't get the same care, and that's a real problem when it all goes wrong, because it can stay in their minds forever, and it might even put them off having children forever. The feeling you get from them is like, oh, you're young, you'll get over it, you can have another one.

Lowri: Afterwards they wanted to have a look, to check that everything was all right, and I really just wanted to be left alone. She [midwife] said, 'Oh let me just have a look, can you lift up your legs for me,' and all that. But the other one was just so heartless, really. She said, 'Well love, I'll tell you, the only good news you'll hear today is that you haven't got to have any stitches.' That just finished me off. [...] She just made me so mad. I thought, 'Oh you are so heartless.' (Lowri, 16 years old, talking with Dilys (her mother who is also pregnant). W)

The 'heartlessness' of midwives, which Lowri's mother attributes to the fact of her daughter's youth, is a recurring theme in the teenagers' narratives. Varying degrees of 'heartlessness' characterised interactions with other maternity staff, although perhaps never quite to the extent where practitioners might be described as adopting the 'totalizing emotional defence against suffering or death' (Radley, 2000: 300) so evident in Lowri's and Luci's accounts. Lowri also draws attention to the normative processes of 'doing' bereavement in contemporary institutionalised maternity settings. This typically involves care providers paying due attention to particular memorialising practices: the bereaved mother is expected to hold her baby, to allow photographs and perhaps a lock of hair to be taken, and to have her dead baby's foot and/or handprints recorded. There is also an autopsy to be agreed and a funeral to be arranged. The bereft mother then makes her way into the world without a baby, but with a collection of mementos. From Lowri's account, it seemed that these aspects of the bereavement ritual assumed greater significance for the midwives than processes associated with her labour and birth. Or, perhaps, it was because these aspects were more clearly defined, and midwives were more comfortable dealing with the physicality of death, rather than the emotional aftermath. It is also possible that Lowri had lost all trust in the midwives and her refusal to conform to their expectations may be read as an expression of her displeasure and disappointment.

In the next chapter I consider the immediate postpartum period – the first few hours and days following birth when the teenagers became acquainted with their newborn infants and initiated processes associated with mothering them. I describe the multiple ways in which these young mothers were further disadvantaged by the hostile reception many received from midwives and sometimes other mothers following transfer to postnatal wards. I discuss routine medical interventions in the lives of postpartum women and the impact of maternity events on teenagers' mental and physical health, especially those whose general health status was already compromised by smoking, inadequate access to nutritional food and/or living in poor-quality, unsafe accommodation. I examine how the teenagers (re)negotiated their on-going maternal identities within their respective social worlds after they rejoined their families and communities as new mothers, and the helps and hindrances they encountered en route; personal agency and access to a plentiful store of 'identity capital' (Côté, 1996) were key motifs in, and essential features of, their quests. I also ask why the teenagers' attempts to establish everyday routines, including those associated with feeding, sleeping and discipline, often provoked considerable tension, not least because these were often sites for 'turf wars' between the teenagers and their mothers, and others with vested interests including health visitors. Finally I consider the intergenerational transmission of parenting norms, a theme I explore further in Chapter 7.

6

'Chucked in the Deep End': Mothering in the Early Postnatal Period

Familiarity with childrearing practices is relatively rare for new (middle-class) mothers in late modernity, as the socio-cultural context in which these informal knowledges and skills are acquired is generally not available outside working-class and minority ethnic communities. In this sense, adolescent mothers may be perceived as having an advantage, although this is unlikely to be widely acknowledged.

Learning to mother: the significance of place and the influence of others

Many teenagers reported that their initiation into motherhood was marred by the critical and unhelpful attitudes of maternity staff and older females. Criticism was voiced in the first instance by midwives, and subsequently by health visitors, and some mothers and mothers-in-law. Most young women had already accumulated considerable experience of caring for older infants through their early and repeated involvement with their siblings and other young relatives and, hence, their confidence and skill with managing day-to-day practicalities. While they were in hospital, young women's embodied childrearing knowledge was rendered inaccessible by competing institutional norms. The short periods (between one and three days) spent on postnatal wards were mostly recalled as unpleasant experiences, and narratives confirmed that most teenagers felt generally unsupported by staff:

> I was chucked in the deep end [...] She [midwife] said, 'He needs a feed,' and she gave me this bottle and this teat. You have to take the top off the teat and put it on the bottle but she didn't tell me that. And it was cold milk as well, which I didn't like. So I used to [...]

warm it up. It wasn't totally warm but it wasn't cold cold. It was like luke-ish. So I used to give him his feed and I used to think, 'He's only taken that much, he's going to starve.' I tried to get him to drink all his bottle, but he wouldn't. He would only take a tiny bit and she said, 'Don't feed him again with the same bottle, you have to chuck it away.' I was thinking well that's a real waste, why do they give you such a big bottle when he's only going to take such a little bit? That bottle was that big and he was only having that much. [Alys indicates with her fingers.] And then she said, 'You have to change him.' So I changed him. I knew what to do, 'cos I'd done it loads of times with [younger brother]. I was changing him on the bed, and she came and said, 'Don't change him on the bed, that's where you get an infection. You must change him in the cot.' I was thinking, 'But the cot's only that big!' *All laugh.* (Alys, now 17 years old; son aged two years. W)

As well as feeling judged by midwives, many teenagers felt disapproved of by older mothers on the postnatal wards. A general sense of being expected to 'get it wrong', which most teenagers reported, has been echoed elsewhere (Dykes and Moran, 2003).

You just knew whatever you did it was going to be wrong. You know, 'Oh you don't put the nappy on like *that*' and, 'Oh, is he *still* crying?' It really got on my nerves. (Michelle, 16 years old; son aged two weeks. SY)

During a conversation about this issue some months later, Michelle agreed with my suggestion that the pressures on teenage mothers were similar to those induced by academic exams. Indeed, the anxieties generated in anticipation of (in)adequate performance stimulated negative memories of being back at school again:

Michelle: When I'd had [baby] I remember her [midwife] saying, 'Now I'm going to show you how to bath him,' so she showed me and the next day I had to do it in front of her. Oooh, the sweat were dripping off me! *Laughs.* It were awful. I were completely panicked. I'd never done it in front of anybody before. I remember thinking, 'Oh, shit, I wish I'd gone to them [parentcraft] classes so I'd have known something.' *Laughs.*

HS: Mmm, yeah, but it also sounds a bit like you were doing like a test or something?

Michelle: Yeah it were a bit like that. *Laughs.* It were like I were
back at school again. *Laughs.* It were really awful. I were
so scared of dropping him. (Michelle, 16 years old; son
aged four months. SY)

Experiences on postnatal wards suggested that midwives were generally unable to empathise with teenagers' acute sense of disorientation.
All teenagers returned to the familiarity of their homes at the earliest
opportunity. Family members generally welcomed and celebrated the
new mother and baby and adjusted personal and domestic routines
to accommodate them, although that is not to imply that this was
undemanding with respect to family dynamics. In particular, the issue
of 'ownership' of the baby caused considerable tensions between the
teenage mothers and other female family members:

I hate everyone messin' with her [baby]. It's like [older sister] and
[younger sister], they're always picking her up and holding her, so
she's never sort of quiet, like. It's not even when she's awake or she's
crying. They just come in and pick her up. They never ask me if it's
all right. (Clare, 14 years old; daughter aged nine days. SY)

His [boyfriend's] mum, she acts like the baby's hers […] last night she
wouldn't let me feed her 'cos she said I weren't doing it right. (Lou,
16 years old; daughter aged four days. SY)

For most young women contestations of maternal authority were generally resolved once the 'novelty factor' associated with the arrival of the
new baby dissipated. Lou and Tracey, however, faced more problematic
transitions as their maternal efforts were constantly undermined by
older female relatives who were unwilling to affirm their attempts to
negotiate a personal style of mothering.

Some midwives and health visitors also undermined young women's
efforts to establish a maternal self. This was sometimes unintentional,
for example when they suggested that they 'take it easy' when their
personal circumstances did not permit them to do so:

You know you shouldn't be running about as much as you are, petal.
You've had a major operation. You need to be careful. Remember,
that's major abdominal surgery you've had. You've got to take it easy
or your scar could burst open you know. It needs time to heal properly. You've got to rest up. Let others do things for you a bit more.
(Community midwife Bianca to Tracey, two days after a caesarean for
her second baby. SY)

Tracey's older child was just 13 months old at the time Bianca advised her to 'rest up'. Her boyfriend, with whom she lived, was learning disabled and received incapacity benefit on account of long-standing mental health problems. Tracey's mother lived on the other side of town and her chaotic lifestyle meant that any help she offered was unpredictable and unreliable. Adequate rest was therefore not an option for Tracey, because there was no one to provide the nurturing care the midwife suggested was necessary. She was, nonetheless, admonished.

Discourses on the family as a social unit in need of management and reform have a long history across the health and social service sectors. Health visitors, the key health professionals involved in the lives of new families in the UK, have been described as embodying the combined roles of 'inspector, social worker and teacher' (Symonds, 1991: 256), hence their established position in policing and regulating family life. Research findings are equivocal as to whether unsupported teenage mothers perceive their input to be helpful (Bloomfield et al., 2005), although a recent systematic review (Walker et al., 2008) suggested that targeted visiting may be preventative against later infant health problems. Compared to midwives – whose professional contribution to maternal and infant health generally ceases ten days after birth in the UK – postnatal support from health visitors has been described as too 'businesslike' and 'judgemental' (Hunter, 2004: 25). Continued support from community midwives has thus been reported by new mothers as preferable to that provided by health visitors, because midwives are generally already known to the family and are perceived to be the 'experts' in infant care (ibid.). In my study, teenagers and their loved ones generally viewed the contributions of both professional groups as unhelpful.

A 'classed' dimension to these discourses is evident in the orientation of many policy reforms, where the gaze of reformers is squarely on the working classes, the group traditionally perceived as having greater need for remedial action to improve health outcomes. In this sense, policy formulation can be said to reflect long-held professional preoccupations, rather than addressing the specific needs of marginalised groups. The interface between healthcare providers, recipients and the state is regulated by an ever-expanding armoury of disciplinary technologies which operate to scrutinise family practices and coerce 'wayward' families into compliance with middle-class behavioural norms. The autonomy and privacy of the family are thus increasingly encroached upon.

Wrong(ed) maternal bodies

Many of the teenagers in this study began their mothering careers under the mantle of a wrong(ed) body. For the poorest and most marginalised, including Lou, Tracey, Jade and April, exposure to maternity services simply added to their accumulated sufferings. By contrast, Michelle, Alys and Lowri had all grown up with a sense of being wanted and valued members of their respective families. They presented as sociable, articulate and confident young women who were used to making at least some of their own decisions, or, when in doubt, consulting with respected others. The manner in which interactions were conducted by maternity staff came as something of a shock to these teenagers unaccustomed as they were to 'doing' deference in accordance with the expected norms of 'marginal' persons. Nor did they identify themselves primarily as 'pregnant teenagers' – with all the negative connotations – but rather as young women who had simply encountered a patch of 'bad luck' which they were attempting to deal with as best they could. Nonetheless, some of their mothers considered that midwives generally framed pregnant teenagers negatively, regardless of their personal circumstances.

> When she [Alys] first went to the clinic, after they'd finished with her they just left her hanging about. [...] Once I was there with her, but they didn't know who I was. They didn't know I was her mother. I overheard this one [midwife] saying it was a disgrace to see girls of Alys's age pregnant. It was just a disgrace. They were looking over at Alys and one of them said, 'There are people who shouldn't be mothers and there are people who should be mothers.' I knew she was talking about Alys when she said about the ones who shouldn't be mothers. (Angharad (mother of Alys, aged 15). W)

The following excerpt summarises a midwife's commentary following her visit to April, an extremely poor young mother living in a squalid, cockroach-infested squat, with her nine-month-old baby daughter. April had recently become pregnant with her second child by a different father.

> The community midwife does not wait until we are in her car before she starts listing April's wrongdoings. As we drive away from her house she really lets her have it: Why is she still in her pyjamas when we arrive [at 11.30 a.m.]? Why has she not already made up a feed for her baby? Why is the dog allowed to sleep in the same room as the

baby? And why is the baby also still asleep so late in the morning? The midwife also comments on the dirtiness of the house and the general state of disrepair. When she had undressed the baby [waking it first] the midwife had discovered a weeping rash on her genitals which she insisted was due to her lying too long in a wet nappy. April contested this diagnosis, arguing that the rash was caused by chlorine irritation from taking her swimming the previous day. The midwife's tone of voice suggests strong disapproval of April's style of mothering and, indeed, she later confided that she would liked to have taken April's baby home with her for a bit of 'real mothering'. (Field notes. Non-recorded conversation with community midwife Katy. W)

I observed this midwife on a number of occasions while undertaking research for the 'Informed Choice' project (Kirkham and Stapleton, 2001), accompanying her to the homes of a wide range of women. Her responses to her most disadvantaged clients were similar to those described above, and although I found her criticism difficult, I also appreciated that she was in an impossible situation. While she had a professional duty to protect, and promote, infant welfare, because her poorest clients lacked control over the material circumstances of their lives her role would inevitably be compromised.

Body matters: recovery and surveillance in the early postnatal period

All the teenagers, including Lou and Tracy, both of whom endured long and difficult labours followed by emergency caesarean sections, made speedy recoveries from the physical effects of labour and birth. Midwives and mothers identified youthfulness as being a primary factor in the teenagers' excellent recuperative processes:

HS: I thought Lou made a remarkably quick recovery from the caesarean. What did you think?

Midwife: Yes. Yes, she did pick up very quickly didn't she? [...] I think that might be to do with her age. The younger ones do tend to pick up quicker than the older mums. (Interview with Jocelyn, Labour ward midwife. SY)

I know when you're an older person that you're more likely [to have problems] but at her age, well, they spit them out no problem, don't they? (Angharad (mother of Alys, aged 15.) W)

A number of the teenagers complained about feeling uncomfortable when maternity staff did not appreciate their embodied sensitivities to the norms of clinical routines. Customary practices, including exposing the 'sexed', leaking and/or disrupted aspects of young women's maternal bodies to strangers, especially in settings where privacy could not be guaranteed, caused considerable embarrassment and distress.

They [midwives] came to check my [perineal] stitches all the time. Asking me to lie down and pull my clothes down so they could have a look. That were, that were just so embarrassing. (Clare, 14 years old; daughter aged three weeks. SY)

They didn't care if you were half naked and the curtains were pulled. It was horrible. [...] I were sitting there and she came in and she just pulled my top up to look at my boobs. I nearly smacked her one. *Laughs.* (Jade, 16 years old; two weeks following the birth of her first daughter. SY)

Some young women reported being angry when their consent was not sought for students to undertake, or observe, physical examinations. Two years after this experience, Alys vividly recalls her indignation:

One day she [midwife] brought a student with her [...] She checked my stitches first and then she called the student over to look as well, which I found just so embarrassing. She didn't ask me if I minded, she just asked the student to have a look. I think she should have asked me if I minded first. [...] It was none of the, 'Do you mind if we ...?' (Alys, now 17 years old; son aged two years. W)

Uninvited bodily exposure seemed less problematic during labour, perhaps because women's expectations at this time are somewhat different:

I didn't care when I were in labour, you could have three monkeys in there and I wouldn't have minded who had a look, but afterwards it were just so embarrassing. (Clare, 14 years old; daughter aged three weeks. SY)

It is possible that the presence of mothers and/or significant others during labour may have worked as a protective device mitigating young women's discomfiture, while pain-relieving drugs may have reduced sensitivity to procedures normally perceived as invasive and/or intrusive.

Despite attempts in recent years to encourage maternity staff to be more mindful of their clients' needs for privacy, unannounced intrusions remain commonplace. While it may be relatively uncomplicated to make cosmetic adjustments to the material aspects of the maternity environment, for example by fixing locks to doors and blinds to windows, changing staff habits and attitudes is a rather more complex, and long-term, task.

The six-week postnatal check

All the teenagers visited their GP for a routine postnatal check, generally around six weeks following birth. As a minimum, they anticipated that the doctor would perform a vaginal examination, 'to check everything were all right', and to assess perineal and/or abdominal wounds for signs of satisfactory healing. In the event, GPs rarely appeared to do anything which young women considered to be of value:

HS: Did you have a check-up afterwards with your GP?

Clare: Yeah. He didn't do much though. He just had a feel of my tummy and that were it. It were waste of time really. He didn't do nowt.

HS: So he didn't look at your stitches or ask to do a vaginal exam or anything like that?

Clare: No, nothing. I didn't want internal anyway, so he just says well I won't look at your stitches either, then. I didn't mind if he looked at my stitches, 'cos they were still a bit sore, like, but I didn't want internal, because they really hurt when they did them in labour. [...] He says, 'Oh well we wouldn't have even asked you to have one [an internal] if you didn't want one anyway. We wouldn't force you to have one.' [...] I may as well have not bothered going. [...] It were waste of time really.

HS: Yeah? Was that different from what you thought was going to happen?

Clare: Yeah. Health visitor said I would have to have an internal with me being so young 'n all, and he would look at my stitches as well, but he never did any of them things. (Clare, now 15 years old; daughter aged five months. SY)

Many of the teenagers and their mothers/female relatives voiced expectations about age-appropriate maternity care. Pregnant teenagers were widely perceived as requiring greater input from midwives and other professionals, especially during the early postnatal period. Many were surprised, therefore, to find that they received much the same care as other pregnant women, despite having been identified as 'vulnerable' by service providers. Indeed, compared to their middle-class counterparts, the teenagers I observed often received an inferior standard of care and, in this respect, the 'inverse care law' (Hart, 1971: 405) continues to be not only operational but also influential in the allocation of maternity resources.

Cervical screening in the puerperium: medical bargaining and women's resistance

The UK NHS Cancer Screening Programme currently recommends that women aged between 25 and 64 are offered cervical screening and in the UK financial incentives are offered to encourage medical practitioners to achieve annual targets.

Opinions vary about the appropriateness of undertaking cervical screening in the early postnatal period. From a clinical point of view, smears taken during this time may return an equivocal result, on account of the 'hyperoestrogenic' environment effected by pregnancy and/or breastfeeding. Given that 'best estimates suggest it is only moderately accurate and does not achieve concurrently high sensitivity and specificity' (Nanda et al., 2000: 810), screening undertaken during clinically sub-optimal periods, including the early puerperium, may be less than helpful.

Some teenagers described GPs as pressuring them to undergo a cervical smear, as a prerequisite to obtaining hormone-based contraception. This demand, which has no scientific basis, proved problematic for those wanting to resume early sexual relationships because cervical screening is generally not recommended within three months of giving birth:

> I went to my GP to go back on the pill again, but she said I had to wait until [the baby] was about three months old. She said I had to have a smear first. [...] She was a bit funny with me. She said things like, 'Oh you can't want to have sex again yet anyway, you've only just had a baby.' (Michelle, 16 years old; son aged six weeks. W)

> My doctor wouldn't give me another prescription for pill until I had a smear test. I'd never had one [smear] before, and I didn't really want one, but he said I had to have one or he wouldn't give me pill. (Clare, 14 years old; daughter aged three months. SY)

While the general consensus is that cervical screening should be delayed for at least the first six weeks following delivery, there is currently no specific guidance on this issue. And although cervical screening for teenagers is not incentivised, the widespread stereotyping of this population identifies them as a likely target for opportunistic testing. Hence, Michelle's and Clare's experiences are likely to reflect prevailing practice among GPs in their areas.

Some young women reported their first smear test as being very uncomfortable, not least because it reactivated negative memories of labour:

> It were horrible. [...] I were shakin' 'n shakin' after it. [...] If I'd known it were going to be that horrible I'd have asked my mum to come with me. [...] It felt like when I were in labour and they put my legs in those poles so they could fetch baby out. (Michelle, 16 years old; son aged five months. SY)

Alys was particularly upset when the result of her smear test indicated abnormal cervical cells and need for further investigation. When she returned to the clinic, she did not appreciate that a colposcopy (an examination of the cervix – the neck of the womb – using a specially designed microscope – a colposcope) would be performed and a sample of the affected cervical tissue removed for laboratory examination:

> HS: So you were by yourself – you didn't have anyone with you?
> Alys: No, 'cos like I said, they told me it was just for another smear test. [...] I was terrified. [...] You were sitting on a dentist's chair and they put your legs in stirrups. It felt exactly like the labour room. [...]
> HS: Do you know why your cervix has got these abnormal cells?
> Alys: No. The only thing I can think of is that it's something to do with having him [baby]. I never had trouble before him. (Alys, now 17 years old; son aged two years. W)

Although Alys appears to link her abnormal smear with the birth of her baby, there is no evidence to suggest that these events are causally related.

Health professionals and sexual health messages: contraception, contraception, contraception ...

Health professionals' concerns for young women's health in the postnatal period often did not reflect teenagers' agendas. The one health message which teenagers reported that most health professionals emphasised was that of contraception, although as I have previously explained, this was at odds with the restrictions some GPs imposed on accessing hormonal contraception in the early postnatal period.

HS: Has your doctor been to see you then?

Lou: Yeah. But he were horrible. He were just on 'n on about if I were using contraception. [...] Before I left hospital [24 hours following caesarean section] midwives were banging on 'n on about it as well. *Laughs*. (Lou, 16 years old; two days following an emergency caesarean section under general anaesthetic. SY)

From my observations of midwives undertaking routine postnatal visits, discussions about contraception were often inappropriately timed and improperly presented. At different times throughout my fieldwork I also observed a tendency for midwives to construct the most disadvantaged teenagers as appearing to be singularly focused on sexual intercourse and unregulated reproduction. In the following excerpt, a community midwife shares her suspicion that, in order to present herself in a better light, April 'lied' about her use of contraception:

During the consultation the midwife asks April about her previous history of using contraception. April tells her she was on the pill and that she and her boyfriend were also using condoms. The midwife purses her lips and exhales loudly; her body language suggests that she does not believe her. Later, she tries to trick April into admitting that she had forgotten to take the pill – an accusation which April quickly refutes. After we leave the house the midwife tells me that she thinks April is a 'liar' and that she doubts whether she has ever used any form of contraception: 'You can see she's that type of girl but she has to put the front on for us. You know, 17, pregnant with the second kid, unstable relationship, grotty housing, blah blah blah ...' (Field notes. Interaction between community midwife Loretta, and April, 17 years old and ten weeks pregnant with her second baby. W)

I rarely heard midwives challenging assumptions about the gendered nature of contraception responsibilities, an omission which is reflected in the research literature. For example, a highly successful specialist service operating in the South Tyneside region of the UK for the past 20 years, which currently provides 85 per cent of the service needs for local teenagers, lays emphasis on 'the young *woman* [to feel] *she* has made a well-informed choice about *her* chosen method and that *she* has enough information, knowledge and understanding to take ownership of *her* choice' (Doherty and Smith, 2006: 238; emphasis added). It was generally young women in this study who organised contraception: who took the pill or consented to the administration of injectables. Even when they suffered distressing side effects, including headaches and weight gain, young women generally lacked the authority to persuade boyfriends to use condoms:

HS: So Pete, if you're not wanting another baby right now, what's going on with contraception?

Pete: I don't know, you're [to Lou] the one that goes to doctors. You're the one that gets the pill. I don't go to doctors me. Don't like 'em.

HS: But you don't need to go to the doctors to get condoms?

Pete: Whatever. Don't like using condoms anyway. (Pete (Lou's boyfriend). SY)

When I questioned other young women about the stance their boyfriends adopted on this issue, Pete's response proved typical. The terms of the current NHS contract appear at best unhelpful and at worst discriminatory towards men as GPs are currently financially rewarded for providing contraception services to their female, but not to their male, clients. Additionally, many young men perceive family planning services to be run for, and by, women (SEU, 1999), which may further discourage them from accessing provision and from participating in discussions. The following excerpt from my field notes alerted me to the gendered comparisons midwives make between their own adolescent children, and the young people in their care:

After Jade leaves the room, Nicola (community midwife) waits until the door is closed before she leans back in her chair, sighs, and says, 'Oh, I feel so sorry for her. She's got such a lot to deal with anyway, and that's before the baby's born. [...] It makes me really glad I've only got boys. *Laughs.* I'm really, really grateful I don't have to worry day in day out about whether they're going to come home one day and tell me they're pregnant. (Observation of interaction between community midwife Nicola and Jade, 16 years old and 11 weeks pregnant. SY)

Theoretically, there is no method of contraception which is unsuitable for new mothers, although medical considerations and infant feeding decisions are normally taken into account. The majority of teenagers were initially prescribed Combined Oral Contraception (COC, otherwise known as 'the pill'), but some had rejected this in favour of injectable forms of contraception, including Depo Provera or Noristerat. 'Injectables' were generally preferred by young women because, following administration, they could 'forget about it', attending family planning clinics only for repeat injections. As I have mentioned, however, some of the teenagers were refused requests for hormonal contraception until after they had seen a GP, and completed their six-week postnatal check:

> Well, I remember she went down to make her postnatal appointment and she asked about contraception and he [GP] told her she can't have anything until after she's had her postnatal check-up. I said that was nearly eight weeks away but he still wouldn't give her anything before then. I told her she'd have to cross her legs and not let him [boyfriend] come near her in case she fell pregnant again. *Laughs.* (Angharad (mother of Alys, aged 15). W)

The postnatal check, together with attendance at mother and baby clinics, provided openings for professionals to offer contraception advice and to question teenagers about their sex lives. In the following excerpt, Lou describes a visit to her local clinic for the purpose of having her baby weighed and measured. Although this was a clinic which Lou was expected to attend in her role as a new mother, the midwife erroneously assumed she had attended because she was pregnant again:

> HS: So you went last week to the baby clinic?
> Lou: Yeah, I took 'er [baby] to get weighed, like. I were there 'n then one of 'em [midwives], she says, 'Have you come to see me then?'
> HS: What, you mean she thought you were pregnant again?
> Lou: Yeah, like I got nothing else to do. *Laughs.* I reckon I got me hands full with this 'un. *Laughs.*
> HS: How did you feel when she said that?
> Lou: At first I were, like, cheeky sod, you know? [...] Well, I do want another one but, same as I said to her, like, yeah I want another one but not just yet. [...] I wanna wait till she's a bit more grown up. I wanna feel better in m'self. Not so tired like. (Lou, 16 years old; daughter aged three months. SY)

Jade described a similar response from a midwife she met in her local supermarket:

> She [midwife] goes, 'Are you missing me yet then?' I goes, 'What? What'ya mean?' She goes, 'Oh, I thought you'd have been back to see me by now.' (Jade, 16 years old; first daughter aged ten weeks. SY)

Most of the teenagers, and some of their mothers/significant others, described similar incidents, particularly when they encountered midwives and health visitors in social settings. This was particularly evident among the South Yorkshire cohort, most of whom lived in the same small town as their healthcare providers. While friendly banter may be understood as linguistic convention which eases the difficulty of approaching sensitive topics, the boundaries between ironic commentary and overt stereotyping may be difficult to accurately assess. Jade and Lou, two of the most poorly resourced young women, were least likely to challenge care providers, and hence were more vulnerable to mistreatment and in greater need of protection. Jade did conceive again shortly after her meeting with the aforementioned midwife, although she did not indicate that a desire to re-engage with maternity care providers was a motivating factor.

The side effects of contraception and pregnancy: the 'fat' (postnatal) body

Teenagers were very aware that weight gain was a potential (but most unwelcome) side effect of using hormone-based contraception and they spoke with passion about how best to avoid this consequence. The issue was a particular concern in the early postnatal period when they were struggling to come to terms with a body which they generally abhorred; most were desperate to reclaim and to reinscribe their bodies as 'not pregnant'. While many of the teenagers were wearing their preferred styles of clothing very soon – sometimes within hours – after giving birth, and most quickly returned to their pre-pregnant weight, a return to pre-pregnant *shape* was rather more elusive for some. Like many childbearing women, some of the teenagers including Clare continued to struggle with the extra weight she had gained, and six months after the birth of her son she was still very unhappy with her body:

> Only side effect [of Depo] were I put on weight. [...] Only time I were ever heavier than eight stone two [pounds] were when I were carrying him. Now I'm nine stone six [pounds]. It's horrible. (Clare, now 15 years old; daughter aged six months. SY)

Research evidence confirms that gestational weight retention is common among postpartum women and that this is most keenly felt in the first year after delivery; younger age and a short interval from menarche to first ever birth are particular risk factors (Gunderson and Abrams, 2000). Failure to lose weight is also associated with the use of hormonal contraception, particularly injectable preparations.

Some young women reported being distressed by boyfriends' comments about their changed body shape:

Susan: He [boyfriend] hates it when I'm fat but I keep telling him
         I can't help it. I told him he should try having a baby and
         then taking the pill and see what happens to him. *Laughs.*
         [...] I hate it when he teases me about being fat. It makes
         me really nervous. *Laughs.* I think, Oh he's gonna leave me
         if I stay looking like this.
HS: How does your body feel to you? Do you feel fat?
Susan: *Starts crying.* Yeah, yeah I do. I hate myself. I can't fit any
         of my clothes so I'm still wearing the horrible ones I were
         wearing at end of pregnancy. [...] like my trackkies [track-
         suit bottoms] 'n that. [...] My stomach's totally revolting.
         [...] No one told me I were gonna end up looking like this.
         Still crying. (Susan, 15 years old; son aged two months. SY)

Adolescent females are susceptible to media, fashion and social pressures to conform to a stereotype of femininity which valorises thinness over most other attributes, including intellectual excellence (Tiggemann et al., 2000). It is of note, however, that concerns about looking attractive to males, and having the 'right' body shape to wear preferred clothing styles, are important issues for most women, irrespective of age and whether they are pregnant or have recently given birth (Earle, 1998; Longhurst, 2001).

Mental (ill) health: social and biological factors

The over-representation of women in conventional and feminist writings on mental health issues has been noted (Ussher, 1991), notwithstanding explanations which differentiate biological from social aetiologies (Stoppard, 1997). The historical belief that women's hormones are a primary cause of depression is not supported by research, although women are known to be afflicted across the life course, beginning in adolescence. Depression in women has been linked to low socio-economic status, which, in turn, is linked to their lesser degree of agency, power and status, factors which heighten their predisposition to sexual and psychological abuse. Whether, and to what degree, mental illness in females is socially constructed or 'real', perhaps resulting from material and/or physiological disadvantage, is a complex and unresolved question.

Due consideration must be given to contextual factors in this respect, however, as illnesses are not equally 'weighted'; a diagnosis of mental illness, especially in women, is frequently accompanied by stigmatisation and pathologisation. A considerable body of literature attests to the oppression of women within patriarchal psychiatric systems, both from the perspective of the 'outsider' (Ussher, 1991) and from those who have been incarcerated (Millett, 1991). These texts explore gender subjugation by examining sex-roles and the ways in which they are reinforced, particularly by institutional norms. They also illustrate how mental institutions and medical personnel construct and measure 'insane' female identities in accordance with narrow social norms of femaleness, for example by an insistence on modest clothing and a demure, passive and acquiescent, presentation of self.

Of the six young women in the South Yorkshire cohort, Tracey, Jade and Lou commenced mothering careers with pre-existing mental health problems. Jade's health temporarily improved when she was rehoused in a hostel following eviction from her family home when she became pregnant. With support from her surrogate parents and hostel residents, Jade ceased self-harming, started eating regularly, and substantially reduced her alcohol and cigarette consumption. Her mood also improved and she started to take more interest in her appearance. Following the birth of her second child, Jade and her two daughters were permanently housed in a squalid council bungalow in a rough neighbourhood some distance away from the hostel and the only close friend she had made during the time she lived there. Isolation, loneliness and aggravation from her older sister, who began an affair with the father of her second baby while he was still officially her boyfriend, stimulated a further deterioration in Jade's mental health status.

Lou's long history of poor mental health was almost certainly due to the systematic abuse she had suffered throughout her life. From an early age she endured a succession of care and foster homes which afforded her limited protection, especially from her mentally unstable, and violent, mother; the experience of being a 'looked-after' child appeared only marginally better than the 'care' Lou received from her biological mother, during the brief intervals she spent at home. By the time Lou became a mother herself, she was severely asthmatic and her respiratory health was further compromised by heavy smoking. She suffered from panic attacks, chronic insomnia, migraines and a moderate degree of agoraphobia. She had no close friends and relied entirely on her boyfriend and his family for all her support needs.

Tracey's family background categorised her as vulnerable and fragile and, hence, predisposed to mental ill health. At an early age Tracey witnessed the violent death of her younger sister and she herself had been subjected to periods of physical and sexual abuse. She had been hospitalised on a number of occasions and had undergone investigations for a range of conditions without a cause having been identified. A psychiatric report referred to her as a 'Munchausen-prone personality'. Although she had not previously attempted to harm herself, she voiced intentions to 'top' herself during the latter part of my study. Aged 14 at the time of her first conception, Tracey was also one of the youngest of the teenagers I recruited. Despite all the hardships and traumas she had endured, however, she repeatedly demonstrated greater resilience and capacity than either Lou or Jade.

Although the socio-economic, cultural and familial circumstances of children and young people's lives have long been implicated in adult ill health, the data contributing research of this kind are largely derived from retrospective accounts in adulthood. These 'straightforward causal explanations' (Backett-Milburn et al., 2003: 621) have been increasingly challenged by the findings from child-focused research, in which children and young people have located inequalities 'as much in relationships and social life as in material concerns' (ibid.). In this respect, poverty in childhood may be understood to act 'in the same way as other adversities. By itself, it is only a statistical risk factor for psychological sequelae, with most people being resilient to its effects. As with other adversities cumulative risks are more pathogenic: the combination of poverty and severe family dysfunction are a potent toxin for children' (Paris, 2000: 25).

The structuring (and abuse) of power within their social environments was an important and ever-present aspect of teenagers' lives. Previous experience of powerlessness, exposure to family violence, early parental separation and/or divorce, and difficult relationships with parents or substitutes, are strongly associated with maternal depression (Reading and Reynolds, 2001), especially among teenage mothers (Quinlivan et al., 2004; Walters, 2005). Arguments have also been made for the 'classed' aspects of power relationships to be recognised in mental illness: 'it [class] is seen to taint everything we do, how we speak, who we know, where, what and how we eat, where and what we learn, the kind of job we do, the size, type and location of our home [...] It is more than economic deprivation, it's about constantly looking up or down at each other to see who is superior or inferior to us. [...] The most devastating blows fall on working-class people' (Hagan and Smail, 1997: 260). Finally, mental health problems are more prevalent among 'cared-for' children and young people, those from poorer backgrounds and those who have witnessed domestic violence (British Medical Association, 2006).

A classic study of the social origins of depression in women (Brown and Harris, 1978) revealed that depressed patients had twice the rate of pregnancy and birth events than those who were not depressed. And although this association had previously been recognised, Brown and Harris covered new ground by questioning the prevailing tendency to identify cause and effect by implication. They found no evidence that the events of childbearing *per se* are causally linked with postnatal depression, except for those women who became severely ill with psychotic-like symptoms within the first few weeks of birth. The authors could find no *physical* trigger for depression, and suggested it was often the *social* circumstances in women's lives which provoked their illnesses: grossly inadequate housing, poor marriages that failed to support the newborn child/ren, and pregnancy losses (including those sustained through forced abortion). Brown and Harris concluded that 'it is the meaning of events that is usually crucial: pregnancy and birth, like other crises, can bring home to a woman the disappointment and hopelessness of her position – her aspirations are made more distant or she becomes even more dependent on an uncertain relationship' (Brown and Harris, 1978: 141). This reiterates an important point made by these same authors, that 'by and large, clinical depression arises because of the *meaningfulness* of experience' (ibid.; emphasis added). The links between economic hardship and women's health are clearly articulated in a later study by an internationally renowned expert in the field:

> hardship frames and constrains what mothers can do for their children [...] low income affects not only the quality of the home but living standards within it. For mothers struggling to make ends meet, the drive to economise means cutting back on items that they know are important for health [...] food [...] fuel and transport, clothes and toys. Poverty does more than restrict access to material resources. It also restricts access to the events and experiences which make

up the everyday lives of most children in Britain. School trips and family outings, bus journeys and meals out are sacrificed as mothers struggle both to protect basic necessities and service household debts [...] caring on less than you need drains the energy of mothers. It leaves them searching for ways of keeping themselves as well as their families going, ways which – ironically – are often health damaging. (Graham, 1993a: 185)

Psychological factors, including depression, continue to be leading causes of maternal death in the UK (CEMACH, 2004), although 'negative cognitions' are also experienced by mothers who are not clinically depressed (Hall and Wittkowski, 2006).

While the majority of the young women described feeling 'low' and/ or tearful, often for some months following childbirth, Lou was alone in being prescribed antidepressants; her repeated requests for sleeping pills were consistently refused by her GP:

HS: Are you still taking the antidepressants?
Lou: I'm on antidepressants, yeah, 'n I'm taking 'em. I've asked her [GP] for some sleeping pills as well, but she won't give me any. She says I'll get addicted to them. (Lou, now 17 years old; daughter aged 15 months. SY)

Immediately after the birth of her baby, Lou's domestic situation significantly deteriorated and she faced greater difficulties at this time than perhaps any of the other teenagers. The council housing which had been promised had not materialised and hence, on discharge from hospital, Lou and her newborn baby had no option but to return to her unstable and unsafe family household. Within two days she was forced to flee to her boyfriend's home, following an attempted rape by one of her mother's boyfriends.

There is some evidence to suggest that social support in the perinatal period, including that provided by professionals, may be preventative against maternal depression, but even when teenagers in this study were well supported, many nonetheless often reported being unable to initiate routine activities and/or control their emotional lability:

When I'm here on my own I just get really really depressed [...] I have to keep doing something because if I just sit around doing nothing, I end up in tears all the time. My phone bill's sky high. [...] Before I was pregnant I could control my emotions but now I can't.

I just end up bursting into tears at the slightest thing. (Nia, 18 years old; son aged six weeks. W)

Alys: [Boyfriend] used to say to me, 'Come on, come to the shops with me and get something to drink or let's go down to get the papers or something?' But I was like, no, no, you go. I was just crying and crying. It was horrible.

Mother: Yes, she was very very low for a long time afterwards. (Alys, now 17 years old talking with her mother, two years following birth. W)

In addition to feeling generally miserable, most of the teenage mothers complained about feeling chronically tired, often from interrupted sleep. Those who had continued to live in the parental home were generally helped by their mothers during the 'night shift', especially in the immediate period following birth when babies were often very restless. Teenagers planning an early return to education or employment considered the help mothers provided to be invaluable, not least because it ensured that they were sufficiently well rested to cope with these additional demands. Young mothers living with their boyfriends generally assumed greater responsibility for attending to their baby's needs, especially during the night. This was true regardless of whether or not young men were employed, or had other daytime commitments.

For the seven teenagers whose relationships survived the disorienting, and disruptive, effects of pregnancy and birth, becoming a parent presented a new set of challenges. Working arrangements and financial pressures meant that young couples often had no option but to live apart, usually in their respective parental homes, which were sometimes quite a distance apart. Separation from a partner increased the stresses:

We don't see much of each other. Not as much as we like to. It really stresses me out. *Starts crying.* It's too far to go [to see boyfriend] every day and he's too tired after work to come here. [...] He's saving so we can get a place for ourselves to live. [...] Because he works so much and then he comes here to see me and him [baby], the only time we have to go out is if my mam looks after him or his mam looks after him. So we don't see each other alone very much. (Alys, now 17 years old; son aged two years. W)

Like other young parents who remained in the parental home following the baby's birth, Alys and her boyfriend enjoyed little time in each other's sole company. Privacy within domestic environments was rarely available because these spaces were normally overcrowded and communal areas often busy and noisy.

Despite difficult conditions, most of the teenagers assumed their maternal roles with a minimum of fuss; they also managed to retain good relations with their extended families during this challenging transition. Indeed, for many, becoming a mother strengthened their 'relational sense of self' (Bailey, 1999: 344). In ways similar to descriptions of first-time, middle-class mothers (Bailey, 1999), the experience also nurtured mother–daughter communication, deepened kinship networks and increased a sense of belonging to an adult female community.

Naming and registering the baby

The act of naming communicates the 'confluence of historical, cultural, biographical, political, and symbolic themes that express membership in a particular group' (Tanno, 1994: 33). The rituals associated with choosing a name for the baby, and registering its birth, were significant preoccupations for all the teenagers and their significant others. In England and Wales, babies must be registered within 42 days of birth. Visiting the registry office was one of the first social events to be undertaken and was generally arranged within the first week following birth; a small number went directly there following discharge from hospital. The baby was generally registered in the father's surname, even when the couple had already ended their relationship and the father showed no interest in, nor expressed intentions towards, his baby. Jade and April were alone in remaining estranged from the fathers of their children at the time my study ended although Jade had ceded sole parental responsibility by including her ex-partner's name in the birth register.

According to UK law, when parents are not married, only the mother has parental responsibility for her child unless the child is adopted or placed for adoption under a placement order. The term 'parental responsibility' denotes the 'powers, rights and responsibilities of parents with respect to decisions concerning the welfare of their child(ren)' (Stevens, 2004: 314). Traditionally the two routes by which unmarried fathers acquired such responsibilities were by formal legal agreement with the mother or by a court order. As of December 2003, however, the mother may consent to her unmarried partner acquiring parental responsibility by the fact of his being registered as the child's father in the register of births and hence being named on the birth certificate.

In many cases, the decision to register the baby in the father's name was a commonsensical response that anticipated future marriage – at which point young women intended to relinquish their own surnames and assume that of their spouse:

Susan: He's going to be registered under [boyfriend's] name because we're going to get married anyway, so it doesn't matter if the baby has his name in the meantime.
HS: You wouldn't have a double-barrelled name – say have your name and his name?
Susan: No. I don't see the point of it really. My name's going to change to his anyway when we get married so what's the point? (Susan, 15 years old; son aged three days. SY)

Even when teenagers no longer wanted a relationship with their former partners, and they assumed full parental responsibilities on their behalf, they did not necessarily wish to deny him access to his child and hence agreed to enter his details in the birth register, despite their mothers' sometimes vehement objections. Very few teenagers expressed doubt about providing boyfriends or partners with rights of access. Clare, for example, initially refused to accommodate her partner's request to include his details but finally conceded when her baby was about a year old, but then only to avoid further harassment. This process, termed 're-registration', enables the biological father to be included in the birth register; new birth registration details are subsequently issued.

I've only done it to keep him happy. I were fed up with him going on 'n on about it. *Laughs.* I've not changed her surname to his. No way I'd do that. He can walk away anytime he wants, surname or no surname. I can't walk away. I don't want him walking off and her staying here with me with his surname. (Clare, now 15 years old; daughter aged 14 months. SY)

This quotation illustrates that while acknowledging the limits to her boyfriend's parental claim, Clare simultaneously voices her resentment that his freedoms are at the expense of her responsibilities. Relieved of the monotony and responsibility of childcare, young men were generally viewed as having 'the best of both worlds'. Outside of work commitments they were free to 'come and go as they pleased', confident in the knowledge that girlfriends and/or mothers would continue to service their domestic needs, and look after the baby.

Infant feeding practices

In many Western societies, breastfeeding generally denotes 'good' mothering while formula-feeding tends to be constructed as an inferior practice – at least by the middle classes and maternity experts. Paediatrician and psychoanalyst Donald Winnicott, the originator of the term 'good-enough' mother, suggested, however, that 'it is not impossible for a mother to be a good-enough mother (in my way of putting it) with a bottle for the actual feeding' (Winnicott, 1971: 11). The increasing tendency for both mothers and maternity professionals to question infant feeding choices confirms that this area of maternal decision-making is indeed a 'highly accountable matter' (Murphy, 1999: 205), weighted with significant 'moral baggage' (ibid.), and set against broader ideologies and conceptualisations of 'appropriate' parenting. The young women in this study approached infant feeding decisions in a pragmatic manner; after an initial 'flirtation' with breastfeeding all of the South Yorkshire cohort switched to formula-feeding in accordance with local norms.

Infant feeding has become something of a contested practice in recent years with increased social, medical, and more recently political, pressures on childbearing women to breastfeed their infants (and women's strategies of avoidance). Polarised debates tend to ignore the material circumstances of women's lives and the impact of feeding decisions, in particular the lack of attention to socio-cultural conditions which has encouraged a misperception that breastfeeding, as it is practised by women living in 'traditional societies', may be regarded as a homogeneous event to be exported as an example of good practice for Western women (another supposed homogeneous category) to emulate.

Recent guidelines from the World Health Organization and the United Nations Children's Fund recommend exclusive breastfeeding for a minimum of six months, followed by partial breastfeeding for two years or more. Prevalence rates in the UK, however, currently fall well below these targets, with only 21 per cent of women still breastfeeding at six months and only 13 per cent continuing at nine months (Department of Health, 2005; Hamlyn et al., 2002). Although an increase in breastfeeding initiation rates for women in lower social classes has been reported (D'Souza and Garcia, 2003), they are still much less likely than their better-educated peers to breastfeed. Little is known about how to increase breastfeeding among teenagers, although targeted interventions with low-income women in the United States, another population with traditionally low uptake rates, have demonstrated effectiveness (Dyson et al., 2005).

Negative associations with breastfeeding have been consistently reported for mothers who are young, of low social class and/or who leave full-time education at an early age (Foster et al., 1997; Wylie and Verber, 1994). Research also suggests that 'embodied', rather than 'cognitive', knowledge – for example as might be accessed through an apprenticeship style of learning experience – may be more influential on breastfeeding decisions for these groups of women (Hoddinott and Pill, 1999). Although breastfeeding is widely promulgated as *the* morally superior choice, statistics confirm that new mothers, especially those who are young and impoverished, experience considerable difficulty overcoming deeply entrenched socio-cultural, economic and practical barriers.

All six young women from the South Yorkshire cohort signalled an initial interest in breastfeeding, and Clare, Michelle, Jade and Louise briefly suckled their babies after giving birth. Susan remained undecided. Having fed her baby formula milk in hospital, she changed her mind when she returned home and expressed a desire to begin breastfeeding. A community midwife dissuaded her from taking this initiative, however, suggesting that the baby would become 'confused' as it had already become accustomed to feeding from a bottle. Tracey expressed an intention to breastfeed but was unable to follow this through when her son was born prematurely and was admitted to a Neonatal Intensive Care Unit. Both Jade and Tracey formula-fed their second babies from birth.

Of the young women in the Welsh cohort whose infant feeding practices were known to me, Alys opted to formula-feed her baby, while Nia was fully breastfeeding when I interviewed her six weeks following birth. Regarding young women's mothers, Dilys (Lowri's mother) and Polly (Michelle's mother) both breastfed at least some of their children for substantial periods, while Marg (Susan's mother) and Chris (Clare's mother) both initiated, but did not sustain, breastfeeding with some of their children.

Reiterating earlier research in this area (Earle, 2000), most of the teenagers were very knowledgeable about the benefits of breastfeeding and they voiced a keen interest in transmitting these benefits to their babies. However, those who opted to bottle-feed did not downplay their knowledge by playing 'dumb' (Murphy, 1999: 195), or otherwise feigning ignorance about the benefits of breastfeeding. Rather, their narratives suggested 'that they are at pains to assert that they *do* know that breastfeeding is reputed to be healthier for their babies' (ibid.; emphasis added) but that they proceeded with bottle-feeding because this was the customary practice within their families and local communities.

Young women who initiated breastfeeding despite prevailing norms to formula-feed their infants from birth, struggled to find adequate, and appropriate, midwifery support:

> When [daughter] were born, I weren't actually sure she were going to breastfeed even though I wanted her to. [...] There were no one to help me except for one [midwife] but she only stayed for coupla minutes after she were born. She made sure she were on me [breast] right, and then she left. [...] I mean, I know it's good 'n all to leave you do it yourself, but when you don't know what you're doing, and you're only 15. (Clare, 14 years old; daughter aged ten days. SY)

Clare breastfed her baby for a total of ten days. She persisted despite being in considerable pain, initially from engorged breasts, and subsequently from raw and bleeding nipples. When I asked her why she persevered, she stated her desire to give her daughter the 'best start', before other demands, including returning to education, claimed more of her time and energy:

> HS: But you kept on with it even though it really hurt?
> Clare: Yeah.
> HS: Why? How come you managed to do that?
> Clare: 'Cos it's best for her. That's what all books said. That's what everyone said. My mum said it would be really good for her if I start her off on breastfeeding. And I thought, well, I'm not really gonna be giving her much while I'm at school and college 'n all, so if I can give her best start now, then at least I'm doing something for her when she's young. (Clare, now 15 years old; daughter aged five months. SY)

In the following excerpt, I am interested to know whether Rhian, who expressed an intention to breastfeed, considers it beneficial or burdensome for midwives to discuss controversial information about this issue. Rhian's response confirms her considerable knowledge base and also reiterates earlier research (Dykes and Moran, 2003) emphasising the need for good support if adolescents are to successfully realise breastfeeding intentions:

> HS: Do you think it's useful for midwives to give you information [about breastfeeding] which is, like, a bit open to question. Like here in this ['Informed Choice'] leaflet it says there might be a link between breastfeeding and the baby's IQ.

Rhian: Yeah, I read that, but things like that don't really bother me. You're either intelligent or you're not. I don't believe breastfeeding makes that much difference. It's like I wasn't breastfed and I just passed ten GCSEs. *Laughs*. It's other things that make the difference, like if you have someone to help you, to cook your dinner so you can sit and just breast-feed. [...] No, I'm breastfeeding 'cos it's better for the baby, there's things like antibodies and for me there's less chance I'll get breast cancer and my womb contracts quicker as well so I'll lose weight. *Laughs*. (Rhian, 15 years old; 37 weeks pregnant. W)

The positive effects of breastfeeding on children's intelligence have, in fact, been challenged by research findings which reported that pur-ported benefits are accounted for by maternal characteristics, including higher maternal IQ (Der et el., 2006).

Younger mothers' experiences of breastfeeding are comparable with older first-time mothers, although teenagers may require additional support to initiate and sustain breastfeeding, especially in environments lacking a socio-cultural precedent. Contemporary midwives are in a dif-ficult position with respect to advising pregnant women about infant feeding. On the one hand, they must strive to be 'with' women (and the 'bad' choices they make which go against government policy) but, on the other hand, they 'are caught up in the disciplinary technologies to which they contribute' (Murphy, 2003: 458) and, as such, are expected to vigorously promote breastfeeding. Within this contested territory the preferences of individual childbearing women may be easily overlooked as midwives struggle to be facilitators, rather than coercers, of choice.

Infant feeding decisions tended to be made early in pregnancy, some-times in anticipation of a prompt return to (low-paid) work, and/or a desire to enlist help from partners and significant others:

To be honest I never even thought about breastfeeding anyway, 'cos I'm planning to go back to work, only for four hours a week but that's an extra 15 quid isn't it? (Elenor, 18 years old; 23 weeks pregnant. W)

Susan: I'm going to bottle-feed him. I was going to breastfeed him, but I won't have time now, 'cos I need to go back to work.
HS: Would you have liked to give breastfeeding a go?

Susan: Yeah, but I can't now we've moved here. We worked out
          how much money we need just to pay rent 'n bills 'n all. I'll
          have to go back to work for us to afford it.
HS: What about just breastfeeding at night?
Susan: Yeah, but they can get attached, can't they? I thought then
          he might not take to the bottle from Joe [boyfriend] 'n then
          I'm going to be in a right state when I need to go to work.
          (Susan, 15 years old; 26 weeks pregnant. SY)

My research reiterates the findings of previous work in this area
(Hoddinott and Pill, 1999) which documented women's reluctance to
breastfeed in front of others, including family members; the teenagers
singled out males, especially fathers and brothers, as being particularly
problematic in this regard. The private/public distinction between
domestic and non-domestic environments also influenced decisions:

HS: Do you think Megan would breastfeed in front of her dad?
Mother: Oh no, she'd never do that.
HS: And what about outside home, say in places like cafes?
Mother: No I don't think so. [...] She'd probably do it in front
          of me, but anyone else, I think no. (Anwen (mother of
          Megan, aged 14). W)

I'd really like to [breastfeed] but I wouldn't feel ... I'd feel so self-
conscious I couldn't do it. Not here at home with all my brothers
and their mates around. I just couldn't. (Alys, 15 years old; 30 weeks
pregnant. W)

I like walking round the street and sitting in the cafe and things like
that. If I'm going to do that it'll be easier to have a bottle. I'd never
breastfeed outside home. (Catrin, 18 years old; 16 weeks pregnant. W)

Interestingly, Clare's mother identified the community midwife as
being someone in whose company her daughter did not feel comfortable breastfeeding:

Midwife, she just come in and of course the baby were a bit grizzly
then, and it were about time for her to be fed, but Clare, she doesn't
like doing it in front of people. She's all right in front of me, but not
anybody else. So [midwife] she's just stood there, waiting for her to

feed baby. 'Well, come on then', she says, 'I haven't got all day. Feed her!' I were thinking, 'She will do, she's just waiting for you to get out ...!' *Laughs.* I mean, I thought it were really comical. Of all the people she don't want to feed in front of, I can understand, but she were the midwife ... But it's their attitude isn't it? If they put you off, then you don't want to feed in front of 'em. *Laughs.* (Chris (mother of Clare, aged 14). SY)

Infant feeding decisions are undoubtedly value-laden consumption practices (Stapleton and Keenan, 2009). Unlike many older mothers who strive to project a morally sound representation of 'good' mothering, however, the teenagers in this study did not appear to 'do' guilt in relation to breastfeeding. They were disinclined to endure prolonged discomfort in order to demonstrate allegiance to a politically correct (breastfeeding) 'cause', and when their circumstances changed and they were unable, or unwilling, to continue breastfeeding, they switched to formula-feeding with little evidence of regret or disappointment. In effect, their attitudes reflected their pragmatic mothering styles: they tended to 'get on with the job' of looking after their infants with little heed to the moral messages emphasising the 'oughts' and 'shoulds' of mothering practices.

Introducing solids

The mothers of childbearing women also influence infant feeding, including weaning, decisions and uphold cultural norms regarding the timing of solids and the choice of food the infant is offered. In this study, young babies from poorer households were frequently offered food and drink that would generally be considered unhealthy and inappropriate, particularly for this age group. The following excerpt is both typical and illustrative:

Jasmine: I'll get you some little Milky Bars [white chocolate], for when he's [three-month-old baby] a bit better, aye? [To Tracey]

HS: Has he been having much of that kind of thing – Milky Bars, 'n stuff like that?

Jasmine: Yeah. But not now ... Not while he's mardy [= moody/upset]. Not till he's eating proper meals again, like.

Tracey: He had one [Milky Bar] this morning, but he just sicked it all back up.

Jasmine: Yeah, well he would wouldn't he? I told you not to give 'em to 'im when he's mardy. [To me] Every now and again we give him one. Just for a treat like. (Jasmine (mother of Tracey, aged 14). First son aged three months. SY)

In this study, other family members were also influential in decisions regarding the foods offered to infants:

> I am invited to eat lunch with the family. As a 'good' researcher I feel that I should accept the invitation but I decline, because I am very fussy about food and the meal which I can see about to be served, consisting of baked beans, sausages, fried eggs and small chunks of something brownish sprinkled over the top, does not appeal to me. A vast pile of white bread and a large tub of margarine have been set in the middle of the battered pink formica table. [...] Pete's dad mashes up a portion of his meal, which he has covered in ketchup, and offers it to the baby – who is not quite six weeks old. [...] Later, Pete takes the baby on his knee and spoons warm, heavily sugared tea from his mug into the baby's mouth. On a previous occasion, when the baby was barely three weeks old, I observed Pete's dad making a similar offering with his coffee. (Field notes. Observation of family mealtime with Lou and Pete, daughter aged five weeks. SY)

A number of young women reported that they struggled to assert their authority when they disagreed about food items offered to their child. This was particularly so when they perceived it would have a negative effect on the child's behaviour, or was detrimental to their health:

> Jade: Soon as we walked in door he [surrogate father] turns round and says, 'Do you want some chocolate?' Well of course she does, doesn't she, so then that's it, chocolate was in her hands, in her hair, it was everywhere, and I thought, 'Oh no, oh my God ...'
>
> HS: Was it the mess you were worried about?
>
> Jade: No, it weren't mess. I'm not bothered about that. *Laughs.* It were chocolate. She's very, very hyper after she's had chocolate. She goes haywire. Completely mad she is after she's had it. I keep telling 'em all not to give it her, but they think it's a joke when she flips out. It's all right for them, they don't have it all night. (Jade, now 17 years old; first daughter aged six months. SY)

At three months most babies were reported to be enjoying a variety of food and drink. Items were generally offered in response to the child's preferences, and the extent to which the young parents, and their extended families, wished to encourage the baby to sample a wider range of tastes and textures:

> He's had some mashed potatoes but that's all so far. He's not that bothered on proper foods [i.e. the same as that eaten by Susan and her boyfriend]. I started him on some baby yogurts, but then I read on the label you shouldn't give them before four months old. I told health visitor, but she just said, 'Oh, don't matter, he's nearly four months now anyway and if he's hungry, he's hungry. You have to give him more.' (Susan, 15 years old; son aged three months. SY)

Young women who had moved out of the family home, and who lacked consistent, and trustworthy, support from their mothers, were most likely to seek nutrition-related advice from health professionals:

> HS: How about things like rusks – are you giving those to him?
> Tracey: No. I were, but then health visitor said I shouldn't be givin' 'im stuff like that, 'cos it's got too much sugar in. She said he'll get too fat, so I ain't givin' 'im them any more. (Tracey, 14 years old; first son aged three months. SY)

Tracey's response is interesting in light of the earlier reference to her mother's habit of feeding the baby Milky Bars, with their much higher sugar and fat content. Tracey rarely directly challenged her mother, however, even when she disagreed with her opinions.

Feeding older children

Food purchasing, preparation and family feeding routines are designated 'women's work' (DeVault, 1991: 95). Compared to adult family members, who have 'bodily licence' (Bell and Valentine, 1997: 34) to eat food of their own choosing, children must generally accept the food which is offered to them. Hence, food and feeding practices are potentially important media through which mothers may exercise power over their children, at least until such time as they develop strategies of resistance. The feeding-related activities of older children were widely reported as stress-provoking occasions for most of the teenage mothers; fussy or picky children especially taxed their mothers' patience:

> HS: How's he doing with his eating at the moment? Is he eating what you give him?

Susan: No. *Laughs*. He's a right pain with that. He's so fussy. He won't eat anything. I try and make him eat it but he just screams and spits it everywhere. *Laughs*. He does eat a lot of fruit though. He loves his fruit, so I s'pose that's one good thing. (Susan, now 16 years old; son aged 16 months. SY)

Toddlers who refused to eat, especially when food was freshly prepared from raw ingredients, rather than extracted from a tin or jar, were viewed as particularly vexing. The teenage mothers who had grown up in environments where eating 'proper' meals was a regular feature of family life, expressed a wish to reproduce this pattern in their newly constituted family. Most of these young women cooked 'proper dinners' for their children and were upset by children's food refusals, or when they expressed preferences for junk food. Children's fathers and grandmothers often acted as mediators between children and their agitated mothers:

HS: What causes you the most stress with him [toddler] right now?

Michelle: It's him not wanting to eat the food I cook him! *Laughs*. I cook him a proper dinner every day – like yesterday I made him vegetable lasagne – but he just wants junk food all the time. He just loves it. *Laughs*. I know it's only a phase but some days I get really upset when that's all he'll eat. Ryan [boyfriend] tells me off. He says I should stop fussing so much, that he'll eat when he's hungry. [...] When we're down at my mum's on a Sunday, he eats all his dinner for her no trouble. He makes out I'm a right liar, he does ...! *Laughs*. (Michelle, now 17 years old; son aged 16 months. SY)

More than two decades ago, Anne Murcott (1982) described the social significance of the 'cooked dinner' produced by women for their families. In this research, cooked dinners were often unaffordable, and thus unavailable, to children in poorer households. Lou and Pete, for example, frequently had insufficient money to buy enough food for themselves, even before their daughter was born. Had it not been for the regular mealtime invitations extended to the young family by Pete's parents, the hunger they occasionally experienced might have been a more regular feature of their lives:

I mean, over the past week, she [toddler] loves her cooked dinners, and we haven't had a cooked dinner for ages, and that's what she's missing. She went round to [mother-in-law] other day 'n she gave her a cooked dinner, 'n she ate the whole lot she did. [...] I give her Frosties in morning, like, 'cos that's all we've got left. That 'n potatoes, but she were having them all week, so she were a bit fed up with 'em. That's why she ate all her cooked dinner. (Lou, now 17 years old; daughter aged 15 months. SY)

The impact of poverty on family feeding practices and, hence, as a significant constraint on childhood development, is well documented (D'Souza and Garcia, 2003; Nelson, 2000). Despite regular reportage from the tabloid press to the contrary, there is evidence to suggest that the problems which arise in households with inadequate food supplies occur because there is insufficient money available to spend on food, not because money is being spent unwisely (Nelson, 2000).

In the next (penultimate) chapter I describe the teenagers' adjustment to their mothering roles and the processes and practices associated with the 'doing' of motherhood, particularly for those who were most physically, emotionally and socially impoverished. I discuss how the teenagers' emergent maternal personas were supported, or undermined, by family and kinship, and/or maternity professionals, and how the impact of domestic, including childcare, responsibilities affected young mothers' intimate relationships. I also examine the availability of employment and educational opportunities and the constraints which operated to limit teenagers' preferred choices. Disciplinary practices which would ensure 'appropriate' infant behaviour and, hence, the formation of 'good' future citizens, were highly regarded; obedient and well-mannered children also enhanced the teenagers' maternal reputations and demonstrated their ability to be 'good' mothers. The teenagers who opted to do things differently from their mothers, and/or from socially accepted norms, risked censure. The trials and tribulations of everyday life provided teenagers' mothers with a mixture of opportunities and challenges; those who were well supported demonstrated their adaptive capacities, in stark contrast to those who were struggling alone. Finally, I discuss the teenagers' mothering activities, and the gendering of domestic responsibilities within the context of family life, wherever this was located.

7
Mothering in Early Childhood: Everyday Practices and Identity Formation

Women who 'choose' motherhood are pressured by multiple, and oppositional, forces. At a material level, the very visible, and highly persuasive, advertising industries aggressively promote the latest 'must have' products and rely on children's 'pester power' to reduce adult resistance. At the corporeal level, women-as-mothers are targeted by health-promotion campaigns to recognise the importance of a 'healthy' diet and of correct sleeping arrangements for infants, and the need for appropriate disciplinary measures for older children. All the while, mothers are charged with conveying the 'right' messages to children, especially their (sexually adventurous) adolescents, encouraging them to complete their education and make a successful transition to the workforce and, later, to stable and loving relationships unmarked by police, or maternity, records. Hence, mothers are routinely positioned as the moral arbiters of the family's behavioural and social practices and are harshly judged when individual members fail to meet approved standards of conduct. The mothers of childbearing teenagers tend to be identified as failures in this respect.

Formulating adolescent maternal identities: class, age and agency

Teenage motherhood disrupts dominant (patriarchal) discourses about sexuality because childbearing is not class neutral: girls who become pregnant and go on to become mothers, do so because the life course they inherit is pre-inscribed with disadvantage and inequality. Power relationships, and the multiple ways in which these may be enacted, also have consequences for women in so far as men assume significant control over many aspects of women's reproductive lives

(Blanc, 2001; Dudgeon and Inhorn, 2004). The exercise of personal power in sexual relationships is anyway more limited for girls, especially those born into impoverished circumstances, not least because it is often 'neither the only, nor the most salient, site of struggle and negotiation' (Woollett et al., 1998: 371). Gender-based power, derived from social meanings underpinning biological differences between men and women, and expectations regarding (sexual) behavioural norms, reinforces a sexual double standard whereby men's greater sexual freedoms, and their rights to sexual self-determination, are in sharp contrast to the denial of such rights for women, especially during their adolescent years.

Stereotyped images and tabloid accounts of motherhood frequently depict children as dichotomised images in the form of monsters or angels; as 'unnatural' products of inadequate (lone/poor/teenage) mothering, or the well-behaved, and socially competent, offspring of economically stable families. With respect to 'monster' children, two who are arguably conceived in the UK public imagination as being notorious in this respect are Robert Thompson and Jon Venables, the ten-year-olds convicted for the abduction and murder of a two-year-old child – James Bulger – in the north of England in 1993 (see Morrison (1997) for a thoughtful, and provocative, literary account of this event).

As I have previously stated, teenage parenthood also tends to be presented in terms of dichotomous, insider/outsider discourses. Outsider views, usually from 'authoritative' elders, focus on issues of dependency, while insider views, from teen mothers and their kinship groups, are more concerned with identifying markers of independence. Age was a defining factor which categorised and set the teenagers in this study apart. While it was normally health professionals who were most divisive, teenagers themselves also made negative judgements about their peers on the basis of (younger) maternal age. Some were particularly concerned that association with teenage mothers might spoil their own reputations:

> A lot of girls round here, they've got young babies and some of them they're girls a lot younger than me. I mean, I look at them and to be honest they don't always look after the babies all that well. I mean sometimes their babies look a bit uncared for and the way they treat them and whatever is not always good. That's my opinion anyway. [...] I think they [midwives] just assumed that was me. That would be me as well, that I'd be exactly the same because I was 15, not married or anything. (Rhian, 15 years old; 37 weeks pregnant. W)

The combination of adolescence and impending parenthood was problematic because these categories were often conflated by power-holders:

Mother: The midwives in the clinic, now, they're like, 'Oh you're too young to be pregnant,' but then they say, 'You're old enough to know better.' Now what are you? Are you old enough to know better or are you too young to get pregnant? You can't be both, can you? I think they must be old enough, because, well, they *are* pregnant aren't they, so they should be treating them as old enough.

Alys: Yeah … It's, like, you can't win and they don't want you to win. […] You're stuck in the middle. You don't know where you are with 'em. (Alys, 15 years old and 20 weeks pregnant, talking with Angharad, her mother. W)

Mothers expressed ambivalence about whether adolescent motherhood conferred more, or less, adult status on their daughters, reflecting the tensions expressed in tabloid and academic discourses, where teenage mothers are depicted either as immature dependants unable to survive without the benefits of a welfare state, or as young adults struggling to assert mature and self-sufficient identities. At different times and in different circumstances individuals are considered variably proficient in the presentation of an independent and autonomous self. Faced with rapidly changing environments in which the 'rules of the game' are not always clear, but where moral judgements are nonetheless operating, regression to a more psychologically dependent state is not unusual. Daughters switching between a mature, and an evolving, identity was a frequently articulated theme in mothers' narratives:

She's not one for asking for herself. Before we go [to the clinic] she says, 'Mum, don't forget to ask about so 'n so will ya?' She's like that with everything though. She won't phone hairdressers to make an appointment. She won't phone doctors or nowt for herself, she just goes through me. I think it's an age thing, isn't it? (Polly (mother of Michelle, aged 16). SY)

Many of the young women participating in this study were not in the habit of maintaining personal diaries and neither did they arrange their own appointments, relying instead on their mothers' organisational skills. At this stage in their development then, most accessed adult status through the agency of their mothers.

In contrast to mother–daughter relationships, which were generally very sensitive to nuances in the dependency-autonomy continuum, maternity staff were rather more rigid in their interactions with their young clients. The fieldwork for the 'Informed Choice' study (Kirkham and Stapleton, 2001) provided an exceptional opportunity to observe a wide range of maternity professionals interacting with a broad cross-section of childbearing women. A recurring feature in this study was the high value attributed to traditional female characteristics such as passivity and compliance. This was most evident when a significant hierarchical gap, largely accounted for by age and social class, but intensified by gender differences, existed between client and professional. Few mothers, however, anticipated the degree to which their daughters' teenage status would be perceived as problematic by maternity staff, especially midwives. Although mothers did not necessarily remember their own childbearing experiences as enjoyable events, most nonetheless offered more positive comparisons of their relationships with maternity staff. Dilys was pregnant at the same time as her daughter, and when she compared their parallel experiences of maternity care, she suggested her older age automatically commanded greater respect:

> I've been with her [daughter] to the clinic and I've seen the way she's been treated and it's made me so angry. They treat her like she's stupid, like she's irresponsible. She was brushed away from the start. [...] When I go to the clinic I'm treated like a proper person, like an adult. I'm sure the only difference is our age. And if that's how they treat her at 16, God knows how they treat the younger ones. (Dilys (mother of Lowri), who was pregnant at the same time as her daughter. W)

Legitimate access to the title 'Mrs' increased a pregnant teenager's status and appeared to improve the likelihood of her being treated more humanely by antenatal staff. It was unclear, however, whether women who were addressed in this way were actually married or whether some simply claimed marital status in order to protect themselves from negative attitudes. It is also possible that staff automatically used this form of address for pregnant women they identified as 'older' and, therefore, 'respectable'.

They'd call them ones out properly. They call out, 'Mrs X please', and then they'd call out, 'Alys'. They wouldn't call her, 'Miss X'. She could have been married as well for all they knew, but they'd still have called out, 'Alys', just so they could rub it in, isn't it? (Angharad (mother of Alys, aged 15). W)

Attending for maternity care may be a unique opportunity for pregnant teenagers to have a sense of agency reflected back to them; to be legitimated as 'mothers in the making', with all the potential for personal growth and development associated with assuming a maternal role. Such recognition might serve to enhance their transition to, and status as, teenage mothers, although this would also require maternity staff to keep pace with their alternating needs for dependency and autonomy.

Motherhood and mothering practices

As with children and young people, images of mothers are also often portrayed as stereotypes: the composed and serene medieval Madonna with her baby nestling in her arms or contentedly suckling her breast; the aristocratic mothers of earlier periods who abandoned their offspring to wet nurses or fosterage (and of course their contemporary counterparts whose children are bundled off to boarding schools); the (feckless) working-class mother with insufficient means to provide for, and control, her (too many) children; the 'modern' mother juggling a busy career with the pressure to spend 'quality time' with her family; the (surrogate) mother-as-incubator whose reproductive efforts are intended for (an)other. Young mothers are portrayed as 'pramface' mums (Kehily and Nayak, 2008; McRobbie, 2009) or 'chav' mums (Tyler, 2008), while the plight of the 'Mothers of the Disappeared' (Ruddick, 1989) has given a public face to the grief of mothers caught up in the machinery of military regimes.

Although many of the practices associated with motherhood have changed over time, psychoanalytic approaches continue to emphasise an 'ideal' (middle-class) mother, whose (unconditional) love for, and attachment to, her child(ren) is seen as fundamental to their healthy development; hence the reification of a particular ('classed') representation of motherhood. Modern (middle-class) motherhood parallels aspects of women's professional lives in so far as 'good' mothers and 'good' workers must be seen to 'be there' in order to demonstrate role potential and capacity. And whether 'there' is a staff meeting scheduled outside working hours, or kids' sports days or Christmas concerts, attendance signifies commitment to a normative 'truth' of mother-hood as a happy and fulfilling enterprise. These idealised versions of mothering tend to obliterate depictions of the everyday pain and suffering of 'ordinary' (working-class) mothers. Perhaps *because* there is so little (conceptual) space within which women's unhappy accounts of their mothering experiences might be made available, explanatory frameworks are mobilised which fit the dominant discourses. Hence diagnoses of 'postnatal depression' or 'traumatic stress disorder' as (medical) explanations for maternal distress.

The term 'mother' is weighted with multiple contradictions, functioning as a conduit for debates on a range of contentious issues including family values, health and well-being, the significance of nature and culture, and the place of nurture in the development of gender roles and identities, employment rights and notions of citizenship. Regardless of whether women are biological, social, surrogate or adoptive mothers, representations of motherhood reverberate with the perceptions individual women hold of their own maternal bonds and their infantile experiences of being mothered. Understandings of motherhood are thus multifaceted, rooted in socio-cultural concerns, and integral to economic and political deliberations and reforms. In addition, the status of motherhood in any society is intimately linked to the general status of women and to understandings of female roles and identities, which in turn are irrevocably bound up with interpretations about the construction of gender. In contrast to *biologically* derived motherhood, *social* mothering does not require a biologically derived child-object as the focus of (maternal) attention, but may include the nurturing and befriending of chosen others. Maternity as a biological fact, grounded in the female body through the act of giving birth, is therefore differently understood from the (culturally constructed) activity of *mothering*, which is grounded in specific historical and cultural practices.

Feminist academics such as Ann Oakley ([1974] 1985) have long refuted assertions that women *need* to become mothers simply because they are biologically equipped to do so, but insist that most do so because of social and cultural conditioning, and a lack of alternative opportunities. In defence of her arguments, Oakley (ibid.) cites studies showing that women who had been abused were more likely to abuse or neglect their own children; and women who had not seen their own mothers breastfeeding were unlikely to adopt this practice themselves. These observations, grounded in empirical studies, suggest that mothers, and their capacity for mothering, are made, not born – which reiterates a claim made two decades earlier with reference to the defining processes involved in the construction of 'woman' (de Beauvoir, 1953). Mothering has been defined as:

> the maternal behaviour learned in interaction with a particular child, beginning in the process of achieving a maternal role identity and continuing to evolve throughout the child's development. [...] the blend of nurturing, caring, teaching, guiding, protecting, and loving that enhances the infant's physical, emotional, social, and cognitive development to adulthood. [...] derived from the mother's resources and extensive knowledge of each individual child that enables her to meet the child's needs in unlimited situations and conditions from a very expert and creative base. (Mercer, 1995: 1)

To situate this perfectly reasonable, but arguably unachievable, list of desirable attributes in a less idealised context, maternal practice can only ever respond 'to the historical reality of a biological child in a particular social world' (Ruddick, 1980: 348). As is evident from the snapshots of the teenagers' lives presented in this book, the social worlds and future prospects for the most impoverished were very grim indeed. They were badly resourced, both materially and psychologically, and hence their attention to their child's developmental needs was often secondary to meeting more basic needs, including hunger, warmth and physical safety. The effects of poverty severely limit options, making 'interested maternal practice and therefore maternal thinking nearly impossible' (ibid.: 349).

In common with other first-time mothers, the narratives of the teenagers who contributed to this study reflect a diversity of experiences. The absence of a universal maternal script for the way in which mothering was individually performed, from a 'matrix of images, meanings, sentiments, and practices that are everywhere socially and culturally produced' (Scheper-Hughes, 1992: 341), allows for a 'pragmatic' rather than a 'poetic' approach to the everyday aspects of 'doing' mothering. This echoes what David Morgan has referred to as an increased 'fluidity' in family life and family practices (Morgan, 1999).

Doing mothering differently: young women's mothers as role models?

Mothering practices are embedded within a social context in which relationships with others are a fundamental aspect; young women's experiences of relationships inevitably influenced, and cumulatively affected, their capacity as mothers. Hence the importance of identifying relevant classed and other socialisation processes not least because 'Behaviours we associate with a specific life stage may more truly reflect the conditions through which a group has lived collectively, such as its access to education, than biological age' (Monk and Katz, 1993: 20). When I asked the teenagers if they intended raising their children similarly to, or differently from, how they had been raised, their replies tended to reflect their individual experiences of being mothered. In effect, this reiterates a point made some 25 years ago: 'what happens to women when they become mothers reflects what has already happened to them as they became women' (Oakley, [1979] 1986: 11). A historical perspective insists that 'women are seen not only as mothers, wives and workers, but also in relation to other generations – as daughters, grandmothers, aunts and so on – and in domains outside the family and workplace and their wider community of friends, as well as in relation to various social and political institutions' (Monk and Katz, 1993: 20). Over the life course, then, women's circumstances may undergo profound changes which, in turn, will influence their maternally derived relationships.

Observing their daughters' mothering efforts prompted mothers to reflect on their own experiences of childrearing and to protect their daughters from repeating the 'mistakes' they perceived themselves to have made, especially with their first-born infants. Mothers often disagreed with how their daughters managed socialisation processes with their grandchildren and this provoked considerable tensions for both parties. Although many of the teenagers articulated a desire to 'do' mothering differently from the patterns they 'inherited', the majority conformed to the intergenerational patterns described over 40 years ago by Josephine Klein (1965) in her study of 'Ashton', a fictional community in the heart of the Yorkshire coalfields. The most emotionally deprived teenagers in my research mirrored the behaviours of parents in Klein's study, for example by stressing their children's material, rather than psychological, well-being, which accentuated 'the taboo on tenderness and [...] concentration on the outward signs – new clothes, new toys' (ibid.: 115). External appearances were especially important to the poorest teenagers and most strove to maintain a façade of plenty which they hoped would protect them from negative appraisal by others. Living with debt was a common experience and some young families went without food and other essential items in order to afford status symbols such as expensive toys and designer clothes for their children.

Mothers played a central role in the formation of daughters' characters and, hence, in shaping their mothering potential. As narratives throughout this book have demonstrated, the quality of mother–daughter relationships varied greatly and although some daughters complained about their mothers, they nonetheless made frequent reference to them. If they were estranged they agonised over whether, and on what terms, they might re-establish contact; the volatile nature of mother–daughter bonds was thus evident but also ambiguously manifested 'with bitterness masquerading as love, and bondage masquerading as attachment' (Apter, 1990: 7). Young women who had enjoyed a stable and nurturing upbringing generally expressed a desire to emulate at least some of the parenting practices to which they themselves had been exposed. In this way the 'inherited' self is woven into a pattern of cyclical transmission, with the potential for the child to make of its past what it will; continuity and change thus reflect the parenting styles of each generation.

As I have already mentioned, Michelle's modelling career necessitated her travelling to European locations for fashion shoots, where she was exposed to the glamour and allure of lifestyles she had only previously encountered in glossy magazines. She was earning a wage far in excess of that earned by anyone she knew and she was beginning to get a feel for, and to enjoy, the independence and status associated with her emerging identity as a 'high flyer'. Her mother, Polly, provided a useful point for comparative reference and offered the necessary emotional support which enabled Michelle to do mothering differently: to have a career *and* be a good mother:

HS:　　　Do you think the way you're a mother to Daniel is very different from how your mother was with you?

Michelle:　Yes, I think so. I'm very different from my mother.

HS:　　　Tell me more – in what way would you say you're different?

Michelle:　Well, for a start, I'm not putting my life on hold the way she did for us. I don't want to be mad with Daniel when he's older for taking chances away from me. I don't mean I don't get upset when I'm away from him – I do. I was really upset when I went to Greece [on a modelling contract] but my mum told me that lots of mums go out to work now and that it's something he'll get used to. She said it doesn't mean I don't love him just because I want a life of my own. (Michelle, now 17 years old; son aged 16 months. SY)

Polly encouraged her daughter to maximise the opportunities afforded by her new career and usually looked after her grandson when Michelle worked abroad. Although she was disappointed that both her eldest and youngest daughters had become teenage mothers, Polly viewed these events as temporary setbacks which would resolve when her grandchildren commenced schooling and her daughters became more independent.

The teenagers whose childhoods had been disrupted by violence and/or multiple changes in family structure expressed no inclination to replicate their parents' childrearing patterns and, indeed, some were very concerned lest they inadvertently reproduce these practices. Hence, with respect to mothering potential, systems of 'inheritance' may be both benign and threatening, with the latter having specific, and potentially troublesome, repercussions for daughters. The expression 'matrophobia' – the fear of becoming (too) like one's own mother (Rich, 1977) – has been employed to describe the unwelcome intrusion of socially (classed) and genetically acquired maternal characteristics into the minds and bodies of daughters. The reproduction of 'inherited' characteristics, or the fear of this occurring, may be detrimental to the creation of mothering identities:

> I don't want to turn out like my [alcoholic] mum and end up being a bad mum like her. That's what I'm worried about the most. [...] I'm scared I'll turn out just like her no matter how hard I try not to be like her. *Starts crying.* I just couldn't bear it. I'd rather have a termination. I can't bear the thought of doing that to my child. [...] She was the worst mother you can imagine. Vile, she was, vile. (Catrin, 18 years old; 28 weeks pregnant. W)

A personal experience of negative mothering, then, provided Catrin with embodied knowledge about how she did *not* want to be as a mother. Exposed to chaos and uncertainty from an early age, Catrin talked at length, and at an early stage in pregnancy, about her fear of reproducing her mother's 'vile' parenting style. Her experiences of being mothered were largely conflictual and adversarial, and in the absence of alternative examples of mothering, Catrin's parenting skills will have to be learned. In this respect she will become a 'self-developed' mother (SmithBattle, 2000: 87).

Clare, who endured her mother's early separation and subsequent divorce from her alcoholic father, followed soon afterwards by the sudden early deaths (from suicide and cancer) of her only two uncles, was well aware of the impact of tragedy on family cohesiveness. She expressed an intention to protect her daughter from the emotional distress of such events:

> I think my mum has been, like, a really good mum, but I wouldn't go round saying, 'Oh I want to be a mum like my mum,' 'cos my mum's had a really rough time, wi' me dad and her brothers 'n everything, and I think that's, like, affected me as well. […] I don't want my kids having to grow up wi' all that going off. It's too hard. I think that's what's made [younger sister] go off the rails is all that stuff that happened when we was younger. (Clare, now 16 years old; daughter aged two years. SY)

Jade frequently articulated a desire to be more emotionally consistent with her daughters than she had experienced in her family of origin. On a number of occasions throughout the study, she alternated between despair and anger when she described differences in the relationship between herself and her mother, and between her mother and Josie, her older sister – according to Jade, the favoured daughter. Jade's intention to demonstrate a more equal relationship with her own daughters may thus be interpreted as a desire to 'disinherit' her mother's parenting legacy. Her intentions were fuelled by her mother's acceptance of, and support for, Josie who became pregnant at 15, and her rejection of Jade in similar circumstances two years later.

> HS: Do you think the way you're a mother to Janey and Gemma is different from how your mother was with you?
>
> Jade: Yeah, 'cos, like, my mum, she favoured Josie. She were always down on me for everything. I'm trying to treat both of these equal, like, so I'm definitely different from her in that way. (Jade, now 18 years old; daughters aged 18 months and four months respectively. SY)

At the time Jade made the above claim, however, she had already arranged for her younger daughter, Gemma, to live with Josie and Tom (Gemma's father and Jade's ex-boyfriend with whom Josie was now living). Despite Jade's intentions to do mothering differently, her relationships with her daughters replicated the very pattern she was trying to avoid: that of distancing herself from her younger daughter, just as her mother had done with her.

In the following excerpt, Lou is reminded by her partner that even seemingly small gains in parenting status nonetheless deserve to be recognised and celebrated:

> HS: What about you Lou, are you being a mum in a different way to what your mum was like with you?
>
> Lou: I dunno, 'cos when I were Amy's age, I were in care weren't I? Yeah, I were 'n all.
>
> Pete: Well then, that proves you *are* doing better job then, 'cos like, if she's [daughter] still here then you must be. You were in care and she's still here so that proves it, doesn't it? (Pete and Lou, now 17 years old; daughter aged 15 months. SY)

At the end of the study period, apart from occasional 'glitches', Michelle, Clare and Susan maintained close and caring relationships with their mothers, and Jade and her mother had re-established contact and were in the process of initiating a reconciliation process. Lou remained estranged from her mother and, following her daughter's birth, successfully sought legal aid to obtain a court order banning her from further contact.

Childcare: formal and informal provision and access

Childcare was a gendered activity which most young women who were in a position to do so shared with their mothers, at least during the time they continued to live at home. When daughters moved into rented accommodation, usually with male partners, mothers generally continued to support them, albeit sometimes on different terms. Continued family support is crucial to teenage mothers, especially at the point of exiting the family home. Indeed, research suggests that during the first year of living away a sizeable number continue to spend considerable amounts of time in the parental home, returning to their newly acquired residences only to sleep (Speak et al., 1995). Mothers and mothers-in-law often assumed, or indeed were offered, a considerable role in childminding activities. Offers of help were sometimes resisted, because the 'natural' order of established domestic hierarchies tended to make it all too easy for older female relatives to usurp younger women's attempts to establish their own maternal identities. As I have already explained, however, not all female relatives were willing to assist the young couple with childcare; lack of support added significantly to their feelings of helplessness and distress.

Young mothers who lacked support from their own mothers, and/or who were rehoused at some distance from established family and social support networks, usually had little choice but to accept whatever help was available to them, regardless of the quality or the conditions attached. For example, Lou was economically and socially dependent on her boyfriend's parents and hence had limited bargaining power to challenge her mother-in-law's demands for greater involvement in her granddaughter's life. She repeatedly thwarted Lou's attempts to assert mothering control, for example by refusing to provide childcare if she disagreed with the purpose for which it was requested, and occasionally failing to return her granddaughter at agreed times. As her granddaughter developed from a passive baby to a demanding toddler, she withdrew her support altogether.

Many mothers looked after their own grandchildren in order to help their daughters with their education and/or careers, or simply to take occasional 'time out' to enjoy themselves. In addition to caring for their own kin, a number of mothers also provided childcare for the children of neighbours and friends. Childcare has become increasingly 'corporatized' (Sumsion, 2006) in recent years, with bureaucratic procedures formalising previously casual arrangements between women. Although no formal qualifications are required, prospective childminders in the UK must complete recognised training, including first aid, and return satisfactory clearances from the police and local authorities before being eligible for registration with OFSTED, a UK government agency and the official inspectorate for children and students. In this study, mothers who understood what official registration entailed dismissed suggestions that it was necessarily in their best interests:

HS: Do you think you'll go to the bother then of training and registering [as a childminder]?

Chris: No, it's too much faffing about. I only want to look after my granddaughter, it's not like I want to look after the whole neighbourhood. *Laughs*. And when she goes to school I'll stop doing it anyway, so what's point of stressin m'self, just to look after *one* baby. It's not worth it. [...] I think it's a total con. (Chris (mother of Clare, aged 14). SY)

The requirement to be registered, and to undergo continuing 'professional' development in order to receive the payment to which many mothers felt they were anyway entitled, provoked heated discussions.

Some mothers claimed that an altruistic desire to ensure their grand-children, and the children of friends and neighbours, enjoyed the best possible childcare made them vulnerable to being emotionally and materially manipulated by what they perceived as irrelevant state requirements:

> HS: So, because you're related to [granddaughter], because she is family, then you can only be paid if you register with the local authority?
>
> Polly: That's right, that's what they told me. It's ridiculous. If she [Michelle] were paying for childcare, say in nursery or some-thing, it'd cost her a fortune. [...] Well, she'd not be able to afford it would she? But 'cos I'm related to [granddaughter] then I'm only allowed to look after her if it's for free. *Laughs.* They really make use of you don't they? *Laughs.* We're stupid for doing it 'n all, we are. *Laughs.* (Polly (mother of Michelle, aged 16). SY)

The mothers who are required to submit themselves for formal train-ing in parenting skills are from the working classes, and, in this sense, state controls and regulations increasingly govern the way in which (disadvantaged) children are raised (Gillies, 2005). The introduction of parenting 'standards' also reflects the creeping professionalisation of family life (Furedi, 2001). Mothers in receipt of benefits found it necessary to undertake a comprehensive financial analysis in order to confirm that if they decided to proceed with registration, their earnings would not effect a reduction in benefit payments. This was particularly important for women who had not been in paid employment for many years, some of whom were in considerable debt:

> HS: So are you saying you wouldn't be able to receive any money for childminding anyway, because it would upset your benefits?
>
> Chris: Yes, that's right. Because I'm on benefits I can only earn 15 pound a week [...] When she starts school I'll have to go back on benefits if I can't get a job, but then they might tell me, 'Oh no, you've been working, you can't have benefits.' (Chris (mother of Clare). SY)

The restricted availability of affordable commercial childcare negatively affected some young women's decisions to continue their education.

For example, Susan's and Michelle's intentions to take up college places proved impossible, because the subsidised college crèche only admitted children over the age of two years and neither could afford the fees charged by independent childcare providers. Poor public transport links created additional obstacles for teenage mothers, and as a result some sought employment opportunities rather than returning to education as they had originally intended. Government interventions such as the UK *Care to Learn* initiative (DfES, 2003) were intended to remedy such problems by providing financial assistance with childcare to teenage parents wishing to continue their education, although a 'childcare gap' (National Audit Office, 2004) – that is, the lack of affordable, high-quality care – in the most disadvantaged neighbourhoods remains unresolved. This rather undermines the ideology espoused by social inclusion agendas.

The teenage mothers differed from their older counterparts in that the majority were able to access informal and local childcare arrangements. In the first instance, daughters negotiated with their mothers about the childcare they wanted, and what mothers were prepared to provide. Localised family networks provided additional help, which was flexible and usually available at short notice.

> HS: So, do you like have an agreement with your mum where you both can say, right, I'm off duty now and you're on duty now? Or how does it work out between you?
>
> Alys: *Laughs.* Well it's not, like, I just like tell mum to go away and I'm doing whatever with [son] now. Like, obviously, sometimes I go out and I just leave my mam to carry on. […] My mam doesn't go out much anyway, so she doesn't mind staying in with him. (Alys, now 17 years old; son aged two years. W)

In addition to maintaining their routine domestic responsibilities towards other family members, then, mothers absorbed the additional tasks associated with looking after grandchildren:

> HS: And who does things like getting Chloe's [Clare's daughter] tea for her?
>
> Clare: Sometimes she eats before I get in, if I'm going out like, but if mum knows I'm staying in she probably gives Chloe hers first.
>
> HS: And then you and your mum and [younger sister] all eat together later on?

Clare: Yeah. We usually eat our tea and watch telly.
HS: And who does the cooking and cleaning and, you know, the household stuff?
Clare: Oh, mum. *Laughs.* I can't cook nowt. And I'm totally crap at cleaning. *Laughs.* (Clare, now 16 years old; daughter aged two years. SY)

Although mothers did not expect their daughters to pay them for the childcare they provided, payment in kind was sometimes negotiated. For example, soon after Tracey returned home with her new baby, she resumed the task of collecting her two younger siblings from school each day. Similarly, when Clare passed her driving licence, she took on her mother's role of transporting her younger sister to her social engagements. As soon as they started earning a regular wage, both Clare and Michelle paid their mothers for some of the childcare they provided (which, to some extent, demonstrates the ineffectiveness of government attempts to legislate against informal childcare arrangements). Payment for tasks previously undertaken by women for love, or from a sense of duty or social obligation, reflects the increasing (gendered) commercialisation of many aspects of everyday living.

Disciplining the child: constructing good, future, 'classed' citizens

The project of motherhood is central to the way in which mothers influence their child's development 'in such a way that her child becomes the sort of adult that she can appreciate and others can accept' (Ruddick, 1980: 349). The setting of boundaries, and 'the prevention of naughtiness and the promotion of goodness' (Ribbens, 1994: 174) in children were seen as central to children's successful socialisation and have long been considered as central to the mothering project. Unruly children suggested a dereliction of parental duty, and parents and grandparents were generally of the opinion that bad behaviour should be corrected immediately. The power to exert appropriate control was considered intrinsic to the maternal, but not necessarily to the paternal, role.

Teenagers described the ways in which they exercised disciplinary power in various ways: restricting the child's physical movement by putting it in its room or cot, or by making it sit in a designated place for a set period of time; inflicting physical punishment directly on the child's body ('slaps', 'taps', 'smacks'); depriving the child of favourite toys and routines (bedtime stories); and/or shouting or swearing at it.

Teenagers, and their significant others, were generally very concerned about their child's behaviour and interactions with others; 'proper manners' and 'good behaviour' were highly regarded and, if not spontaneously volunteered by the child, were induced through systems of rewards and punishments. The tendency to blame and discipline the child, as a first response to behaviours considered inappropriate, was more noticeable among poorer parents:

> When [daughter] is with other kids she'll slap them so then I slap her back again to teach her a lesson. She's right wild she is. [...] The dog got her yesterday. It bit her leg. Served her right. She's learned her lesson now. She needed stitches. (April, 17 years old; ten weeks pregnant with her second baby. W)

> You throw that at me again [to toddler] and I'll throw you! [Daughter repeats earlier action of throwing a cushion at Lou.] No! You bad girl, I'm going to smack your bum for that [smacks daughter across buttocks]. (Lou, now 17 years old; daughter aged 15 months. SY)

Psychological theorising (Mercer, 1995) suggests that adolescent mothers are more likely to adopt authoritarian attitudes towards their children and tend to be less tolerant of irksome behaviour. However, research findings often fail to differentiate such behaviour on the basis of participants' social class: middle-class standards have long been the presumed ideal. Working-class parenting methods may thus be considered deviant because they are judged against norms which discount individuals' classed preferences and experiences (Walkerdine and Lucy, 1989). Teenagers, whose personal experiences of parenting were mostly negative, tended to see disobedience in their children as deliberate attempts to undermine their authority, interpreting such childlike behaviours as personal attacks on their maternal authority. Even when alternative explanations were suggested, they were reluctant to change their viewpoint:

> Lou: Every time I pick her up, she's [daughter] slamming her lip back or something stupid. [...] It feels like she's against me for some reason. She's got a right temper on her. She's always trying to get at me. She does it deliberately to wind me up. [...] Yesterday I put her down and she wouldn't settle. She were waving her arms around and one of 'em smacked me across face. She does it to get at me. I know she does. *Starts sobbing.*

HS: Mmm. Yeah I can understand it might feel like a wind up to you but it might be that she's only doing what little kids do normally. She's only expressing herself in the ways she knows.

Pete: Yeah, that's what I think.

Lou: But she won't listen. She won't do nowt to you [Pete]. It's only me she does it to. She knows what she's doing. She's just trying to get at me. *Sobbing.* (Lou, now 17 years old and Pete; daughter aged 15 months. SY)

The above excerpt also illuminates the degree of agency which Lou confers upon her child, which is in marked contrast to that which she claims for herself. In the following excerpt, Jade demonstrates a similar parenting style:

Jade: [To Janey, her elder daughter] Your mamma don't have a life, it's just you 'n your sister. That's my life. That's about it.

HS: Do you get angry with them for that, for putting you in that situation?

Jade: No, it's not their fault. Sayin' that, sometimes I've been scared of what I might do to her [Janey] 'cos I get so angry at her sometimes. She winds me up 'n sometimes I just get so mad.

HS: Have you ever wanted to take it out on her, like you know, hit her or something like that?

Jade: No. Sometimes I've thought about it but I ain't ever done it though. No! Not with Gemma [younger daughter] either. I've left her in her room when she's roarin' her eyes out and givin' me a headache. I've left 'em both in the room for that. Their cryin' does my head in, so sometimes I just put 'em in there 'n shut the bedroom door 'n leave 'em in there to cry.

HS: Right.

Jade: I've never, ever wanted to hit her. Or Gemma.

HS: Right, OK.

Jade: I've smacked her [Janey's] bum when she's like gone off or whatever, not hard though. Enough to teach her a lesson. It's just been like a tap, you know, I just tap her on bum or whatever. (Jade, now 18 years old; daughters aged 18 months and four months respectively. SY)

As I have previously explained, Lou and Jade both entered motherhood scarred by troubled relationships with their mothers and both young women appeared to be replicating, at least in part, the mothering styles to which they themselves had been exposed. The teenagers who entered motherhood without such troubled legacies appeared to be more patient in their interactions with their children, offered more sophisticated rationales for their child's (mis)conduct, and were less likely to resort to physical violence when disciplining children for unacceptable behaviour:

Clare: Well, if she's naughty I make her sit on the chair and she's not allowed to move until I tell her, so she has to sit there and do nothing till I tell her she can get up.

HS: And how does she respond to you telling her to do that?

Clare: Oh it depends. *Laughs.* Sometimes she just laughs. Or she'll kick and scream, and then sometimes she'll just get up after about five minutes and walk away so I say 'Get back on that chair,' but then she'll just laugh at you and go, 'Funny, funny, mummy's funny.'

HS: And what do you then?

Clare: I put her back on chair. But then she'll get off as soon as I'm not looking. So if I want her to stay in chair I have to sit with her and then she just thinks I'm playing a game. (Clare, now 16 years old; daughter aged 18 months. SY)

When mothers were respected, daughters tended to express positive sentiments about the contributions they made to their grandchild's care; such grandmothers were seen as emotionally capable and more able to tolerate a wider range of mischievous behaviours:

I think my mum's more patient than me. She's really good with him. Even when he winds her up I don't think I've ever really seen mum shout at him. (Susan, now 16 years old; son aged 16 months. SY)

And these mothers praised their daughters' mothering efforts:

HS: How's Michelle coping with Daniel's temper tantrums?

Polly: Oh, she copes marvellous. She does. [...] Michelle doesn't, like, expect him to always be on best behaviour, you know, to know how to behave, 'cos after all he is just a baby. She's not like some young mothers in that way, 'cos some of them do expect their kids to behave like little adults almost, don't they? (Polly (mother of Michelle, now aged 17). SY)

The age at which young women started disciplining their children, and the methods they used, varied considerably. That said, all children were subjected to some form of discipline by the age of six months; being 'soft' on meting out punishment was poorly tolerated. In older children, temper tantrums, biting and kicking, and refusal to obey adult commands, were viewed as serious violations of behavioural norms, requiring immediate correction and possible punishment.

Most mothers experience the daily grind of caring for a small infant as stressful and tiring, and the teenagers in this study were no exception. During particularly tough times when children's refusals and temper tantrums exhausted their patience, male partners were called on to provide solace and support; crying provided an outlet for emotional distress:

> Michelle: He has lots of tantrums now when he doesn't get his own way. He just screams and lays himself on floor 'n kicks 'n all, if you don't let him do something he wants. Last week he did it in shop and that were really embarrassing. *Laughs.*
>
> HS: How do you cope with him when he's like that?
>
> Michelle: Oh I just ignore him. *Laughs.* If I'm at home I just go into other room and leave him till he quiets down.
>
> HS: Mmm, that sounds like a sensible thing to do. Do you get angry with him as well? You know, do you yell at him or hit him, or anything like that?
>
> Michelle: No, not really.
>
> HS: No?
>
> Michelle: No, 'cos usually I've always got Ryan [boyfriend] here, so he can sort it out. He's a right daddy's boy he is. *Laughs.* He'll do anything for Ryan, so that makes it easier. *Laughs.* [...] No, I don't get angry with him. I do cry a lot though. *Laughs.* (Michelle, 16 years old; son aged ten months. SY)

But children's behaviours were not uniformly perceived as problematic across the sample:

> HS: Is there anything that [daughter] does that really winds you up?
>
> Clare: No, not really. No, there's nothing really. She's good as gold. She's no problem really. She's just pleasure on legs. *Laughs.* (Clare, now 16 years old; daughter aged two years. SY)

Mothers and daughters frequently disagreed about the need for, and the type of, punishment considered appropriate for children. When relationships between mothers and daughters were affable and accommodating, responses to behavioural infringements were broadly similar and did not need additional discussion. On the rare occasions one party was perceived by the other to have overstepped the mark and applied a punishment thought to be inappropriately harsh, reconciliation was quickly effected. Children's behaviours which infringed on the personal 'space' of others were particularly disapproved of: being excessively noisy, refusing to sleep (alone) and throwing objects at others. Daughters who disregarded their mothers' advice on disciplinary matters were seen as lacking judgement, as 'spoiling' their children and hence as reducing opportunities for the future enactment of socially acceptable behaviour. Daughters, however, tended to live 'in the moment' and looked for immediate resolutions to problems:

> When he [toddler] can't move about, 'n get what he wants, he just goes mad. He starts screamin', shoutin'. [...] He goes on 'n on, till you give it 'im. Me mum says I shouldn't give in to 'im all time. She says I'm spoiling 'im, but I can't stand the noise he makes! *Laughs.* It's well, give in to 'im or leave 'im making noise. (Susan, 15 years old; son aged three months. SY)

When mothers and daughters were less kindly disposed towards one another, differences of opinion about discipline were not easily resolved, were more likely to escalate, to endure longer and to 'spill over' into other areas of the relationship. Among these mother–daughter dyads, disagreements which initially focused on discrete aspects of the child's behaviour often rapidly escalated to involve the extended family, some of whom exercised considerable influence over disciplinary decisions:

> Jasmine: You can't tell Tracey [daughter] owt. That's thing that really annoys me with her, is she's got it all mapped out.
> HS: How do you mean?
> Jasmine: Well it's like she thinks you can just tell kids what to do and they'll do it automatic, like. I told her look, Tracey, you can't just tell 'em what to do, like little Hitlers. [...] She brings in his [boyfriend's] mother to sort things out, 'n then he [boyfriend] brings his sisters in on it as well, 'n they don't know nowt about bringin' up kids [...] But he rules her, do you know what I mean? So then I said

> to Tracey, 'Well good luck to you both then. If it works
> out that's fine, but I think you're making a big mistake.'
> (Jasmine (mother of Tracey, aged 14). SY)

There is now a sizeable body of literature elaborating Donald Winnicott's original concept of 'good-enough' mothering – the style of mothering provided by the 'ordinary' and 'devoted' mother who makes 'active adaptation to the infant's needs' (Winnicott, 1971: 10). While the mothering provided by 'good-enough' mothers (not necessarily the infant's biological mother, as Winnicott points out) may be flawed and imperfect, it nonetheless is usually sufficient to provide the child with the security needed for the development of an autonomous ego. In Eriksonian terms, 'good-enough' mothering enables the child to develop a basic sense of trust in the world (Erikson, [1950] 1963). While the good–bad dichotomy may be a rational response to unknown and unpredictable circumstances, it reduces options for mothers-to-be, good *and* bad, sometimes simultaneously. The concept is seriously flawed, however, as the research did not involve a cross-section of families and ethnicities, but only middle-class families with mothers generally not engaged in paid work but supported by wage-earning husbands. How then, to compare mothering within the context of a more co-operative endeavour which includes not a wage-earning, but an absent father, and parenting contributions provided by extended family and kinship networks? Within a 'classed' context then, the meaning of 'good-enough' mothering must be re-examined in the light of the 'terrible burden on women who, having been "let go of" and "let down" so often themselves, as well as left "holding the baby" are sometimes unable to summon up the extraordinary courage needed to "hold on" or "hold fast"' (Scheper-Hughes, 1992: 361) when relationships between themselves and their child/ren falter. Although the 'good-enough' maternal status was an attempt to repudiate the good–bad dichotomy, it was not intended to gloss over the fact that some mothering is actually quite bad, at least some of the time.

Sleeping practices and arrangements

Mothers and daughters often argued about babies' sleeping routines, including bed-sharing, the 'right' time to settle a baby for the night and the appropriate age when a daytime nap might be abandoned. A mother's advice to her daughter often reflected her own experiential learning, including perceived 'mistakes'. Practical arrangements, however, rather than 'ideals', were more likely to influence young mothers' decisions, particularly in the early postnatal period. The practice of bed-sharing was universally frowned upon by teenagers' mothers, largely because of concerns about the infant becoming 'excessively' attached and 'clingy' and, as a result, less likely to sleep separately. Allowing the infant to share the parental bed was therefore understood to encourage 'bad' habits, including an overly dependent child, and was widely discouraged for this reason.

When young women remained in the family home, rather than leave the baby to cry at night and disturb other family members, they usually brought them into their own beds. As some young women were already sharing their (single) beds with their partners, however, accommodating an additional body, even that of a baby, was difficult, and frequently meant one or other partner slept on the floor or on a sofa:

HS: Is it OK having [son] in the bed with you?

Susan: Mmm. It's all right when it's only me but when [boyfriend's] here as well it's not very good, 'cos he's [baby] very wriggly, so one of us usually ends up sleeping on floor, or coming down here and sleeping on settee.

HS: Are you in a single bed?

Susan: Yeah, so it's not what you'd call comfortable. *Laughs*. (Susan, 15 years old; son aged two months. SY)

Narratives of bed-sharing with infants generated 'horror stories' about parents rolling onto the baby and accidentally suffocating it. Although no one volunteered that they personally knew anyone who had suffered this calamity, the fear of it happening deterred some of the teenagers from adopting this practice. Mothers were largely critical when daughters succumbed to the demands of their infants and initiated shared sleeping arrangements. Most saw in their daughters' actions a repeat of earlier 'mistakes' they themselves had made in their own mothering practices, especially with first-born children:

Jasmine: But like with Tracey [daughter] she's done similar things to what I've done, putting [younger child] in bed with her. I used to do the same thing, because it were easier. Mistakes you make. *Laughs*.

HS: Things you regret afterwards?

Jasmine: Yeah, exactly. Things you think, oh no, why didn't someone tell me. But you can't be told. Not with your first.

> You have to learn the hard way. [...] I've said to her, 'Oh
> you shouldn't have him in bed,' but then, like I've said to
> Tracey, that's what people used to say to me and I never
> listened, but now I've learned. [...] They shouldn't be in
> bed with you. Start that and you never stop. Rod for your
> own back. I learned hard way. I had no mum to tell me
> owt. She's got me to tell her but she won't listen. (Jasmine
> (mother of Tracey, aged 14). SY)

First-time mothers were considered particularly prone to making errors
of judgement because expertise in childrearing was understood to accu-
mulate through previous mothering experiences.

Decisions about infant sleeping arrangements often seemed to reflect
the degree of intimacy available in the original mother–daughter relationship. Daughters whose relationships with their mothers were problematic tended to show greater determination to control sleeping spaces
and, unless a child was ill or a special occasion was being marked, discouraged their child/ren from sharing 'adult' bed space:

> HS: So she's [daughter] sleeping in her own room now?
> Lou: Yeah yeah, she has been for ages.
> HS: Did she ever sleep in bed with you?
> Lou: No. No, she never sleeps in our bed. Never has done. [...] She
>   stayed in our room when she were really little, 'cos health
>   visitor said she shouldn't sleep by herself. But she were always
>   in cot. We moved her into her own room pretty quick.
> HS: Would you ever let her come into your bed?
> Lou: No. Oh, on occasion in morning, yeah we do. Yeah, well like
>   we brought her in other morning. It were just for like a treat
>   like. It were my birthday. (Lou, now 17 years old; daughter
>   aged nine months. SY)

Even when children were restless and kept them awake, most of the
teenage mothers continued to sleep separately. They encouraged independence in the child and valued it as a positive attribute; most were
of the opinion that parental bed-sharing promoted 'mardy' or 'clingy'
behaviour which they sought to discourage.

> Jade: She's [older daughter] a right pain at the minute. She just will
>   not sleep. So then I don't sleep either. Last night I were up
>   and down to her all night.

HS: Would you ever think about having her in bed with you?

Jade: No. No way. Not to sleep. I don't want her getting too clingy, so then she won't sleep on her own. (Jade, now 17 years old; first daughter aged five months. SY)

He were in our bed for first few weeks but now he sleeps on the top bit of his pram. [...] He's going in the cot soon, so he gets used to it from the start. They get right mardy if you leave it too long to get 'em in their own bed. (Susan, 15 years old; son aged three months. SY)

Exceptionally, Michelle's son continued to sleep with his parents from birth until the close of the study, when he was 16 months old. Michelle considered herself 'too soft' to exert the necessary discipline needed to change what had become an established pattern. The following excerpt also suggests that Michelle's decision rested as much on pragmatic concerns about protecting the quality of her own, and her employed partner's, sleep, as on concerns about fostering (bad) habits in her son:

I wanted him [son] in his own room by three months, but that didn't happen. It's 'cos I'm too soft. *Laughs.* [...] It started after he were born, when he were only a few weeks old. I'd just put him on the settee or on our bed till he went to sleep, and then I'd put him in his crib, but now it's just got that he'll like fall asleep down here on the settee and I'll take him up to bed and he'll sleep in his crib for about an hour, but then he knows, he must know somehow he's not in bed with anyone, so then he wakes up, and then I'll just put him in our bed and he'll sleep then till half eight, nine in morning. *Laughs.* [...] Only way we get any sleep is to let him come in bed with us. My mum thinks we're mad but Ryan [partner] has to get up at half four, so we can't spend half the night trying to settle him down. He gets upset if you put him in his own room and then me and Ryan get upset and we can't sleep 'cos he's upset. *Laughs.* So what's point? He's only little. He's got his own bedroom, but he's never been in it yet! *Laughs.* (Michelle, now 17 years old; son aged 16 months. SY)

Routinely acceding to babies' demands was not welcomed by young women's mothers, with most of the opinion that parents had a duty to set firm boundaries and that children had to learn that they could not manipulate their parents beyond these defined limits by resorting to 'paddies and tantrums':

> I think the one thing that both girls have got wrong is the bedtime routines because none of the children will go to bed at night. All three [grandchildren] rule 'em at bedtime. None of 'em go to bed till they [parents] go up. [...] He [Michelle's son] will not go in that lovely cot he's got in his own room, he just sits in it to play in, but he will not go in it to sleep in it. He paddies and tantrums and I say, 'Look, all you've got to do is have a couple of nights of paddies and tantrums and when he learns he's not coming back down, then he won't do it, but they won't let him cry.' [...] They're both working and they say they never have any time on their own but I say, well, look, this is your own doing, this is your own fault. You've made the rod for your own back. (Polly (mother of Michelle, now aged 17). SY)

The more confident teenage mothers such as Michelle, Alys and Clare shared easy and relaxed relationships with their mothers and relied on them for advice, although they did not necessarily feel obliged to act on it. They were also more able to tolerate their mothers' criticisms of their childrearing practices. These young women exhibited more flexible and responsive attitudes to their child's needs, for example for comfort and reassurance when they were frightened at night:

> HS: So [daughter] has her own room and normally she'd sleep by herself?
>
> Clare: Yeah, but sleeping, at the moment she not so good on that. She's sleeping wi' me 'cos she says she's scared of dark. [...] I think she must be going through a phase or summat. [...] Sometimes she'll go to sleep in her own bed wi' the light on, but if she wakes up and she sees light is off she'll come running into my room. [...] I've been trying to move her, when she gets to sleep, but she wakes up so it's not worth it, you end up getting up and down all night. (Clare, now 16 years old; daughter aged two years. SY)

Teenagers were overjoyed when their infants finally started sleeping through the night because this meant that they, too, were assured of sleep. Most were fully cognisant of contemporary risk discourses with respect to 'approved' infant sleeping practices, including positioning the baby on its back and well down towards the bottom of the bed, and not sleeping with the baby following the consumption of drugs or alcohol. Some circumvented these official discourses, however, by creating 'exceptional' circumstances whereby the child's refusal to sleep alone could be excused. Examples which were offered included children's expressed fears or anxieties of the dark, or parental anxieties about impending ill health in their infant, as perhaps indicated by a raised temperature or cough.

Everyday life on the motherhood continuum: harsh realities and rewarding pleasures

Once the 'novelty effect' of the new baby had diminished, young mothers encountered the monotony and hard work associated with motherhood. Teenagers with supportive kinship networks, and whose living arrangements provided stability and security, fared best in their new roles and enjoyed time with their infants. A few planned their engagements and/or weddings and talked excitedly, and often at length, about saving to buy their own homes. Motherhood as a rite of passage for these teenagers appeared to be both a strengthening and an empowering experience.

Impoverished teenage mothers had the odds stacked against them in the shape of poor-quality housing on 'sink' estates, an absence of friendship and kinship networks, and few relationship or employment/educational opportunities. Parenting responsibilities weighed heavily on them and most were immobilised rather than enabled by the challenges they faced; teenage motherhood for this less resilient, and poorly resourced, group of teenagers often accentuated maladaptive behaviours. The following excerpt from my field notes summarises Jade's situation:

> I ask Jade how things have been. There is a heavy silence before she announces that she is, 'Bored ... bored ... bored ... I get up every day. I get these ones dressed. I come over here 'n I feed them 'n then I go back over road [to her small bedroom in the hostel accommodation where she has lived for the past 15 months]. I watch telly till it's time to put them to bed. I'm so fuckin' bored. I did the same thing yesterday and I'll do the same tomorrow and the next day and day after ...' Josie, Jade's sister, interrupts to suggest they could go away for a day in the summer. Jade stares at her, curls her lip in a gesture of contempt and responds, 'Yeah, yeah great idea. Where d'ya think

I'm gonna get money for bus fares? It'll cost at least ten quid [approx. US$14] for me and then there's kids.' (Field notes. Non-recorded discussion with Jade, now 18 years old; daughters aged 16 months and two months respectively. SY)

Although Jade's circumstances were difficult when she became a mother for the first time, they had worsened considerably by the time her second daughter, Gemma, was born. Shortly after this event, Jade was rehoused on a crime-ridden council estate, some distance from the centrally located accommodation where she had previously lived, and where she was well liked and well supported. Her new neighbourhood lacked basic amenities and was poorly served by public transport. At the time, Jade was still 'mad in love' with Tom, father of Gemma, although her affections changed when he and her sister Josie started 'having it off' with each other. Tom subsequently moved in with Josie and her five-year-old daughter. Shortly afterwards, Jade agreed to relinquish Gemma into Josie and Tom's care.

Michelle was at the opposite end of the mothering spectrum from Jade – at least on the surface. When her son was three months old, Michelle moved from her family home into rented accommodation with her boyfriend, Ryan. Michelle's mother, Polly, put aside her concerns about Ryan, which had emerged following his assault on Michelle early in their relationship, and helped the young couple set up home. She offered practical and financial assistance, organised cleaning and decorating parties, and brought them essential household items. At the end of the first year, Michelle appeared happy and well adjusted. She had resumed her education and had achieved the A levels she required to undertake a nursing degree, although she then put her university place on hold after she was talent spotted by a modelling agency and started earning 'fantastic' money on fashion shoots in UK and European locations. Ryan secured more hours with his industrial warehouse employer and, on the basis of Michelle's income, the young couple purchased their first home. Most Sundays, Michelle and her newly constituted family returned home for a traditional roast lunch. For Michelle, balancing her professional life with the demands of motherhood, her on-going relationships with her partner and her close-knit family, was a demanding, but satisfying, set of challenges. Educational and social differences between herself and Ryan, although substantial, did not initially hinder their capacity for mutual respect and nor did these differences prevent them from sharing parenting responsibilities:

If I'm at home [from a fashion shoot] I get up with Ryan around 4.30 [a.m.] and get his breakfast ready and do his packed lunch, then I go back to bed with [son]. He usually wakes up round half seven/ eight. We play a bit in bed and sometimes I read him a story. [...] He can't say sentences yet but he loves his words. *Laughs.* I've always loved books. I think that's rubbing off on him. *Laughs.* We read to him every night. Ryan can't read very well – he can just about keep up with [son]. *Laughs.* But he makes it up if he can't understand it. *Laughs.* We always had books around and our parents always read to us. Ryan's didn't. [...] Ryan finishes work at lunchtime so then he looks after him in the afternoons. He's much better at playing with him than I am. And [son] adores his dad. [...] Being a mother is so exhausting. *Laughs.* I feel sorry for girls who haven't got their mums. (Field notes. Non-recorded discussion with Michelle, now 17 years old; son aged 16 months. SY)

Towards the end of the study I received a phone call from Polly requesting my help. Michelle and Ryan had separated some months previously and Ryan was currently awaiting trial for charges relating to his repeated assaults on Michelle, whose modelling career was in tatters because her face had borne the brunt of his violence. Ryan was subsequently convicted and received a custodial sentence. Michelle was forced to sell the house and split the proceeds of the sale with Ryan: although she had advanced the deposit and paid the mortgage, only his name was entered on the mortgage contract because her earnings, although substantial, were deemed insufficiently reliable to access a mortgage in her own right. In a final conversation with Michelle she reported that things had improved slightly: she had a new boyfriend and she was no longer taking sleeping pills and antidepressants. The scarring from her facial surgery had healed better than expected and she was hopeful her modelling contract would be renewed. She still intended to study nursing but was delaying her application until her modelling career was definitely over.

I positioned Clare and Alys towards the middle of the mothering continuum. Following childbirth, both young women continued to live in the family home, where they were well supported. Both enjoyed time with their boyfriends, although Clare's relationship, by her own admission, was more 'off' than 'on', not least because of his jealousy:

We're still together and my mum still hates him. *Laughs.* [...] They say mothers can get depressed after they've had a baby but I think it's him [boyfriend] that's depressed. [...] I think he's jealous of me. He's drinking and smoking loads. He's still living with his gran but they don't get on. [...] I passed my driving licence and mum's letting me borrow her car, 'n it's, like, now I've got this really great job 'n my mum's always helping me with stuff 'n he hasn't got anything. Not really. (Clare, now 16 years old; final interview when her daughter was two years old. SY)

When her daughter was six months old Clare had returned to college to study child psychology. She abandoned her course, however, after her boyfriend complained that her coursework was 'coming between us'. Around this time she briefly moved into rented accommodation with her boyfriend and her daughter but returned home after a few months, complaining that she 'was doing all the work while he just lays about'. Following a frustrating period of employment interviews and repeated rejections – ostensibly due to lack of work experience although Clare suspected that 'the real reason's 'cos I'm a teenage mum' – she finally secured a full-time job with a local marketing firm. Her employers invited new staff to consent to psychometric testing and when Clare was assessed as 'very bright', she was offered, and accepted, a fully funded day-release scheme studying business skills.

Alys decided to delay a return to education until her son was eligible for state nursery provision. Meanwhile, her boyfriend remained in the same low-paid job and continued to live with his parents some distance away. The young couple visited one another's homes and stayed overnight on alternate weekends, sleeping in separate rooms at his house and sharing her single mattress in her mother's more liberal household. Alys expressed considerably more ambivalence about being a mother than did some of the other teenagers:

Before I had him I had my life cut out. *Laughs.* I'm not much of a stay-at-home. I mean, I like staying in, but if I had the option, I'd rather go out down the pub or go out socialising. But I don't do that as often as I'd like. Not like I woulda done if I'd not had him. I'd probably be a lot richer now if I didn't have him as well. *Laughs.* Don't get me wrong. I love him to pieces but he has changed my life. [...] I'd probably be in my own job. I probably wouldn't even be living here [at home]. I'd probably have moved in with [boyfriend and father of baby] by now. [...] As soon as he's old enough for nursery I'm going to college. (Alys, now 17 years old; final interview when her son was two years old. W)

The constraints of motherhood, especially those imposed by childcare, weighed heavily on Alys. She missed socialising with friends and having regular contact with her boyfriend and looked forward to a time in the future when she could return to activities which were less child-focused.

Reflections on young motherhood

At the final interview, I asked all the young mothers to imagine describing their new lives to an unknown person. Although most admitted that the transition to motherhood had been a difficult process, even the poorest and most marginalised young mother responded affirmatively and positively with reference to her child/ren. This echoes the findings of a systematic review of qualitative studies in this area which reported that, despite the constraining affects of poverty and stigma, many teenage mothers demonstrate resilience and pragmatism in using available resources to best advantage (McDermott and Graham, 2005).

Although some of the teenagers voiced regrets about having become pregnant, few regrets were expressed about having had sex, and those who did so mainly focused on the less than perfect circumstances in which sex occurred (lack of privacy and time constraints) and/or inadequacies with respect to aspects of 'performance' (boys being 'rough' and girls feeling insufficiently 'warmed up'). All the teenagers spoke at length, and with eloquence and passion, about the significance of having a baby at a young age and the need to behave 'appropriately' as a mother; role modelling was considered a practical and effective device in challenging negative public attitudes. Narratives changed over time, and with increasing distance from the events of pregnancy and childbirth, the 'big deal' which had previously foregrounded the initial shock was superseded by the pragmatic demands of motherhood:

It's [motherhood] not as bad as I expected. [...] If I could have not got pregnant, I wouldn't have got pregnant. Definitely not. Having sex were OK but not getting pregnant. *Laughs.* No, that were a mistake. But that's behind me now. I've got a baby and I'm responsible for her. I'm her mum. (Clare, now 16 years old; daughter aged 12 months. SY)

It's not like it's a big deal any more that I got pregnant when I was only 15. It's more like, well now I'm 17 and I'm his mum, so what's the big deal, you know? You just have to get on with it. (Alys, now 17 years old; son aged two years. W)

Although most of the teenagers looked to the future with a sense of hope and ambition for themselves and their child/ren, isolated and penniless young women such as Jade, who had been abandoned by her mother, the fathers of both her babies and her sister, anticipated a bleak and miserable existence:

HS: How do you see your future, Jade?
Jade: Future? *Laughs.* What future? I ain't got no future far as I can see it. Not with two kids 'n no money 'n no boyfriend 'n no mum. I ain't got nowt have I? I ain't even got a sister any more. *Laughs.* (Jade, now 18 years old; daughters aged 18 months and four months respectively. SY)

And while leaving the parental home to live with a boyfriend was eagerly anticipated by most young women, some mothers anticipated this event with trepidation:

I don't know what I'll do when these two [daughter and baby] move out. I'll be feeling lonely then all right, I will. But as long as they don't move too far, it'll be all right. As long as it's in the area. (Angharad (mother of Alys). W)

While living independently from mothers and away from the parental home was usually interpreted as an expression of autonomy for the young mothers in this study, it often constituted a breach in maternal identity for their mothers as they struggled to adjust to the 'loss' of both a daughter and a grandchild.

As I have mentioned, towards the end of my study a number of the teenagers became engaged and some set dates for the wedding ceremony. Others informed me they were delaying these events until their children were of an age when they could act as bridesmaids and pageboys. For working-class women, although partnership and marriage tend to be a primary objective, with young women's lives directed towards these ends, this is despite 'the wealth of evidence that it is within their intimate relationships with men that they are most likely to be molested and raped, beaten up and driven mad, de-skilled and required to work long hours, after hours' (Cain, 1989: 12). While many of the teenagers demonstrated ample evidence that they were replicating intergenerational patterns of 'doing' motherhood, at least in some aspects of family life, as this chapter has illustrated, a small number also described practices that were at variance with their personal experiences of being mothered.

In the next, and final, chapter I gather the sometimes disparate, but always complex, narratives from all the teenagers, their mothers and significant others, and elaborate key themes and major concerns. I also acknowledge the limitations of my study and make suggestions for furthering research in this area.

8
Looking Back and Looking Forward

This study of teenage pregnancy and motherhood was complicated by a number of tensions which manifested in different ways. On a personal level, I often found myself caught between conflicting loyalties and at times experienced considerable difficulty maintaining a neutral stance. For instance, I was sometimes overly critical of midwives' interactions with the teenagers and/or their significant others, forgetting that I had once been in their shoes and had similarly experienced the frustration of being confronted with, and horrified by, the circumstances of clients' lives. I too had been on the receiving end of violent and abusive behaviour from clients and had observed similar conduct in their interpersonal and familial relationships. As a practitioner, I had witnessed the appalling neglect some mothers visited upon their children and I had passed judgements on mothers I had deemed unfit, requesting intervention by social services and/or the police. I had justified my actions by invoking the mantra of professional accountability, aware that failing to act could be interpreted as a dereliction of duty.

In my role as a researcher and an observer of midwives' practices, however, I sometimes reacted as if my former identity had been obliterated. I blamed midwives for what I judged to be their inappropriate responses, although I also knew that many of the situations they faced were complex and irresolvable, at least in the short term. On the occasions that midwives voiced their frustrations about clients, I was sometimes too quick to interpret this as evidence of prejudice, rather than a need to simply 'let off steam'. I had forgotten what it was like to be on call 24/7, to feel crazed with sleep deprivation, and/or to be consumed with grief and guilt about a birth gone wrong. I was also out of touch with how it felt to be responsible for delivering a service which was inadequately resourced, especially for the most marginalised women. While I found the experience of being confronted by the deprivation and adversity which characterised the lives of the poorest teenagers extremely difficult to tolerate, I expected midwives to be somehow magically endowed with the capacity to rise above their personal feelings on these issues. I held double standards: blithely uncritical when the teenagers behaved badly, but hypercritical when midwives voiced their disapproval of behaviours which I also experienced as offensive. Perhaps in an effort to conceal my feelings of inadequacy, I projected unrealistic expectations onto midwives but, in passing judgement, I emulated the very behaviours I was criticising.

How had I become so far removed from the everyday worlds of midwives? How had I become so duplicitous, encouraging midwives to regard me as a confidante, only to betray them by over-interpreting their comments about their clients as other than what they often were: spontaneous and benign outbursts of helplessness and frustration? It was as if the research environment had dulled my awareness to the harsher side of childbearing and rearing practices, to the raw emotions and crude responses which are so powerfully present and which cannot always be contained or explained by clinicians (or researchers). In some ways, I now think my own attitudes were closer to my midwifery colleagues than I had wanted to believe and, in distancing myself from my professional roots, I reduced my empathic capacity.

An additional tension that bothered me was the need to establish equitable and trusting relationships with the teenagers, and simultaneously with their mothers. Initially this was complicated by the fact that I was entering the lives of both parties at an acutely sensitive time, when family relationships had often been temporarily fractured by disclosures of pregnancy. Perhaps because I was closer in age to the teenagers' mothers, and indeed to many of the midwives, some young women initially regarded me as a maternal/midwifery ally rather than as someone who might want to form an independent relationship with them. Although I am a daughter, I have never experienced being a mother, and while I had previously worked with teenagers in a professional capacity, I have had only sporadic contact in my personal life. I suspect that my lack of embodied understanding in both these dimensions thus reinforced my sense of distance and separateness and this occasionally created difficulties in positioning myself appropriately, and interpreting my data accurately.

Limitations of the research

My personal limitations are bound up with other constraints which restricted the scope of this study. Although anyway not an explicit focus of this study, disquiet about appearing overly intrusive prevented me from asking in-depth questions about the teenagers' sexual experiences and, hence, 'sex talk' tended to remain at the level of the superficial and the mundane. That said, the one teenager who spontaneously volunteered information on this topic reported that her first experience of sex was 'crap', which perhaps hints at the ordinary and commonplace positioning of this activity in young people's lives and minds. As Michelle suggested, 'it wasn't at all what it's cracked up to be'.

Personal shortcomings aside, this study, like all research, has its limitations. Although I did not investigate health as a primary focus of young women's maternal transitions, teenagers and their mothers frequently reported concerns about general health issues. Such concerns tended to be dismissed by maternity staff, however, who seemed unable to frame explanations for, and understandings of, 'unwellness' beyond what might be expected in the context of pregnancy. The health-related effects of growing up in poverty and disadvantage, and the potential impact on pregnancy, were seldom mentioned in the narratives provided by maternity staff – which is somewhat surprising given the substantial evidence base. Further research could usefully identify, and clarify, intersections of health, deprivation and maternal–infant outcomes in teenagers across a range of indices, and evaluate the support provided by mothers and other female kin, especially with respect to improving health outcomes.

I did not actively seek to include the experiences of young women of black and minority ethnic (BME) origin, and nor did I include non-English-speaking teenagers. Hence my findings are population-specific and can only be interpreted in relation to the socio-cultural characteristics of the sample, rather than being seen as generalisable to all teenage mothers. Research which has examined the experiences of BME young parents (Higginbottom et al., 2006) supports the broad findings from my research: that adolescent parenting experiences are diverse, and that early motherhood is a normal, rather than problematic, event for some social groups.

Daughters' maternity experiences often prompted mothers to reflect on, and discuss, their own experiences of childbirth with me, and some confided that this was the first time they had disclosed their feelings about these events. Mothers who had experienced a traumatic childbirth worried that their daughters might suffer similarly. Some suggested that they might protect themselves from further distress by refusing to be present when their daughters were in labour; such decisions were generally misinterpreted by staff and they invariably upset daughters. As the focus of my research was the maternity experiences of teenagers, however, I was unable to do justice to mothers' historical accounts and the possible consequences of their negative experiences on their daughters' transitions to motherhood.

Finally, spatial arrangements and organisational procedures within maternity units restricted the number, and timing, of visitors. While these arrangements may have helped maximise clinical efficiency, they substantially increased the teenagers' sense of isolation and disorientation, especially at critical points such as the onset of labour. As my fieldwork did not include observations of labour, however, I cannot comment on the possible impact of these arrangements.

Concluding thoughts

The categories of teenage pregnancy and young motherhood are not homogeneous and uniform but contain wide variation among individuals and their experiences; this diversity makes it difficult to consider universal solutions to the problems confronting young parents. It also confirms that while those identified as socially excluded have received considerable policy and research attention in recent years, the 'black box' (Jones, 2003: 197) of family life, in its most varied forms, remains largely unexamined. Alternative understandings of 'lone' motherhood and 'lone-parent' families are urgently needed, however, not least because, in the public imagination at least, they tend to be viewed as 'less-than' families lacking a father figure, rather than as social groups constructed in response to particular circumstances.

The fact that all of the young women in this study embarked on their mothering careers with bodies and psyches marked by experiences of being mothered themselves cannot be overlooked. The teenagers who embraced motherhood with the least difficulty had been raised in households which fostered warm and loving relationships, and this provided them with a robust capacity to embrace, sometimes even to enjoy, the challenges of parenting. The teenagers who fared badly were those scarred by early, and repeated, experiences of rejection, violence and family disruption; these young women (and some of their male partners) brought with them to parenthood a sense of 'unwantedness' which severely inhibited their ability to adapt to their new roles. Thus, for Alys, Clare, Nia and Susan, becoming a mother during adolescence was largely an affirming and empowering experience, while for Lou, April and Jade, it was primarily undermining and disempowering. Michelle's maternity career was marked by extremes of good and bad fortune, and without the unwavering support of her mother, it is unlikely that she would have weathered her difficulties as well as she did. It is clear that poverty, class and/or disadvantage are not necessarily, in themselves, instrumental in the production of unhappy childhoods, but, rather, it is the cumulative effect of these experiences impacting on 'a predisposed and vulnerable minority' (Paris, 2000: xv) which is problematic.

Although the boundaries between that considered 'legitimate and taboo ... honourable and shameful' (West, 1999: 543) are being redrawn, the context in which young women become mothers cannot be over-looked. In geographically discrete areas of the UK with high teenage pregnancy/fertility rates, early childbearing is a relatively normal, rather than deviant, event. Many teenagers had siblings and/or mothers who were, or had been, teenage mothers; all of them lived within areas of the UK marked by disadvantage and the risks associated with early childbearing. Hence, they became teenage mothers within a particular socio-cultural context which supported childbearing at an earlier age, and the transmission of powerful maternity norms made termination of pregnancy an unlikely proposition within this subculture. While some teenagers moved out of their localities when they became mothers and subsequently became more dependent on fewer people, the majority continued to live within their communities of origin, where they could access extensive family and kinship networks for advice and support. This enabled young women such as Michelle and Clare to pursue employment and educational opportunities. In this respect my findings echo those of a recent systematic review of qualitative research in this area: 'for a significant number of young, working-class women, identity and belonging are secured through informal rather than formal modes of participation' (Graham and McDermott, 2005: 33).

Most of the teenagers were accustomed to their mothers attending to their everyday needs, especially regarding food provision, laundry and transport services, and arranging their personal appointments. Moving out of home to rented accommodation, usually with a male partner, disrupted established domestic routines, and forced individual teenagers to become more self-reliant and better organised. It also pressured them to acquire sophisticated negotiation skills in order to manage the some-times complex relationships with family and friends, and with health (and other) professionals. Some of the teenagers handled these multiple demands with ease and good humour while others anticipated a 'poverty of expectations' (Jones, 2003: 201) which reflected their low self-esteem and socially excluded status. The latter group, which included Jade, Lou and April, did not cope well with the demands of motherhood and it was difficult to see how they might avoid becoming increasingly marginalised. As I have previously mentioned, however, the lives of these young women were already spoiled before the events of early childbearing. Having been chronically deprived of affection, and lacking the most basic of support structures, it is probable that in the absence of pregnancy, a catastrophe of a similar magnitude might have occurred, changing their life courses with equally damaging results.

On-going media, policy and public health attention to teenage pregnancy may be understood to represent largely unexpressed concerns about the supposed dissolution of moral values and the disintegration of family life. The focus on teenagers is significant in this context because, as a group, they are not viewed as fully adult, as 'full' subjects, but rather as subjects-in-the-making, constrained by parental and societal jurisdictions. Their bodies are not (yet) expected to reflect a mature adult subject position, but rather to occupy a developmental phase in the life cycle, somewhere between autonomy and dependence; in this sense, 'sexual citizenship, then, is connected to wider issues of equality and the conditions under which personhood and self-determination are possible' (West, 1999: 543).

The rhetorical framing of teenage pregnancy and young motherhood as 'deviant' (Wilson and Huntington, 2006) obscures the fact that some young women actually plan their pregnancy and view early motherhood as a chance to create a new identity which will change their life course for the better. Indeed, once the initial hurdles are behind them, many actually do rather well and, where this is not the case, it is usually against a backdrop of considerable material and psychological deprivation. Punitive attitudes to young motherhood are unjustifiable and may even be counterproductive. They almost certainly distract attention from the more pressing need for society to reconcile itself to the implications associated with long-term changes in family and kinship formation, relations and obligations. In this context, teenage pregnancy may be a manifestation, rather than a root cause, of social malaise and, as such, will require a concerted focus to address the factors which create, and reinforce, the bleak and empty lives denoted by early, and repeated, childbearing (Selman, 2003).

The transition from childhood to adulthood has been cited as 'the most dangerous period of a woman's life' (Reekie, 1998: 207). Risks may be amplified in contemporary Western societies which are largely devoid of the institutional arrangements and supports which might adequately protect the sexual reputations of the most vulnerable throughout this increasingly protracted transition. The identification of 'vulnerability' is not straightforward, however, and current policy often does not distinguish between that which requires strategic intervention, and that which does not. Nor does it discriminate between risks which are acceptable, and indeed necessary for the process of identity construction and maturation, and risks from which young people need to be protected. Perhaps because teenage pregnancy 'interrupts the lines between adult/child, [...] asexual/ sexual' (Pillow, 2003: 153), policy makers tend to focus on strategies which attempt to control and mould young women's (but not young men's) maternal bodies in ways which reflect political ideals. The emphasis on these particular bodies, however, 'implodes and interrupts the supposed neutrality of policy studies, forefronts policy's role in regulating bodies and exposes the lived experiences of subjects of policy' (ibid.: 156).

Adult status may be attained or conferred, and may be self-defined or 'other' defined, but 'the resultant boundaries to the category are, in the main, simply boundaries of *exclusion, rather than inclusion*' (James, 1986: 156; emphasis added). From the mid-twentieth century onwards, the period of transition from childhood to adulthood has lengthened, resulting in longer periods of dependence and the emergence of discrete stages (e.g. 'adolescence') marking the separation of child and adult categories. Understandings of dependence have also been reconfigured in recent years, shifting from pre-industrial interpretations denoting hierarchical relations of inequality, to contemporary notions of personal pathology, including behavioural syndromes. The transition to parenthood is widely construed as a marker of adult status, although in many Western societies the status of young parents tends to be disregarded by policy makers and health professionals alike. With few exceptions, the teenagers in this study were not regarded by maternity staff and authoritative others as adults, as mothers-in-the-making, with the potential for personal growth and role development. This is perhaps unsurprising as such recognition would require a significant cultural shift, a respect for the shifting identities and transitional status of young parents, and an acknowledgement of their complex, and alternating, needs for dependence and autonomy.

Many of the teenagers, however, had already internalised a degree of adult status through events connected with death, prolonged family disruption and/or the responsibilities involved with becoming a surrogate parent to younger siblings. Hence, most understood the transition to adulthood as a process of *becoming*; one of gradual maturation evidenced by a constellation of on-going events. While they may have been 'just messing around' at the point when pregnancy became an inescapable reality, by the time the study was complete the consensus of opinion was that: 'as soon as you have a child, you've got to grow up. You've got to be a bit more mature.' Young women perceived themselves, and were generally perceived by others, as further along the child–adult continuum than their male partners, regardless of the older age of the latter. The arrival of a baby forced a reappraisal of social relations, including those with male partners, whose habitual behaviours and attitudes were often negatively reinterpreted by their female partners as 'selfish and babyish'.

Young men's attempts to participate in maternity care arrangements were generally negative; a combination of pragmatic and attitudinal factors contributed to their invisibilisation and left most feeling unwanted and overlooked. Those who managed to secure waged work were generally engaged in low-paid, low-status jobs and lacked the necessary bargaining power to negotiate time off work to attend antenatal consultations. Even when they were present, however, midwives generally failed to include them in proceedings and this contrasted with the somewhat prurient interest some showed in other aspects of their lives, including whether they were being 'faithful' to their female partners, and if they intended to 'stick around' after the baby was born. Midwives' attitudes to their young male clients contrasted with their approach to the male partners of older, middle-class women, whom they treated with a deferential respect similar to that accorded to male obstetricians and others of authoritative rank.

Besides attitudinal barriers, the dearth of facilities within local communities prevented some young fathers from actively engaging with their children in social settings, because activities for children typically focused on the needs of young mothers. Hence *inclusionary* practices for one category of young parents (mothers) were perceived as *exclusionary* for another group (fathers). At a societal level, the exclusion of (young) men from maternity-related proceedings may be seen as reinforcing the low expectations of fathers in general, and of working-class fathers in particular. It also, of course, emphasises the gendered division of childrearing, which sees mothers as primarily responsible for the behaviour and welfare of children, and for ensuring their socialisation into law-abiding, and productive, future citizens. Indeed, it has been suggested that there exists an 'inequitable gender division of labour at the scale of the day-to-day, the local and the body that should (but rarely does) guide local and political imaginaries' (Aitken, 1999: 123).

Further, there are generic aspects of childbearing and rearing – and their constraints – which are not specific to teenagers but, rather, may be applied to women across the childbearing age range. For example, my research reiterated the gendered nature of adolescent childbearing and rearing, and it was this element which many of the teenagers experienced as most burdensome. Most envied their boyfriends' continued freedom, and their ability to absent themselves from household, including child-care, routines. Although this general sense of unfairness was perhaps most keenly felt by the young mothers who had left the family home, and the plethora of domestic services provided by their mothers, to live with their boyfriends, related research in this area suggests that similar feelings are, in fact, common to many first-time mothers (Barclay et al., 1997).

Restrictions on hospital visiting hours and observance of scheduled visiting times were especially difficult for partners and parents working inflexible or unsocial hours, those without access to private transport and/or those living in areas which were poorly served by public transport; lack of childcare provision for other children was an additional concern. These constraints severely challenged the most impoverished teenagers, exacerbating distress and tension, and disrupting relationships during an already difficult period of transition. Adolescents may be considered particularly vulnerable to suffering psychological distress in these situations because they are less experienced in dealing with institutions and health professionals and, hence, may be expected to have fewer coping strategies. Furthermore, some of the younger women had never spent a night alone away from home and many had never been separated from loved ones for extended periods, especially against their volition. Feelings of abandonment were increased when young women did not know when they might be reunited with their loved ones, as occurred when they arrived at hospital thinking they were in labour but were instead admitted to the antenatal ward (where adherence to visiting hours was strictly imposed) until staff confirmed that labour was 'properly' established. Young women's relatives were often sent home from hospital but, not infrequently, labour progressed more rapidly than predicted and maternity staff recalled family members, sometimes very soon after they had returned home. Those without private transport usually had no option but to pay a return taxi fare, which they could often ill afford. Enforced separation at critical times was particularly difficult for those adolescents who were already damaged by a lifetime of abandonments and difficult interpersonal relations.

Finally, growing up in poverty and disadvantage affects childbearing women across the age range, as does ethnicity, and having no language in common with service providers. Like teenage pregnancy, these categories of potential exclusion may also be expected to impact negatively on individual women's sense of maternal identity and their experiences of maternity care. As I hope this book has demonstrated, working-class teenage mothers are a particularly vulnerable group in this regard, who require support rather than policing, especially from maternity service providers.

Bibliography

Aitken, S.C. (1999) 'Putting parents in their place: Child rearing rights and gender politics', in E.K. Teather (ed.), *Embodied Geographies: Spaces Bodies and Rites of Passage*. London: Routledge.

Alan Guttmacher Institute, The (1999) *Teen Sex and Pregnancy*. www.agi-usa.org.

Allen, I., Bourke Dowling, S. and Rolfe, H. (eds) (1998) *Teenage Mothers: Decisions and Outcomes*. London: Policy Studies Institute.

Ancel, P.Y., Saurel-Cubizolles, M.J., Di Renzo, G.C., Papiernik, E. and Breart, G. (1999) 'Very and moderate preterm births: are the risk factors different?', *British Journal of Obstetrics and Gynaecology*, 106(11): 1162–70.

Apter, T. (1990) *Altered Loves: Mothers and Daughters during Adolescence*. Hemel Hempstead: Harvester Wheatsheaf.

Arai, L. (2003) 'Low expectations, sexual attitudes and knowledge: explaining teenager pregnancy and fertility in English communities. Insights from qualitative research', *Sociological Review*, 51(2): 199–217.

Armstrong, D. (1983) 'The fabrication of nurse–patient relationships', *Social Science and Medicine*, 17(8): 457–60.

Arney, W. and Bergen, B. (1984) 'Power and visibility: the invention of teenage pregnancy', *Social Science and Medicine*, 18(1): 11–19.

Ashton, J. and Seymour, H. (eds) (1993) *The New Public Health: The Liverpool Experience*. Milton Keynes: Open University Press.

Attree, P. (2004) '"It was like my little acorn, and it's going to grow into a big tree": a qualitative study of a community support project', *Health and Social Care in the Community*, 12(2): 155–61.

Backett-Milburn, K., Cunningham-Burley, S. and Davis, J. (2003) 'Contrasting lives, contrasting views? Understandings of health inequalities from children in differing social circumstances', *Social Science and Medicine*, 57(4): 613–23.

Bailey, L. (1999) 'Refracted selves? A study of changes in self-identity in the transition to motherhood', *Sociology*, 33(2): 335–52.

Baker, K. (1999) 'Young, pregnant … and pleased', *MIDIRS Midwifery Digest*, 9(3): 94–6.

Barclay, L., Everitt, L., Rogan, F., Schmied, V. and Wyllie, A. (1997) 'Becoming a mother: an analysis of women's experience of early motherhood', *Journal of Advanced Nursing*, 25: 719–28.

Bartlett, E.E. (2004) 'The effects of fatherhood on the health of men: a review of the literature', *Journal of Men's Health and Gender*, 1(2): 159–69.

Beale, V. (2002) 'Fashioning the pregnant body: dressing pregnant bodies', unpublished Ph.D. thesis, University of Sheffield.

Bell, D. and Valentine, G. (1997) *Consuming Geographies: We Are Where We Eat*. London: Routledge.

Bell, J., Clisby, S., Craig, G., Measor, L., Petrie, S. and Stanley, N. (2004) *Living on the Edge: Sexual Behaviour and Young Parenthood in Seaside and Rural Areas*. London: Department of Health, Teenage Pregnancy Unit. www.dfes.gov.uk/teenagepregnancy/dsp_showDoc.cfm?FileName=seaside%2Epdf.

Belsky, J., Melhuish, E., Barnes, J., Leyland, A.H., Romaniuk, H. and The National Evaluation of Sure Start Research Team (2006) 'Effects of Sure Start local programmes on children and families: early findings from a quasi-experimental, cross sectional study', *British Medical Journal*, 332(7556): 1476–82.

Berger, J. (1989) *A Fortunate Man*. Cambridge: Granta Books.

Berthoud, R. (2001) 'Teenage births to ethnic minority women', *Population Trends*, Summer (104): 12–17.

Bewley, S. (2005) 'Which career first?', *British Medical Journal*, 331(7517): 588–9.

Bewley, S., Ledger, W. and Nikolaou, D. (eds) (2009) *Reproductive Ageing*. RCOG Reproductive Ageing Study Group. London: RCOG Press.

Biehal, N., Clayden, J., Stein, M. and Wade, J. (1995) *Moving On: Young People and Leaving Care Schemes*. London: HMSO.

Bingley, P.J., Douek, I.F., Rogers, C.A. and Gale, E.A.M. (2000) 'Influence of maternal age at delivery and birth order on risk of type 1 diabetes in childhood: prospective population based family study', *British Medical Journal*, 321(7258): 420–4.

Blair, P., Fleming, P., Bensley, D., Bacon, C., Taylor, E., Berry, J., Golding, J. and Tripp, J. (1996) 'Smoking and the sudden infant death syndrome: Results from 1993–5 case-control study for confidential inquiry into stillbirths and deaths in infancy', *British Medical Journal*, 313: 195–8.

Blanc, A. (2001) 'The effect of power in sexual relationships on sexual and reproductive health: an examination of the evidence', *Studies in Family Planning*, 32(3): 189–213.

Bloomfield, L., Kendall, S., Applin, L., Dearnley, K., Edwards, L., Hinshelwood, L., Lloyd, P. and Newcombe, T. (2005) 'A qualitative study exploring the experiences and views of mothers, health visitors and family support centre workers on the challenges and difficulties of parenting', *Health and Social Care in the Community*, 13(1): 46–55.

Bloustein, G. (2003) *Girl Making: A Cross-Cultural Ethnography on the Process of Growing Up Female*. New York and Oxford: Berghahn Books.

BMRB International (2003) *Evaluation of the Teenage Pregnancy Strategy: Tracking Survey. Report of Results of Nine Waves of Research*. London: BMRB International.

Bonell, C., Strange, V., Stephenson, J., Oakley, A., Copas, A., Forrest, S., Johnson, A. and Black, S. (2003) 'Effect of social exclusion on the risk of teenage pregnancy: development of hypotheses using baseline data from a randomised trial of sex education', *Journal of Epidemiology and Community Health*, 57(11): 871–6.

Boseley, S. (1999) 'British teenagers have the worst sexual health in Europe', *Guardian*, 14 May: 1.

Botting, B., Rosato, M. and Wood, R. (1998) 'Teenage mothers and the health of their children', *ONS Population Trends*, No. 93.

Bottorff, J.L., Oliffe, J., Kalaw, C., Carey, J. and Mroz, L. (2006) 'Men's constructions of smoking in the context of women's tobacco reduction during pregnancy and postpartum', *Social Science and Medicine*, 62(12): 3096–108.

Brewer, M., Browne, J., Joyce, R. and Sutherland, H. (2009) 'Micro-simulating child poverty in 2010 and 2020', London: Institute for Fiscal Studies. www.ifs. org.uk/comms/comm108.pdf.

British Medical Association (2006) *Child and Adolescent Mental Health: A Guide for Health Professionals*. London: British Medical Association www.bma.org.

uk/ap.nsf/AttachmentsByTitle/PDFChildAdolescentMentalHealth/$FILE/Child AdolescentMentalHealth.pdf.

Brown, G.W. and Harris, T. (1978) *The Social Origins of Depression: A Study of Psychiatric Disorder in Women*. London: Tavistock Publications.

Bukowski, R., Smith, G.C.S., Malone, F.D., Ball, R.H., Nyberg, D.A., Comstock, C.H. et al. (2007) 'Fetal growth in early pregnancy and risk of delivering low birth weight infant: prospective cohort study', *British Medical Journal*, 334(7598): 807–8.

Butler, J. (1990) *Gender Trouble: Feminism and the Subversion of Identity*. London: Routledge.

Byrne, D. (2005) *Social Exclusion*, 2nd edn. Milton Keynes: Open University Press.

Cain, M. (ed.) (1989) *Growing Up Good: Policing the Behaviour of Girls in Europe*. London: Sage.

Carabine, J. (2000) 'Constituting welfare subjects through discourses of sexuality and social policy', in G. Lewis, S. Gewirtz and J. Clarke (eds), *Rethinking Social Policy*. London: Sage, 78–91.

Cassell, J. (1996) 'The woman in the surgeon's body: understanding difference', *American Anthropologist*, 98(1): 41–53.

Cater, S. and Coleman, L. (2006) *'Planned' Teenage Pregnancy: Perspectives of Young Parents from Disadvantaged Backgrounds*. A report for the Joseph Rowntree Foundation. Bristol: Policy Press.

Cecil, R. (1996) 'Introduction: an insignificant event? Literary and anthropological perspectives on pregnancy loss', in R. Cecil (ed.), *The Anthropology of Pregnancy Loss: Comparative Studies in Miscarriage, Stillbirth and Neonatal Death*. Oxford: Berg, 1–16.

CEMACH (Confidential Enquiry into Maternal and Child Health) (2004) *Why Mothers Die 2000–02: The Sixth Report of the Confidential Enquiry into Maternal Deaths in the United Kingdom*. London: RCOG Press.

Chambers, D., Tincknell, E. and Van Loon, J. (2004) 'Peer regulation of teenage sexual identities', *Gender and Education*, 16(3): 397–415.

Chambers, L. (2007) *Misconceptions: Unmarried Motherhood and the Ontario Children of Unmarried Parents Act, 1921–1969*. Ontario: Osgoode Society for Canadian Legal History.

Chess, S. and Thomas, A. (1983) 'Infant bonding: mystique and reality', in S. Chess and A. Thomas (eds), *Annual Progress in Child Psychiatry and Child Development: A Selection of the Year's Outstanding Contributions to the Understanding and Treatment of the Normal and Disturbed Child*. New York: Brunner and Mazel, 48–63.

Christensen, P. (2004) 'The health-promoting family: a conceptual framework for future research', *Social Science and Medicine*, 59(2): 377–87.

Churchill, D., Allen, J., Pringle, M., Hippisley-Cox, J., Ebdon, D., Macpherson, M. and Bradley, S. (2000) 'Consultation patterns and provision of contraception in general practice before teenage pregnancy: case-control study', *British Medical Journal*, 321: 486–9.

Colen, C.G., Geronimus, A.T. and Phipps, M.G. (2006) 'Getting a piece of the pie? The economic boom of the 1990s and declining teen birth rates in the United States', *Social Science and Medicine*, 63(6): 1531–45.

Colls, R. (2004) 'Embodying geographies: clothing consumption and female embodied subjectivities', unpublished Ph.D. thesis, University of Sheffield.

Cook, D. and Strachan, D. (1999) 'Summary of effects of parental smoking on the respiratory health of children and implications for research', *Thorax*, 54(4): 357–66.

Côté, J.E. (1996). 'Sociological perspectives on identity formation: the culture-identity link and identity capital', *Journal of Adolescence*, 19(5): 417–28.

Coulter, A. (2002) *The Autonomous Patient: Ending Paternalism in Medical Care*. London: The Stationery Office.

Coward, R. (1992) *Our Treacherous Hearts: Why Women Let Men Get their Way*. London: Faber and Faber.

Davies, L., McKinnon, M. and Rains, P. (1999) '"On my own": a new discourse of dependence and independence from teen mothers', in J. Wong and D. Checkland (eds), *Teen Pregnancy and Parenting: Social and Ethical Issues*. University of Toronto Press.

Davis-Floyd, R. and Mather, F. (2002) 'The technocratic, humanistic, and holistic paradigms of childbirth', *MIDIRS Midwifery Digest*, 12(4): 500–6.

Davis-Floyd, R. and Sargent, C. (eds) (1997) *Childbirth and Authoritative Knowledge: Cross-Cultural Perspectives*. Berkeley and Los Angeles: University of California Press.

DCSF (Department for Children, Schools and Families) (2009) *The Teenage Pregnancy Independent Advisory Group: Sixth Annual Report 2008–2009*. www.dcsf.gov.uk/everychildmatters/healthandwellbeing/teenagepregnancy/tpiag.

DCSF (Department for Children, Schools and Families) (2010a) *Statutory Guidance for Local Duties on Child Poverty* (Child Poverty Act 2010): e-consultation. www.dcsf.gov.uk/consultations/index.cfm?action=consultationDetails&consultationId=1712&external=no.

DCSF (Department for Children, Schools and Families) (2010b) *Teenage Pregnancy Strategy: Beyond 2010*. London: HMSO. http://publications.everychildmatters.gov.uk/eOrderingDownload/00224-2010DOM-EN.pdf.

de Beauvoir, S. (1953) *The Second Sex*. London: Jonathan Cape.

De Chateau, P. and Wiberg, B. (1977) 'Long-term effect on mother–infant behaviour of extra contact during the first hour post partum, I: First observation at 36 hours', *Acta Paediatrica Scandinavica*, 66: 137–43.

Dekker, G.A., Robillard, P. and Hulsey, T.C. (1998) 'Immune maladaptation in the etiology of pre-eclampsia: a review of corroborative epidemiologic studies', *Obstetrical and Gynecological Survey*, 53(6): 377–82.

Dennison, C. (2004) *Teenage Pregnancy: An Overview of the Research Evidence*. London: Health Development Agency.

Dennison, C. and Coleman, J. (1998) 'Teenage motherhood: experiences and relationships', in S. Clement (ed.) *Psychological Perspectives on Pregnancy and Childbirth*. Edinburgh: Harcourt Brace.

Dennison, C. and Coleman, J. (2000) *Young People and Gender: A Review of Research*. Report submitted to the Women's Unit, Cabinet Office and the Family Policy Unit, Home Office. London: The Women's Unit.

Department of Health (2001) *The Expert Patient: A New Approach to Chronic Disease Management for the 21st Century*. London: Department of Health. www.dh.gov.uk/en/Publicationsandstatistics/Publications/PublicationsPolicyAndGuidance/DH_4006801.

Department of Health (2005) *NHS Maternity Statistics: 2002–2003*. Statistical Bulletin 2005/10. London: Department of Health. www.dh.gov.uk/assetRoot/04/10/70/61/04107061.pdf.

Der, G., Batty, G.D. and Deary, I.J. (2006) 'Effect of breast feeding on intelligence in children: prospective study, sibling pairs analysis, and meta-analysis', *British Medical Journal*, 333(7575): 745–51.

Derdeyn, A. and Wadlington, W. (1977) 'Adoption: the rights of parents versus the best interests of their children', *Journal of American Academy of Child Psychiatry*, 16(2): 238–55.

DeVault, M.L. (1991) *Feeding the Family: The Social Organization of Caring as Gendered Work*. University of Chicago Press.

DfES (Department for Education and Skills) (2003) *Care To Learn*. London: DfES. www.dfes.gov.uk/caretolearn/parents.

DfES (Department for Education and Skills) (2005) *Consequences of Teenage Parenthood: Pathways that Minimise Long-Term Negative Impacts of Teenage Childbearing*. Report RW52. London: The Stationery Office.

DfES (Department for Education and Skills) (2006a) *Teenage Pregnancy Next Steps: Guidance for Local Authorities and Primary Care Trusts on Effective Delivery of Local Strategies*. Nottingham: DfES Publications.

DfES (Department for Education and Skills) (2006b) *Working Together to Safeguard Children*. London: The Stationery Office. www.everychildmatters.gov.uk/.

DfES (Department for Education and Skills) (2007) 'Multi-agency working to support pregnant teenagers: a midwifery guide to partnership working with Connexions and other agencies', *Every Child Matters*. London: The Stationery Office.

Di Blasi, Z., Harkness, E., Ernst, E., Georgiou, A. and Kleijnen, J. (2001) 'Influence of context effects on health outcomes: a systematic review', *Lancet*, 357(9258): 757–62.

Dickson, N., Paul, C., Herbison, P. and Silva, P. (1998) 'First sexual intercourse: age, coercion, and later regrets reported by a birth cohort', *British Medical Journal*, 316(7124): 29–33.

Dietsch, E., Shackleton, P., Davies, C., McLeod, M. and Alston, M. (forthcoming) '"You can drop dead": midwives bullying women', *Women and Birth*.

Doherty, E. and Smith, A. (2006) 'Postnatal contraception planning for young women', *MIDIRS Midwifery Digest*, 16(2): 237–9.

Doja, A. (2005) 'Rethinking the couvade', *Anthropological Quarterly*, 78(4): 917–50.

Donzelot, J. (1979) *The Policing of Families*, trans. from French by Robert Hurley. London: Hutchinson.

Douglas, M. (1999) *Implicit Meanings: Selected Essays in Anthropology*. London: Routledge.

Downe, S. (2006) 'Normal birth focus: engaging with the concept of unique normality in childbirth', *British Journal of Midwifery*, 14(6): 352–4.

Doyal, L. (1995) *What Makes Women Sick: Gender and the Political Economy of Health*. London: Macmillan.

Draper, J. (2002) '"It was a real good show": the ultrasound scan, fathers and the power of visual knowledge', *Sociology of Health and Illness*, 24(6): 771–95.

D'Souza, L. and Garcia, J. (2003) *Access to Care for Low Income Childbearing Women: Limiting the Impact of Poverty and Disadvantage on the Health of Low-Income Pregnant Women. New Mothers and their Babies: A Scoping Exercise*. Oxford and London: National Perinatal Epidemiology Unit and Maternity Alliance.

Dudgeon, M.R. and Inhorn, M.C. (2004) 'Men's influences on women's reproductive health: medical anthropological perspectives', *Social Science and Medicine*, 59(7): 1379–95.

Dwyer, A.E. (2006) 'From private to public bodies: Normalising pregnant bodies in Western culture', *Nexus: Newsletter of the Australian Sociological Association*, 18(3): 18–19.

Dykes, F. and Moran, V.H. (2003) 'Adolescent mothers and breast-feeding: experiences and support needs – an exploratory study', *Journal of Human Lactation*, 19(4): 391–401.

Dyson, L., McCormick, F.M. and Renfrew, M.J. (2005) *Interventions for Promoting the Initiation of Breastfeeding*. Cochrane Database of Systematic Reviews, Issue 2, Art. No. CD001688. DOI: 10.1002/14651858.

Earle, S. (1998) 'The body in pregnancy and childbirth: corporeality and self-identity', unpublished Ph.D. thesis, Coventry University.

Earle, S. (2000) 'Why some women do not breast feed: bottle feeding and fathers' role', *Midwifery*, 16(4): 323–30.

Entwistle, J. (2001) *The Fashioned Body: Fashion, Dress and Modern Social Theory*. Cambridge: Polity Press.

Erikson, E.H. ([1950] 1963) *Childhood and Society*, 2nd edn. New York: W.W. Norton.

Ermisch, J. and Pevalin, D. (2003) *Does a 'Teen-Birth' Have Longer-Term Impacts on the Mother? Evidence from the 1970 British Cohort Study*. Working Paper No. 2003-28. Colchester: University of Essex, Institute for Social and Economic Research. www.iser.essex.ac.uk/pubs/workpaps/pdf/2003-28.pdf.

Esmail, A. (2004) 'The prejudices of good people', *British Medical Journal*, 328(7454): 1448–9.

Etzioni, A. (1993) *The Spirit of Community: Rights, Responsibilities and the Communitarian Agenda*. London: Fontana Press.

Evans, T. (2005) *'Unfortunate Objects': Lone Mothers and Eighteenth-Century London*. Basingstoke: Palgrave Macmillan.

Everingham, C., Stevenson, D. and Warner-Smith, P. (2007) '"Things are getting better all the time"?: Challenging the narrative of women's progress from a generational perspective', *Sociology*, 41(3): 419.

Fahy, K. (1995) 'Marginalised mothers: teenage transition to motherhood and the experience of disciplinary power', unpublished Ph.D. thesis. University of Queensland, Australia.

Fearn, J., Hibbard, B., Laurence, K., Roberts, A. and Robinson, J. (1982) 'Screening for neural-tube defects and maternal anxiety', *British Journal of Obstetrics and Gynaecology*, 89(3): 218–21.

Fessler, K. (2003) 'Social outcomes of early childbearing: important considerations for the provision of clinical care', *Journal of Midwifery and Women's Health*, 48(3): 178–85.

Finch, J. and Mason, J. (eds) (1993) *Negotiating Family Responsibilities*. London: Routledge.

Fine, M. (1988) 'Sexuality, schooling and adolescent females: the missing discourse of desire', *Harvard Educational Review*, 58(1): 29–53.

Firestone, S. (1970) *The Dialectic of Sex*. New York: Bantam Books.

Foster, K., Lader, D. and Cheesbrough, S. (1997) *Infant Feeding 1995*. London: Office for National Statistics.

Foucault, M. (1965) *Madness and Civilization: A History of Insanity in the Age of Reason*. New York: Random House.

Foucault, M. ([1991] 1997) *Discipline and Punish: The Birth of the Prison*. London: Penguin.

Fox, G.L. (1977) '"Nice girl": social control of women through a value construct', *Signs: Journal of Women in Culture*, 2(4): 805–17.

Fraser, N. and Gordon, L. (1994) 'A genealogy of dependency: tracing a key-word of the U.S. welfare state', *Signs: Journal of Women in Culture*, 19(2): 309–36.

Free, C., Lee, R. and Ogden, J. (2002) 'Young women's accounts of factors influencing their use and non-use of emergency contraception: in-depth interview study', *British Medical Journal*, 325(7377): 1393–7.

Freeman, L.M., Timperley, H. and Adair, V. (2003) 'Partnership in midwifery care in New Zealand', *Midwifery*, 20(1): 2–14.

Freidson, E. (1970) *Professional Dominance: The Social Structure of Medical Care*. Chicago: Aldine.

Fricker, M. (2003) 'Epistemic injustice and a role for virtue in the politics of knowing', *Metaphilosophy*, 34(1–2): 154–73.

Frost, L. (2001) *Young Women and the Body: A Feminist Sociology*. Basingstoke: Palgrave.

Frye, M. (1983) *Politics of Reality: Essays in Feminist Theory*. Trumansburg: Crossing Press.

Furedi, F. (1998) *Culture of Fear: Risk-Taking and the Morality of Low Expectation*. London: Cassell.

Furedi, F. (2001) *Paranoid Parenting: Why Ignoring the Experts May Be Best for Your Child*. London: Allen Lane.

Gardosi, J. and Francis, A. (1999) 'Effect of menstrual dating error in the assessment of gestational age in premature babies. Poster Session Iii, 19th Annual Meeting of the Society for Maternal-Fetal Medicine; January 18–23, 1999; San Francisco Hilton, San Francisco, California', *American Journal of Obstetrics and Gynecology*, 180(1S-II), January Supplement.

Geertz, C. ([1983] 2000) *Local Knowledge: Further Essays in Interpretive Anthropology*. Philadelphia: Basic Books.

Gillies, V. (2005) 'Raising the "meritocracy"', *Sociology*, 39(5): 835–53.

Goffman, E. ([1959] 1969) *The Presentation of Self in Everyday Life*. London: Allen Lane.

Gold, M. and Bachrach, L. (2004) 'Contraceptive use in teens: a threat to bone health?', *Journal of Adolescent Health*, 35: 427–9.

Graham, H. (1993a) *Hardship and Health in Women's Lives*. London and New York: Harvester Wheatsheaf.

Graham, H. (1993b) *When Life's a Drag: Women, Smoking and Disadvantage*. London: HMSO.

Graham, H. and McDermott, E. (2005) 'Qualitative research and the evidence base of policy: insights from studies of teenage mothers in the UK', *Journal of Social Policy*, 35: 21–37.

Green, E. (2001) 'Suiting ourselves: women professors using clothes to signal authority', in M. Banim, E. Green and A. Guy (eds), *Through the Wardrobe: Women's Relationship with their Clothes*. Oxford: Berg, 97–116.

Green, J., Baston, H., Easton, S. and McCormick, F. (2003) *Greater Expectations: Inter-relationship between Women's Expectations and Experiences of Decision Making, Continuity, Choice and Control in Labour, and Psychological Outcomes*. Summary report, MIRU No. 2003.42. University of Leeds, Mother and Infant Research Unit.

Green, J.M., Coupland, V.A. and Kitzinger, J.V. (eds) (1998) *Great Expectations: A Prospective Study of Women's Expectations and Experiences of Childbirth*. Hale: Books for Midwives Press.

Green, J.M., Renfrew, M.J. and Curtis, P.A. (1999) 'Continuity of carer: what matters to women? A review of the evidence', *Midwifery*, 16(3): 186–96.

Gunderson, E.P. and Abrams, B. (2000) 'The relative importance of gestational gain and maternal characteristics associated with the risk of becoming overweight after pregnancy', *International Journal of Obesity*, 24: 1660–8.

Gustafson, D.L. (2005) 'The social construction of maternal absence', in D.L. Gustafson (ed.), *Unbecoming Mothers: The Social Production of Maternal Absence*. Binghamton, NY: Haworth Press, 23–50.

Hacking, I. (1990) *The Taming of Chance*. Cambridge University Press.

Hacking, I. (1999) *The Social Construction of What?* Cambridge, MA, and London: Harvard University Press.

Hacking, I. (2003) 'What is social construction? The teenage pregnancy example', in G. Delanty and P. Strydom (eds), *Philosophies of Social Science: The Classic and Contemporary Readings*. Maidenhead: Open University Press.

Hagan, T. and Smail, D. (1997) 'Power-mapping-1: background and basic methodology', *Journal of Community and Applied Social Psychology*, 7: 257–67.

Hall, P.L. and Wittkowski, A. (2006) 'An exploration of negative thoughts as a normal phenomenon after childbirth', *Journal of Midwifery and Women's Health*, 51(5): 321–30.

Hamer, M. (1999) 'Listen to the voice: an interview with Carol Gilligan', *Women: A Cultural Review*, 10(2): 173–84.

Hamlyn, B., Brooker, S., Oleninikova, K. and Wands, S. (eds) (2002) *Infant Feeding Survey 2000*. London: The Stationery Office.

Hansen, S.L., Clark, L. and Foster, J.C. (2002) 'Active pushing versus passive fetal descent in the second stage of labor: a randomized controlled trial', *Obstetrics and Gynecology*, 99(1): 29–34.

Haraway, D. (1997) 'The virtual speculum in the new world order', *Feminist Review*, 55: 22–72.

Hardill, I., Graham, D.T. and Kofman, E. (eds) (2001) *Human Geography of the UK: An Introduction*. London and New York: Routledge.

Harding, S. (1987) 'Is there a feminist method?', in S. Harding (ed.), *Feminism and Methodology*. Milton Keynes: Open University Press, 1–14.

Hart, T. (1971) 'The inverse care law', *Lancet*, 1(7696): 405–12.

Health Protection Agency (2006) *HPA Press Statement: Sexually Transmitted Infections Figures for 2005*. www.hpa.org.uk/hpa/news/articles/press_releases/2006/060704_sti_figures.htm.

Hebdige, D. (1988) 'Hiding in the light: youth surveillance and display', in D. Hebdige (ed.), *Hiding in the Light: On Images and Things*. London: Routledge.

Henshaw, S. (1998) 'Unintended pregnancy in the United States', *Family Planning Perspectives*, 30(1): 24–9 and 46.

Higginbottom, G., Mathers, N., Marsh, P., Kirkham, M. and Owen, J. (2005) *An Exploration of Teenage Parenting Experiences of Black and Minority Ethnic Young People in England*. Final Report to the Teenage Pregnancy Unit. Sheffield: The University of Sheffield.

Higginbottom, G., Mathers, N., Marsh, P., Kirkham, M., Owen, J. and Serrant-Green, L. (2006) 'Young people of minority ethnic origin in England and early parenthood: views from young parents and service providers', *Social Science and Medicine*, 63(4): 858–70.

Hill, R. and Fortenberry, J. (1992) 'Adolescence as a culture-bound syndrome', *Social Science and Medicine*, 35(1): 73–80.

Hippisley-Cox, J., Allen, J., Pringle, M., Ebdon, D., McPhearson, M., Churchill, D. and Bradley, S. (2000) 'Association between teenage pregnancy rates and the age and sex of general practitioners: cross sectional survey in Trent 1994–7', *British Medical Journal*, 320(7238): 842–5.

Hobcraft, J. and Keirnan, K. (1999) *Childhood Poverty, Early Motherhood and Adult Social Exclusion*. Centre for Analysis of Social Exclusion: CASE paper 28. London: London School of Economics.

Hoddinott, P. and Pill, R. (1999) 'Qualitative study of decisions about infant feeding among women in East End of London', *British Medical Journal*, 318(7175): 30–4.

Hodnett, E. (2009) 'Pain and women's satisfaction with the experience of childbirth: a systematic review', *American Journal of Obstetrics and Gynecology*, 186(5): S160–S172.

Howie, L. and Carlisle, C. (2005) 'I felt like they were all kind of staring at me ...', *Midwives, the Journal of the Royal College of Midwives*, 8(7): 304–8.

Hudson, A. (1989) '"Troublesome girls": towards alternative definitions and policies', in M. Cain (ed.), *Growing Up Good: Policing the Behaviour of Girls in Europe*. London: Sage.

Hudson, B. (1984) 'Femininity and adolescence', in A. McRobbie and M. Nava (eds), *Gender and Generation*. Basingstoke: Macmillan, 31–47.

Hunter, L. (2004) 'The views of women and their partners on the support provided by community midwives during postnatal home visits', *Evidence Based Midwifery*, 2(1): 20–7.

Ibbotson, S. (1993) *Teenage Pregnancy in Hull Health Authority Residents*. Hull: Department of Public Health, Hull Health Authority.

Irwin, J.C.E. (2006) 'Beyond abstinence: what we need to do to decrease the risks of sexual behavior during adolescence', *Journal of Adolescent Health*, 38(3): 165–8.

Jacobsson, B., Ladfors, L. and Milsom, I. (2004) 'Advanced maternal age and adverse perinatal outcome', *Obstetrics and Gynecology*, 104(4): 727–33.

James, A. (1986) 'Learning to belong: the boundaries of adolescence', in A.P. Cohen (ed.), *Symbolising Boundaries: Identity and Diversity in British Cultures*. Manchester University Press.

Jenkins, R. (2004) *Social Identity*. London: Routledge.

Jewell, D., Tacchi, J. and Donovan, J. (2000) 'Teenage pregnancy: whose problem is it?', *Family Practice*, 17(6): 522–8.

Jones, G. (2003) 'Youth, dependence and the problem of support', in S. Cunningham-Burley and L. Jamieson (eds), *Families and the State: Changing Relationships*. Basingstoke: Palgrave Macmillan, 187–204.

Jordan, B. (1978) *Birth in Four Cultures: A Crosscultural Investigation of Childbirth in Yucatan, Holland, Sweden, and the United States*. Montreal: Eden Press Women's Publications.

Joseph Rowntree Foundation (1995) *Social Background and Post-Birth Experiences of Young Parents*. York: Joseph Rowntree Foundation.

Kehily, M.J. and Nayak, A. (2008) *Lads, Chavs and Pram-Face Girls: Embodiment and Emotion in Working-Class Youth Cultures*. Emotional Geographies of Education Symposium, Institute of Education, 6 November, University of London.

Kelly, D. (2000) *Pregnant with Meaning.* New York: Peter Lang.

Kidger, J. (2004) 'Including young mothers: limitations to New Labour's strategy for supporting teenage parents', *Critical Social Policy*, 24(3): 291–311.

Kiernan, K. (1992) 'The impact of family disruption in childhood on transitions made in young adult life', *Population Studies*, 46: 213–34.

Kirkham, M. and Stapleton, H. (2001) *Informed Choice in Maternity Care: An Evaluation of Evidence Based Leaflets.* York, University of York: NHS Centre for Reviews and Dissemination.

Klaus, M. and Kennell, J. (eds) (1976) *Maternal–Infant Bonding.* St Louis, MO: Mosby.

Klein, J. (1965) *Samples from English Cultures*, vol. 1: *Three Preliminary Studies: Aspects of Adult Life in England.* London: Routledge and Kegan Paul.

Klumb, P. and Lampert, T. (2004) 'Women, work, and well-being 1950–2000: a review and methodological critique', *Social Science and Medicine*, 58(6): 1007–2004.

Knight, B., Shields, B., Powell, R. and Hattersley, A. (2006) 'Paternal details missing at booking: an identifiable risk factor of lower birthweight', *Evidence Based Midwifery*, 4(2): 41–6.

Kukla, R. (2006) 'Pregnant bodies as public spaces', in S. Hardy and C. Wiedmer (eds), *The Spaces of Motherhood.* Basingstoke: Palgrave Macmillan, 283–305.

Laslett, P. ([1965] 2000) *The World We Have Lost: Further Explored.* London: Routledge.

Laslett, P. (1977) *Family Life and Illicit Love in Earlier Generations.* Cambridge University Press.

Layne, L.L. (2000) '"He was a real baby with baby things": a material culture analysis of personhood, parenthood and pregnancy loss', *Journal of Material Culture*, 5(3): 321–45.

Leap, N. and Hunter, B. (1993) *The Midwife's Tale: An Oral History from Handywoman to Professional Midwife.* London: Scarlet Press.

Lee, E., Clements, S., Ingham, R. and Stone, N. (2004) *A Matter of Choice? Exploring Reasons for Variations in the Proportions of Under 18 Conceptions that are Terminated.* York: The Joseph Rowntree Foundation.

Lees, S. (1989) 'Learning to love: sexual reputation, morality and the social control of girls', in M. Cain (ed.), *Growing Up Good: Policing the Behaviour of Girls in Europe.* London: Sage, 19–37.

Levene, A., Williams, S. and Nutt, T. (eds) (2005) *Illegitimacy in Britain, 1700–1920.* Basingstoke: Palgrave Macmillan.

LeVine, R., Dixon, S., LeVine, S., Richman, A., Leiderman, P., Keefer, C. and Brazelton, T. (eds) (1994) *Child Care and Culture: Lessons from Africa.* Cambridge University Press.

Levitas, R. (2005) *The Inclusive Society? Social Exclusion and New Labour*, 2nd edn. London: Palgrave Macmillan.

Levitas, R., Pantazis, C., Fahmy, E., Gordon, D., Lloyd, E. and Patsios, D. (2007) *The Multidimensional Analysis of Social Exclusion: A Research Report for the Social Exclusion Task Force.* Department of Sociology and School for Social Policy, Townsend Centre for the International Study of Poverty and Bristol Institute for Public Affairs, University of Bristol.

Lister, R. (2002) *Childhood Poverty and Social Exclusion: From a Child's Perspective.* Bristol: Policy Press.

Longhurst, R. (1996) 'Geographies that matter: pregnant bodies and public places', unpublished D.Phil. thesis, University of Waikato, Hamilton, New Zealand/ Aotearoa.

Longhurst, R. (2000) '"Corporeographies" of pregnancy: "bikini babes"', *Environment and Planning D: Society and Space*, 18(4): 453–72.

Longhurst, R. (2001) *Bodies: Exploring Fluid Boundaries*. London: Routledge.

Lupton, D. (1994) *Medicine as Culture: Illness, Disease and the Body in Western Culture*. Newbury Park, CA: Sage.

MacDonald, R. and Marsh, J. (eds) (2005) *Disconnected Youth? Growing Up in Britain's Poor Neighbourhoods*. Basingstoke: Palgrave.

MacLeod, A. and Weaver, S. (2003) 'Teenage pregnancy: attitudes, social support and adjustment to pregnancy during the antenatal period', *Journal of Reproductive and Infant Psychology*, 21(1): 49–59.

Marshall, J.E. (2000) 'Informed consent to intrapartum procedures', *British Journal of Midwifery*, 8(4): 225–7.

Martin, E. (1987) *The Woman in the Body: A Cultural Analysis of Reproduction*. Buckingham: Open University Press.

Mason, J. (2000) 'Midwives "verging on the sadistic" … Why are midwives turning nasty?', *British Journal of Midwifery*, 8(4): 247.

May, V. (2004) 'Meanings of lone motherhood within a broader family context', *Sociological Review*, 52(3): 390–403.

McDermott, E. and Graham, H. (2005) 'Resilient young mothering: social inequalities, late modernity and the "problem" of "teenage" motherhood', *Journal of Youth Studies*, 8(1): 59–79.

McPherson, K., Steel, C.M. and Dixon, J.M. (2000) 'ABC of breast diseases: breast cancer – epidemiology, risk factors, and genetics', *British Medical Journal*, 321(7261): 624–8.

McRobbie, A. (2007) 'Top girls', *Cultural Studies*, 21(4–5): 718–37.

McRobbie, A. (2009) *The Aftermath of Feminism: Gender, Culture and Social Change*. London: Sage.

Mercer, R.T. (1995) *Becoming a Mother: Research on Maternal Identity from Rubin to the Present*. New York: Springer.

Millett, K. (1991) *The Loony Bin Trip*. London: Virago.

Mitchell, E. (1995) 'Smoking: the next major and modifiable risk factor', in T. Rognum (ed.) *Sudden Infant Death Syndrome: New Trends in the Nineties*. Oslo: Scandinavian University Press.

Mitchell, W. and Green, E. (2002) '"I don't know what I'd do without our Mam"; motherhood, identity and support networks', *Sociological Review*, 50(1): 1–22.

Monk, J. and Katz, C. (1993) 'When in the world are women?', in C. Katz and J. Monk (eds), *Full Circles: Geographies of Women over the Life Course*. London: Routledge, 1–26.

Morgan, D. (1999) 'Risk and family practices: accounting for change and fluidity in family life', in E. Silva and C. Smart (eds), *The New Family?* London: Sage, 13–30.

Morgan, J., Lacey, J. and Sedgwick, P. (1999) 'Impact of pregnancy on bulimia nervosa', *British Journal of Psychiatry*, 174(2): 135–40.

Morrison, B. (1997) *As If*. London: Granta.

Murcott, A. (1982) 'On the social significance of the "cooked dinner" in South Wales', *Social Science Information*, 21(4–5): 677–96.

Murnen, S.K. and Wright, C. (2002) 'If "boys will be boys," then girls will be victims? A meta-analytic review of the research that relates masculine ideology to sexual aggression', *Sex Roles*, 46(11–12): 359–75.

Murphy, E. (1999) '"Breast is best": Infant feeding decisions and maternal deviance', *Sociology of Health and Illness*, 21(2): 187–208.

Murphy, E. (2003) 'Expertise and forms of knowledge in the government of families', *Sociological Review*, 51(4): 433–62.

Murphy-Lawless, J. (1998) *Reading Birth and Death: A History of Obstetric Thinking.* Cork University Press.

Murray, L. (1995) 'The politics of attachment', *Soundings*, Autumn, 1: 65–77.

Nanda, K., McCrory, D.C., Myers, E.R., Bastian, L.A., Hasselblad, V., Hickey, J.D. and Matchar, D.B. (2000) 'Accuracy of the Papanicolaou test in screening for and follow-up of cervical cytologic abnormalities: a systematic review', *Annals of Internal Medicine*, 132(10): 810–19.

National Audit Office (2004) 'Early years: progress in developing high quality child care and early education accessible to all', London: National Audit Office. www.nao.org.uk/publications/nao_reports/03-04/0304268.pdf.

Nelson, M. (2000) 'Childhood nutrition and poverty', *Proceedings of the Nutrition Society*, 59: 307–15.

New Policy Institute (2006) *Poverty: Key Facts.* London: The New Policy Institute with support from the Joseph Rowntree Foundation. www.poverty.org.uk/.

Newburn, M. and Hutton, E. (1996) 'Women and midwives: turning the tide', in D. Kroll (ed.), *Midwifery Care for the Future: Meeting the Challenge.* London: Baillière Tindall, 201–36.

Nicoll, A., Catchpole, M., Cliffe, S., Hughes, G., Simms, I. and Thomas, D. (1999) 'Sexual health of teenagers in England and Wales: analysis of national data', *British Medical Journal*, 318(7194): 1321–2.

Oakley, A. ([1974] 1985) *The Sociology of Housework.* Oxford: Basil Blackwell.

Oakley, A. ([1979] 1986) *Becoming a Mother* [later published as *From Here to Maternity*]. Harmondsworth: Penguin.

Oakley, A. (1984) *The Captured Womb: A History of the Medical Care of Pregnant Women.* Oxford: Basil Blackwell.

Oakley, A., Hickey, D., Rajab, L. and Rigby, A. (1996) 'Social support in pregnancy: does it have long-term effects?', *Journal of Reproductive and Infant Psychology*, 14: 7–22.

O'Hara, M. (2009) 'Teenage pregnancy rates rise: Government promises £20m to cut teen pregnancy after first increase in conception rates in five years', *Guardian*, 26 February. www.guardian.co.uk/society/2009/feb/26/teenage-pregnancy-rise.

ONS (Office for National Statistics) (2006, Spring) 'Conceptions in England and Wales 2004', *Health Statistics Quarterly*, 29. www.statistics.gov.uk/downloads/theme_health/HSQ29.pdf.

Osgerby, B. (1998) *Youth in Britain since 1945.* Oxford: Blackwell.

Owen, J., Carroll, C., Cooke, J., Formby, E., Hayter, M., Hirst, J., Lloyd Jones, M., Stapleton, H. and Stevenson, M. (2010) *School-Linked Sexual Health Services for Young People (SSHYP): A Survey and Systematic Review Concerning Current Models, Effectiveness, Cost-Effectiveness and Research Opportunities.* A report to the Health Technology Assessment Panel. www.hta.nhs.uk/project/1662.asp.

Oyěwùmí, O. (2006) 'The invention of women', in H.L. Moore and T. Sanders (eds), *Anthropology in Theory: Issues in Epistemology*. Oxford: Blackwell Publishing, 540–6.

Paris, J. (2000) *Myths of Childhood*. Hove: Brunner/Mazel.

Parkin, F. (1979) *Marxism and Class Theory: A Bourgeois Critique*. London: Tavistock.

Paton, D. (2004) 'Random behaviour or rational choice? Family planning, teenage pregnancy and STIs', paper presented at the Royal Economic Society Conference, Swansea.

Peacock, J. (1986) *The Anthropological Lens: Harsh Light, Soft Focus*. Cambridge University Press.

Pietsch, N. (2002) 'Possession: a feminist phenomenological and post-structuralist analysis of illegitimate pregnancy, pregnant embodiment and adoption', *Women's Health and Urban Life (a journal affiliated with the University of Toronto)*, 1(1): 1–8.

Pillow, W. (2003) '"Bodies are dangerous": using feminist genealogy as policy studies methodology', *Journal of Education Policy*, 18(2): 145–59.

Quinlivan, J.A., Tan, L.H., Steele, A. and Black, K. (2004) 'Impact of demographic factors, early family relationships and depressive symptomatology in teenage pregnancy', *Australian and New Zealand Journal of Psychiatry*, 38(4): 197–203.

Quinton, D., Pollock, S. and Golding, J. (2001) *The Transition to Fatherhood by Young Men: Influences on Commitment*. ESRC Grant No. L134251018. Bristol: University of Bristol.

Radley, A. (2000) 'Health psychology, embodiment, and the question of vulnerability', *Journal of Health Psychology*, 5(3): 297–304.

Reading, R. and Reynolds, S. (2001) 'Debt, social disadvantage and maternal depression', *Social Science and Medicine*, 53(4): 441–53.

Reagan, P.B., Salsberrya, P.J. and Olsena, R.J. (2007) 'Does the measure of economic disadvantage matter? Exploring the effect of individual and relative deprivation on intrauterine growth restriction', *Social Science and Medicine*, 64(10): 2016–29.

Reardon, D.C. and Cougle, J.R. (2002) 'Depression and unintended pregnancy in the National Longitudinal Survey of Youth: a cohort study', *British Medical Journal*, 324(7330): 151–2.

Reekie, G. (1998) *Measuring Immorality: Social Inquiry and the Problem of Illegitimacy*. Cambridge University Press.

Ribbens, J. (1994) *Mothers and their Children: A Feminist Sociology of Childrearing*. London: Sage.

Rich, A. (1977) *Of Woman Born: Motherhood as Experience and Institution*. London: Virago.

Ridge, T. (2005) 'Supporting children? The impact of child support policies on children's wellbeing in the UK and Australia', *Journal of Social Policy*, 34: 121–42.

Rooks, J.P. (1997) *Midwifery and Childbirth in America*. Philadelphia: Temple Press Books.

Rose, G. (1993) 'Speculations on what the future holds in store', *Environment and Planning A, Anniversary Issue*: 26–9.

Royal College of Midwives, The (n.d.) Standards and Practice: National Teenage Pregnancy Midwifery Network. www.rcm.org.uk/college/standards-and-practice/national-teenage-pregnancy-midwifery-network/.

Royal College of Psychiatrists, The (2003) *Bridging the Gaps: Health Services for Adolescents*. Report CR114. www.rcpsych.ac.uk/publications/cr/cr114.htm.

Rozette, C., Houghton-Clemmey, R. and Sullivan, K. (2002) 'A profile of teenage pregnancy: young women's perceptions of the maternity services', *The Practising Midwife*, 3(10): 23–5.

Ruddick, S. (1980) 'Maternal thinking', *Feminist Studies*, 6(2): 342–67.

Ruddick, S. (1989) *Maternal Thinking: Towards a Politics of Peace*. London: The Women's Press.

Sage, L. (2001) *Bad Blood*. London: Fourth Estate.

Salihi, S. and Melrose, E. (2002) 'Revisiting a pilot survey involving contraception and teenage pregnancy in Ayrshire and Arran', *The Journal of Family Planning and Reproductive Health Care*, 28(1): 37–8.

Sarri, R. and Phillips, A. (2004) 'Health and social services for pregnant and parenting high risk teens', *Children and Youth Services Review*, 26: 537–60.

Schaffer, J., Bloom, S., Casey, B., McIntire, D., Nihira, M. and Leveno, K. (2005) 'A randomized trial of the effects of coached vs uncoached maternal pushing during the second stage of labor on postpartum pelvic floor structure and function', *American Journal of Obstetrics and Gynecology*, 192(5): 1692–6.

Schechner, R. (1993) *The Future of Ritual: Writings on Culture and Performance*. London: Routledge.

Scheper-Hughes, N. (1992) *Death without Weeping: The Violence of Everyday Life in Brazil*. Berkeley: University of California Press.

Seamark, C. (2001) 'Design or accident? The natural history of teenage pregnancy', *Journal of the Royal Society of Medicine*, 94(6): 282–5.

Seamark, C. and Lings, P. (2004) 'Positive experiences of teenage motherhood: a qualitative study', *British Journal of General Practice*, 54(508): 813–18.

Selman, P. (2003) 'Scapegoating and moral panics: teenage pregnancy in Britain and the United States', in S. Cunningham-Burley and L. Jamieson (eds), *Families and the State: Changing Relationships*. Basingstoke: Palgrave Macmillan, 159–86.

Seth, V. ([1993] 2004) *A Suitable Boy*. London: Phoenix.

SEU (Social Exclusion Unit) (1999) *Teenage Pregnancy*. Report No. Cm 4342. London: The Stationery Office. www.dfes.gov.uk/teenagepregnancy/dsp_content.cfm?pageID=87.

Sharpe, S. (1987) *Falling for Love: Teenage Mothers Talk*. London: Virago.

Sharpe, S. (1999) 'Bodily speaking: spaces and experiences of childbirth', in E.K. Teather (ed.), *Embodied Geographies: Spaces, Bodies and Rites of Passage*. London: Routledge, 91–104.

Shaw, M., Lawlor, D.A. and Najman, J.M. (2006) 'Teenage children of teenage mothers: psychological, behavioural and health outcomes from an Australian prospective longitudinal study', *Social Science and Medicine*, 62(10): 2526–39.

Shennan, A.H. and Bewley, S. (2006) 'Why should preterm births be rising?', *British Forty Journal*, 332(7547): 924–5.

Sibley, D. (1995) *Geographies of Exclusion: Society and Difference in the West*. London: Routledge.

Silva, E. (ed.) (1996) *Good Enough Mothering?: Feminist Perspectives on Lone Motherhood*. London: Routledge.

Silva, E. and Smart, C. (1999) (eds) *The New Family?* London: Sage.

Sim, F. and Mackie, P. (2006) 'Britain gives up smoking', *Public Health* 120(5): 381–2.

Simpkin, P. (1991) 'Just another day in a woman's life? Women's long-term perceptions of their first birth experience. Part 1', *Birth*, 18(4): 203–10.

Simpson, K.R. and James, D.C. (2005) 'Effects of immediate versus delayed pushing during second-stage labor on fetal well-being: a randomized clinical trial', *Nursing Research*, 54(3): 149–57.

Skeggs, B. (1999) 'Matter out of place: visibility and sexualities in leisure spaces', *Leisure Studies*, 18(3): 213–32.

Skeggs, B. (2005) 'The making of class and gender through visualizing moral subject formation', *Sociology*, 39(5): 965–83.

Skuse, T. (1997) 'Adolescent motherhood: a longitudinal study of teenage and adult mothers over the first year', unpublished Ph.D. thesis, Oxford Brookes University.

Smart, C., Neale, B. and Wade, A. (eds) (2001) *The Changing Experience of Childhood: Families and Divorce*. Cambridge: Polity.

Smith, A. and Jacobson, B. (1988) *The Nation's Health: A Strategy for the 1990s*. London: The King's Fund.

Smith, D. (1992) 'Sociology from women's experience: a reaffirmation', *Sociological Theory*, 10(1): 88–98.

Smith, G.C.S. and Pell, J.P. (2001) 'Teenage pregnancy and risk of adverse perinatal outcomes associated with first and second births: population based retrospective cohort study', *British Medical Journal*, 323(7311): 476–81.

SmithBattle, L. (2000) 'Developing a caregiving tradition in opposition to one's past: lessons from a longitudinal study of teenage mothers', *Public Health Nursing*, 17(2): 85–93.

Sontag, S. (1983) *Illness as Metaphor/AIDS and its Metaphors*. Harmondsworth: Penguin Books.

Speak, S., Cameron, S., Woods, R. and Gilroy, R. (1995) *Young Single Mothers: Barriers to Independent Living*. London: Family Policy Studies Centre. www.jrf.org.uk/KNOWLEDGE/findings/socialpolicy/pdf/sp72.pdf.

Stacey, J. (1988) 'Can there be a feminist ethnography?', *Women's Studies International Forum*, 11(1): 21–7.

Stapleton, H. (1997) 'Choice in the face of uncertainty', in M. Kirkham and L. Perkins (eds), *Reflections in Midwifery*. London: Baillière Tindall, 47–70.

Stapleton, H. (2006) *Childbearing and Eating Disorders: A Qualitative Study of Some Women's Experiences*. Department of Midwifery and Children's Nursing, University of Sheffield.

Stapleton, H., Duerden, J. and Kirkham, M. (1998) *Evaluation of the Impact of the Supervision of Midwives on Professional Practice and the Quality of Midwifery Care*. London: English National Board.

Stapleton, H. and Keenan, J. (2009) '"It depends what you mean by feeding on demand": mothers' accounts of babies' agency in infant feeding relationships', in Allison James, A.-T. Kjørholt and V. Tingstad (eds), *Children, Food and Identity in Everyday Life*. Basingstoke: Palgrave Macmillan.

Statham, H., Green, J. and Kafetsios, K. (1997) 'Who worries that something might be wrong with the baby? A prospective study of 1072 pregnant women', *Birth*, 24(4): 223–33.

Stevens, R. (2004) 'A change in the law on parental responsibility', *Midwives, The Journal of the Royal College of Midwives*, 7(7): 314.

Stewart, F. (1999) '"Once you get a reputation, your life's like ... 'wrecked'": The implications of reputation for young women's sexual health and well-being', *Women's Studies International Forum*, 22(3): 373–83.

Stoppard, J.M. (1997) 'Women's bodies, women's lives and depression: towards a reconciliation of material and discursive accounts', in J.M. Ussher (ed.), *Body Talk: The Material and Discursive Regulation of Sexuality, Madness and Reproduction*. London and New York: Routledge, 10–33.

Summers, A. (2003) *The End of Equality: Work, Babies and Women's Choices in 21st Century Australia*. Sydney: Random House.

Sumsion, J. (2006) 'The corporatization of Australian childcare: towards an ethical audit and research agenda', *Journal of Early Childhood Research*, 4(2): 99–121.

Sutherland, H., Sefton, T. and Piachaud, D. (2003) *Poverty in Britain: The Impact of Government Policy since 1997*. York: The Joseph Rowntree Foundation.

Symonds, A. (1991) 'Angels and interfering busybodies: the social construction of two occupations', *Sociology of Health and Illness*, 13(2): 249–64.

Tanno, D.V. (1994) 'Names, narratives, and the evolution of ethnic identity', in A. González, M. Houston and V. Chen (eds), *Our Voices: Essays in Culture, Ethnicity, and Communication*. Los Angeles: Roxbury, 30–3.

Teixeira, J., Fisk, N. and Glover, V. (1999) 'Association between maternal anxiety in pregnancy and increased uterine artery resistance index: cohort based study', *British Medical Journal*, 318(7177): 153–7.

Thomas, S.G. and Upton, D. (2000) 'Expectant fathers' attitudes towards pregnancy', *British Journal of Midwifery*, 8(4): 218–21.

Tiggemann, M., Gardiner, M. and Slater, A.M.Y. (2000) 'I would rather be size 10 than have straight A's: a focus group study of adolescent girls' wish to be thinner', *Journal of Adolescence*, 23(6): 645–59.

Tolman, D.L. (1994) 'Doing desire: adolescent girls' struggles for/with sexuality', *Gender and Society*, 8(3): 324–42.

Townsend, D. (2004) 'I wasn't told my daughter was going to have a baby ... or that she was keeping it', *Observer*, 16 May. http://observer.guardian.co.uk/focus/story/0,6903,1217958,00.html.

TPU (Teenage Pregnancy Unit) (2007) *Under-18 and Under-16 Conception Statistics 1998–2005*. London: The Stationery Office. www.everychildmatters.gov.uk/teenagepregnancy/.

Treffers, P., Olukoya, A., Ferguson, B. and Liljestrand, J. (2001) 'Care for adolescent pregnancy and childbirth', *International Journal of Gynaecology and Obstetrics*, 75(2): 111–21.

Tripp, J. and Viner, R. (2005) 'Sexual health, contraception, and teenage pregnancy', *British Medical Journal*, 330(7491): 590–3.

Tyler, I. (2008) 'Chav mum chav scum', *Feminist Media Studies*, 8(1): 17–34.

Tylor, E.B. (1889) 'On a method of investigating the development of institutions, applied to laws of marriage and descent', *Journal of the Anthropological Institute of Great Britain and Ireland*, 18: 245–72.

Ussher, J. (1991) *Women's Madness: Misogyny or Mental Illness?* Hemel Hempstead: Harvester Wheatsheaf.

Valentine, G. (1997) '"My son's a bit dizzy", "My wife's a bit soft": gender, children and cultures of parenting', *Gender, Place and Culture*, 4(1): 37–62.

Valentine, G. (2008) 'Contested terrain: teenagers in public space', in T.S. Oakes and P.L. Price (eds), *The Cultural Geography Reader*. Abingdon: Routledge, 395–401.

van der Kolk, B.A. (1989) 'The compulsion to repeat the trauma: re-enactment, revictimisation, and masochism', *Psychiatric Clinics of North America*, 12(2): 389–411.

Wade, A. (2005) *Continuity and Change in Parent–Child Relations over Three Generations*. University of Leeds, ESRC Research Grant No. R000239523.

Walker, A.M., Johnson, R. et al. (2008) 'Targeted home visiting intervention: the impact on mother–infant relationships', *Community Practitioner*, 81(3): 31–4.

Walker, R., Turnbull, D. and Wilkinson, C. (2002) 'Strategies to address global caesarean section rates: a review of the evidence', *Birth*, 29(1): 28–39.

Walkerdine, V. and Lucy, H. (1989) *Democracy in the Kitchen? Regulating Mothers and Socialising Daughters*. London: Virago.

Wallace, C. (1987) *For Richer, For Poorer: Growing Up in and out of Work*. London: Tavistock.

Walters, V. (2005) *Report on Child Health: Background Information for the NSF on Children and Young People*. National Centre for Public Policy, University of Wales, Swansea.

Wellesley, D., Boyle, T., Barber, J. and Howe, D.T. (2002) 'Retrospective audit of different antenatal screening policies for Down's syndrome in eight district general hospitals in one health region', *British Medical Journal*, 325(7354): 15–19.

Wellings, K., Field, J., Johnson, A. and Wadsworth, J. (1994) *Sexual Behaviour in Britain*. London: Penguin.

Wellings, K. and Mitchell, K. (1998) 'Risks associated with early sexual activity and fertility', in D. Roker and J. Coleman (eds), *Teenage Sexuality: Health, Risk and Education*. London: Harworth Academic, 81–100.

Wellings, K., Wilkinson, P., Grundy, C., Kane, R., Lachowycz, K., Jacklin, P., Stevens, M., Gerressu, M. and Parker, R. (2005) *Teenage Pregnancy Strategy Evaluation: Final Report Synthesis. Report: RW38*. London: Teenage Pregnancy Unit. www.everychildmatters.gov.uk/_files/94C1FA2E9D4C9717E5D0AF1413A329A4.pdf.

West, J. (1999) '(Not) talking about sex: youth, identity and sexuality', *The Sociological Review*, 47(3): 525–47.

Wheeler, R. (2006) 'Gillick or Fraser? A plea for consistency over competence in children', *British Medical Journal*, 332(7545): 807.

Wight, D., Henderson, M., Raab, G., Abraham, C., Buston, K., Scott, S. and Hart, G. (2000) 'Extent of regretted sexual intercourse among young teenagers in Scotland: a cross sectional survey', *British Medical Journal*, 320(7244): 1243–4.

Wilson, H. and Huntington, A. (2006) 'Deviant (m)others: the construction of teenage motherhood in contemporary discourse', *Journal of Social Policy*, 35: 59–76.

Winnicott, D. (1971) *Playing and Reality*. London: Routledge.

Winterson, J. (2004) 'An interview with Jeanette Winterson', *Guardian*, 29 May.

Wong, J. (1997) 'The "making" of teenage pregnancy', *International Studies in the Philosophy of Science*, 11(3): 273–86.

Wong, J. and Checkland, D. (eds) (1999) *Teen Pregnancy and Parenting: Social and Ethical Issues*. University of Toronto Press.

Woollett, A., Marshall, H. and Stenner, P. (1998) 'Young women's accounts of sexual activity and sexual/reproductive health', *Journal of Health Psychology*, 3(3): 369–81.

Wylie, J. and Verber, I. (1994) 'Why women fail to breast feed: a prospective study from booking to 28 days post partum', *Journal of Nutrition and Dietetics*, 7: 115–20.

Wynn, L.L., Foster, A.M. and Russell, J. (2009) 'Can I get pregnant from oral sex? Sexual health misconceptions in e-mails to a reproductive health website', *Contraception*, 79(2): 91–7.

Young, M. and Wilmot, P. (1957) *Family and Kinship in East London*. London: Routledge and Kegan Paul.

Index